EARLY CHILDHOOD EDUCATION SERIES

NANCY K. FILE & CHRISTOPHER P. BROWN, EDITORS

Resisting the Kinder-Race: Restoring Joy to Early Learning
CHRISTOPHER P. BROWN

Reshaping Universal Preschool: Critical Perspectives on Power and Policy
LUCINDA GRACE HEIMER & ANN ELIZABETH RAMMINGER, WITH KATHERINE K. DELANEY, SARAH GALANTER-GUZIEWSKI, LACEY PETERS, & KRISTIN WHYTE

Pre-K Stories: Playing with Authorship and Integrating Curriculum in Early Childhood
DANA FRANTZ BENTLEY & MARIANA SOUTO-MANNING

Ready or Not: Early Care and Education's Leadership Choices—12 Years Later, 2nd Ed.
STACIE G. GOFFIN & VALORA WASHINGTON

Teaching STEM in the Preschool Classroom: Exploring Big Ideas with 3- to 5-Year-Olds
ALISSA A. LANGE, KIMBERLY BRENNEMAN, & HAGIT MANO

High-Quality Early Learning for a Changing World: What Educators Need to Know and Do
BEVERLY FALK

Guiding Principles for the New Early Childhood Professional: Building on Strength and Competence
VALORA WASHINGTON & BRENDA GADSON

Leading for Change in Early Care and Education: Cultivating Leadership from Within
ANNE L. DOUGLASS

When Pre-K Comes to School: Policy, Partnerships, and the Early Childhood Education Workforce
BETHANY WILINSKI

Young Investigators: The Project Approach in the Early Years, 3rd Ed.
JUDY HARRIS HELM & LILIAN G. KATZ

Continuity in Children's Worlds: Choices and Consequences for Early Childhood Settings
MELISSA M. JOZWIAK, BETSY J. CAHILL, & RACHEL THEILHEIMER

The Early Intervention Guidebook for Families and Professionals: Partnering for Success, 2nd Ed.
BONNIE KEILTY

STEM Learning with Young Children: Inquiry Teaching with Ramps and Pathways
SHELLY COUNSELL ET AL.

Courageous Leadership in Early Childhood Education: Taking a Stand for Social Justice
SUSI LONG, MARIANA SOUTO-MANNING, & VIVIAN MARIA VASQUEZ, EDS.

Teaching Kindergarten: Learner-Centered Classrooms for the 21st Century
JULIE DIAMOND, BETSY GROB, & FRETTA REITZES, EDS.

Healthy Learners: A Whole Child Approach to Reducing Disparities in Early Education
ROBERT CROSNOE, CLAUDE BONAZZO, & NINA WU

The New Early Childhood Professional: A Step-by-Step Guide to Overcoming Goliath
VALORA WASHINGTON, BRENDA GADSON, & KATHRYN L. AMEL

Eight Essential Techniques for Teaching with Intention: What Makes Reggio and Other Inspired Approaches Effective
ANN LEWIN-BENHAM

Teaching and Learning in a Diverse World, 4th Ed.
PATRICIA G. RAMSEY

In the Spirit of the Studio: Learning from the *Atelier* of Reggio Emilia, 2nd Ed.
LELLA GANDINI ET AL., EDS.

Leading Anti-Bias Early Childhood Programs: A Guide for Change
LOUISE DERMAN-SPARKS, DEBBIE LEEKEENAN, & JOHN NIMMO

Exploring Mathematics Through Play in the Early Childhood Classroom
AMY NOELLE PARKS

Becoming Young Thinkers: Deep Project Work in the Classroom
JUDY HARRIS HELM

The Early Years Matter: Education, Care, and the Well-Being of Children, Birth to 8
MARILOU HYSON & HEATHER BIGGAR TOMLINSON

Thinking Critically About Environments for Young Children
LISA P. KUH, ED.

To look for other titles in this series, visit www.tcpress.com

continued

Standing Up for Something Every Day
BEATRICE S. FENNIMORE

FirstSchool
SHARON RITCHIE & LAURA GUTMANN, EDS.

The States of Child Care
SARA GABLE

Early Childhood Education for a New Era
STACIE G. GOFFIN

Everyday Artists
DANA FRANTZ BENTLEY

Multicultural Teaching in the Early Childhood Classroom
MARIANA SOUTO-MANNING

Inclusion in the Early Childhood Classroom
SUSAN L. RECCHIA & YOON-JOO LEE

Language Building Blocks
ANITA PANDEY

Understanding the Language Development and Early Education of Hispanic Children
EUGENE E. GARCÍA & ERMINDA H. GARCÍA

Moral Classrooms, Moral Children, 2nd Ed.
RHETA DEVRIES & BETTY ZAN

Defending Childhood
BEVERLY FALK, ED.

Don't Leave the Story in the Book
MARY HYNES-BERRY

Starting with Their Strengths
DEBORAH C. LICKEY & DENISE J. POWERS

The Play's the Thing
ELIZABETH JONES & GRETCHEN REYNOLDS

Twelve Best Practices for Early Childhood Education
ANN LEWIN-BENHAM

Big Science for Growing Minds
JACQUELINE GRENNON BROOKS

What If All the Kids Are White? 2nd Ed.
LOUISE DERMAN-SPARKS & PATRICIA G. RAMSEY

Seen and Heard
ELLEN LYNN HALL & JENNIFER KOFKIN RUDKIN

Supporting Boys' Learning
BARBARA SPRUNG ET AL.

Young English Language Learners
EUGENE E. GARCÍA & ELLEN C. FREDE, EDS.

Connecting Emergent Curriculum and Standards in the Early Childhood Classroom
SYDNEY L. SCHWARTZ & SHERRY M. COPELAND

Infants and Toddlers at Work
ANN LEWIN-BENHAM

The View from the Little Chair in the Corner
CINDY RZASA BESS

Culture and Child Development in Early Childhood Programs
CAROLLEE HOWES

Educating and Caring for Very Young Children, 2nd Ed.
DORIS BERGEN ET AL.

Beginning School
RICHARD M. CLIFFORD & GISELE M. CRAWFORD, EDS.

Emergent Curriculum in the Primary Classroom
CAROL ANNE WIEN, ED.

Enthusiastic and Engaged Learners
MARILOU HYSON

Powerful Children
ANN LEWIN-BENHAM

The Early Care and Education Teaching Workforce at the Fulcrum
SHARON LYNN KAGAN ET AL.

Windows on Learning, 2nd Ed.
JUDY HARRIS HELM ET AL.

Supervision in Early Childhood Education, 3rd Ed.
JOSEPH J. CARUSO WITH M. TEMPLE FAWCETT

Guiding Children's Behavior
EILEEN S. FLICKER & JANET ANDRON HOFFMAN

The War Play Dilemma, 2nd Ed.
DIANE E. LEVIN & NANCY CARLSSON-PAIGE

Possible Schools
ANN LEWIN-BENHAM

Everyday Goodbyes
NANCY BALABAN

Playing to Get Smart
ELIZABETH JONES & RENATTA M. COOPER

The Emotional Development of Young Children, 2nd Ed.
MARILOU HYSON

Young Children Continue to Reinvent Arithmetic—2nd Grade, 2nd Ed.
CONSTANCE KAMII

Bringing Learning to Life
LOUISE BOYD CADWELL

The Colors of Learning
ROSEMARY ALTHOUSE ET AL.

A Matter of Trust
CAROLLEE HOWES & SHARON RITCHIE

Embracing Identities in Early Childhood Education
SUSAN GRIESHABER & GAILE S. CANNELLA, EDS.

Bambini
LELLA GANDINI & CAROLYN POPE EDWARDS, EDS.

Serious Players in the Primary Classroom, 2nd Ed.
SELMA WASSERMANN

Young Children Reinvent Arithmetic, 2nd Ed.
CONSTANCE KAMII

Bringing Reggio Emilia Home
LOUISE BOYD CADWELL

RESISTING the KINDER-RACE

RESTORING JOY TO EARLY LEARNING

Christopher P. Brown

TEACHERS COLLEGE PRESS
TEACHERS COLLEGE | COLUMBIA UNIVERSITY
NEW YORK AND LONDON

Published by Teachers College Press,® 1234 Amsterdam Avenue, New York, NY 10027

Cover design by adam c. bohannon. Photo by Kai Keisuke / Shutterstock.

Library of Congress Cataloging-in-Publication Data

Names: Brown, Christopher Pierce, author.
Title: Resisting the kinder-race : restoring joy to early learning / Christopher P. Brown.
Description: New York, NY : Teachers College Press, 2021. | Series: Early childhood education series | Includes bibliographical references and index.
Identifiers: LCCN 2021009106 (print) | LCCN 2021009107 (ebook) | ISBN 9780807765609 (paperback) | ISBN 9780807765616 (hardcover) | ISBN 9780807779705 (ebook)
Subjects: LCSH: Early childhood education—United States. | Kindergarten—United States. | Democracy and education—United States. | Educational change—United States.
Classification: LCC LB1139.25 .B77 2021 (print) | LCC LB1139.25 (ebook) | DDC 372.210973—dc23
LC record available at https://lccn.loc.gov/2021009106
LC ebook record available at https://lccn.loc.gov/2021009107

ISBN 978-0-8077-6560-9 (paper)
ISBN 978-0-8077-6561-6 (hardcover)
ISBN 978-0-8077-7970-5 (ebook)

Printed on acid-free paper
Manufactured in the United States of America

To my family and friends
for accepting me for who I am
while challenging me to be a better
person, husband, father, friend, educator, and researcher

Contents

Acknowledgments

Personally, thank you to my wife, Michele, for her belief in me and for her continued love and support over the past 24 years of marriage, and to our three daughters, Camille, Vivienne, and Lucille, for always reminding me what's important in life and the significance of kindergarten in the lives of all children. Thanks to all the family members and friends who have helped me get to this point in my life, including my parents, their partners, my siblings, and their families. Thank you to Mark and Beth Jernigan and their family, Mark Bixby and his family, and Jack Morrison for their varied levels of support as I finished up this book.

Professionally, I owe thanks to my former preschool and elementary school colleagues and the many students and their families who helped me "live" the realities of kindergarten and schooling in general on a daily basis as a teacher—particularly Ruby Gordon and Susan Turner. Also, thanks to all the participants in the larger study, whose knowledge, insight, and honesty helped me to understand the complexity of the Kinder-Race, particularly Ms. Cutler, who allowed me to spend so much time with her and her students. I truly treasure her kindness, honesty, and support over the years as I share what I learned from my time with her and her students.

Thank you to Natalie Weber for being the first person to listen to my ideas for this study and for providing me with the critical feedback needed to move forward with this work. Natalie also provided many other levels of support (too many to name) throughout this project. The same goes for Dr. Joanna Englehardt, who helped me tighten up my argument before recruiting a site and participants for this study and also provided other forms of support over the years. I owe a deep level of gratitude to Dr. Melissa Sherfinski for her willingness to support me in making sense of the West Virginia schooling context, as well as for assisting me in recruiting stakeholders in West Virginia for this study. Also, thank you to Cody Summerville and Elizabeth Holstein for their assistance in recruiting participants for this study in Texas. I want to thank Dr. Jennifer Adair for talking with me about Tobin et al.'s (1991, 2009, 2013) VCME method after I submitted several grant proposals for this study and for securing a research site, and thank you for lending me a camera and filming with me for a day in Ms. Cutler's classroom.

I owe much gratitude to David Barry and Da Hei Ku, as well as Dr. Joanna Englehardt, for their assistance in coding, analyzing, and writing up findings about the changed kindergarten in several research articles, as well as for pushing my thinking forward in ways I never imagined. Thank you to the preservice teachers and doctoral students at The University of Texas at Austin with whom I've had the opportunity to work over the years, including Kate Puckett, Hye Ryung Won, Dr. Beth Feger, Dr. Brian Mowry, Dr. Yi-Chin Lan, and many others. Each has shaped me as an educator in ways they'll never know. I also would like to thank Robert Donald for assisting with the creation and editing of the film using Adobe Premier Pro; Dr. Karen French for helping me to share the video securely; and Liz Kogan for submitting many grant applications on my behalf.

Speaking of grants, many thanks to the Spencer Foundation Small Grants Program (Reference # 201700116) and the Big XII Faculty Fellowship Program for their support of the study that led to this book.

Thank you to those who provided me with and worked alongside me as I went through my educational experiences at Sewanee, New Mexico State University, and the University of Wisconsin–Madison; each pushed me to think and write about teaching and learning in kindergarten and beyond in more complex ways.

Thank you to Dr. Elizabeth M. Graue (Beth) for expanding my understanding of the complexity of school readiness as well as for introducing me to and assisting my growth of understanding of Bakhtin's work and Holland et al.'s (1998) construct of figured worlds, and for introducing to me the construct of agency through Holland et al.

Thanks to the groups of early childhood researchers and teacher educators at such organizations as the Early Education and Child Development and Critical Perspectives in Early Childhood SIGs of AERA, the National Association of Early Childhood Teacher Educators, and RECE for allowing me to share and develop my work across multiple venues and outlets.

I owe many thanks to Sarah Biondello at TC Press for her support in putting my book proposal and this text together, as well as Dr. Nancy File for being such a good friend and great sounding board during the writing process. I'd also like to thank Karl Nyberg at TC Press for taking me and this book through the production process, Nancy Power and Emily Freyer for working on the marketing of it, and Myra Cleary for her insightful editing of this text. I also owe thanks to the two anonymous reviewers of my original book proposal; both offered suggestions for improving what has become this manuscript.

Lastly, I do apologize if I forgot to mention or thank any of the many folks who have supported me throughout the years.

CHAPTER 1

Why Examine the Changed Kindergarten?

> There's more pressure in kindergarten today to have the kids perform at a higher level academically. The students are expected to do more and produce more. The kids see the pressure. They feel the pressure. No matter how much you try to hide it, they know it's there.
>
> —Ms. Cutler[1], a kindergarten teacher in Texas

> If you want policy change, you have to be really intentional and strategic because there are so many other forces pulling state policymakers this way and that. The force that is consistently here at the capitol ends up getting it done. It seems urgent because they're always here. Remember, there are all these groups that exist for school choice, for school finance, or teacher protections, but where is the group that is literally just working on changing what's taking place in the classroom on a daily basis—be it kindergarten or any grade? Without that, without a strategy that has someone here every day advocating for that change, things will not change.
>
> —Member of the Texas House of Representatives and House Education Committee

These two statements provide a glimpse into the complexity of the current cultural enactment of kindergarten in the United States. Ms. Cutler speaks directly to the pressure to perform academically that she and her kindergartners feel on a daily basis. Such pressure makes it difficult for Ms. Cutler to engage in instructional practices that support the personal, sociocultural, developmental, and linguistic talents her students bring to the classroom on a daily basis. The Texas representative speaks to what needs to be done if this pressure is to be reduced through reforming the daily practices that occur in kindergarten and public education in Texas, and possibly the rest of the nation.

Combined, these statements capture my more than 20-year concern over the impact of national, state, and local policymakers' high-stakes, standards-based accountability (SBA) reforms, such as the No Child Left Behind Act (NCLB), on kindergarten classrooms and the entire structure of public schooling in the United States (e.g., Brown, 2005b). High-stakes SBA reforms are policies that prioritize the use of standardized instructional practices so that students in public education systems demonstrate on academic achievement tests that they possess a state-mandated set of knowledge and skills (O'Day, 2002). Students' test scores often are used to determine such things as whether students can move to the next grade level and/or the effectiveness of their teachers, school administrators, and/or the school district. These SBA reforms have altered the processes and practices of not only kindergarten (e.g., Minicozzi, 2016) but also of public preschool programs (such as pre-K) and the rest of the prekindergarten through grade 12 (pre-K–12) education system (Brown, 2005a; Brown & Gasko, 2012; Brown & Weber, 2016a).

ORIGINS OF MY INTEREST IN THE CHANGED KINDERGARTEN

My interest in the impact of policymakers' SBA reforms on kindergarten specifically and public education in general emerged when I was a kindergarten teacher in Virginia in the late 1990s. What I experienced and witnessed on a day-to-day basis in my own classroom and my school led me to question whether my colleagues and I were to teach the child or the standard. These concerns, which included the pressure to perform that Ms. Cutler referred to above, led me to further my education so that I might be able to speak back to these issues. When I applied for graduate school, I told prospective universities and professors that I wanted to pursue my PhD because:

> Over the past 3 years, I have been working in school systems that possess standards (state and local) that each classroom teacher must ensure his or her students are meeting—accountability for ECED classrooms being rooted in statewide assessments that are given in grade 3. These standards were established by politicians, and the assessments being used to measure these standards were not standardized, which causes one to question the reliability and validity of the tests themselves. As a researcher, I would like to examine the effects of these standards and tests on the early childhood classroom and its curriculum. I believe there are many issues that need be researched in order to determine if these standards are creating successful learners in the classroom.
>
> Some of the educational issues that I believe need to be examined are: Whose standards are teachers teaching? Do these standards

> create a situation for failure for some students? What are the effects of standards on students' performance in school? What are the effects of these standards on students' views of learning? How has curriculum changed? Are teachers teaching to the test rather than teaching students how to be independent learners and thinkers? How do teachers meet the needs of students when they have to meet specific standards? How do standards affect readiness for school? How do standards affect the relationship between parents, teachers, and schools? and Do the standards take into account what research and professional educators know about how children learn and develop? (Application to the University of Wisconsin–Madison, November 1999)

As you can see, I wanted to know why policymakers believed their reforms would improve school; how school personnel, which includes administrators and teachers, were making sense of these reforms; how they implemented them; and what this meant for the learning and development of children and their families. It has been *more than 20 years* since I first put those thoughts to paper, and those concerns and the continued impact of policymakers' SBA reforms on the kindergarten classroom *have not changed*.

In this book, I present what I've learned recently from studying stakeholders' sensemaking of the changed kindergarten (e.g., Brown, Englehardt, Barry, & Ku, 2019a), alongside the knowledge I gained from conducting a dozen other studies that have examined the impact of policymakers' reforms on classrooms, teachers, students, families, preservice teachers (or what some might call teachers-in-training), graduate students in early childhood education, school and district administrators, teacher educators, and other education stakeholders. By examining these issues empirically, practically, and theoretically in relation to what I and others term *the changed kindergarten* (e.g., Graue, 2011), I illuminate what currently is occurring in kindergarten and other early childhood classrooms across the United States. In doing so, I make apparent how the current process of schooling that frames public education through economic, rather than democratic, terms is fundamentally flawed and why it must change (Brown, Englehardt, Barry, & Ku, 2019b). I end by providing a range of strategies that education stakeholders can employ in their everyday interactions with children, teachers, or schools, as well as use to push policymakers to pay attention to the day-to-day practices of kindergarten and the larger public education system so these programs produce the next generation of educated and engaged democratic citizens.

WHY THIS BOOK?

Debates over what kindergarten is and/or should be are not new (Martin, 1985; Powell, 1969). Furthermore, there was a time, when policymakers'

SBA reforms first were being implemented, that researchers, practitioners, and others—including myself—thought that kindergarten teachers and policymakers' SBA reforms could coexist so that all students would succeed in school (Brown, 2007a; Brown & Mowry, 2009; Goldstein, 2007). However, as policymaker demands for academic achievement and accountability increased, such positive responses were short-lived. Researchers began to demonstrate how these policies were negatively impacting the practices of teachers (Brown et al., 2015) and the learning experiences of children (Brown, 2015). Moreover, it became increasingly apparent that these policies framed teaching and learning (Brown, 2007b) as well as assessment and performance (Brown, 2011) in fundamentally different ways that could not be easily reconciled (Brown, 2009b). Essentially, teachers who employ developmentally appropriate practices (DAP) pivot their instructional decisionmaking off the needs of the children in their classrooms to foster a democratic learning community (Copple & Bredekamp, 2009). Yet, under SBA reforms, teachers must employ an economic (neoliberal) logic centered on the production of particular outcomes, which leads them to pivot their instructional decisions off the knowledge and skills that policymakers have mandated all children must learn at each grade level.

Additionally, in recent years, much of the research in ECE (the research area typically investigating kindergarten) has turned its gaze away from what happens in elementary school. Instead, many researchers and those who fund their work have focused on preschool and are examining how teachers and programs can ready children for the academic and social demands that await them in kindergarten (e.g., Bustamante & Hindman, 2019). Researchers have examined such issues as how to do SBA reform better by analyzing curricular alignment between preschool and elementary school (e.g., Cohen-Vogel et al., 2020) or examining the grade level of content being taught to children (e.g., Engel et al., 2016). Such work seeks to ensure simply that children across the United States are experiencing the same sets of learning opportunities as they progress through school so that they are on a trajectory for success by the time they take the high-stakes exams that await them in the later grades (Brown & Englehardt, 2017). In doing so, the system that has failed and continues to fail a range of children remains intact, and this gets to my last point.

HOW NO CHILD LEFT BEHIND HAS FAILED

It has been 20 years since the implementation of NCLB, and yet policymakers' SBA reforms have not created democratic systems of public education in which all children are academically successful (Ladd, 2017). This is evident for those students who are not White, who may not have what Alim (2005) termed "White dialects of English" as their primary language, and/or who live in families classified as low-income. This is particularly disconcerting because these populations will constitute the majority of students enrolled in U.S. public schools by 2027 (McFarland et al., 2018). Furthermore, the passage of the Every Student Succeeds Act (ESSA) in 2015, which replaced NCLB, sought to empower states to rethink schooling, allowing them greater flexibility in developing their own systems of standards and accountability. Policymakers in some states (e.g., Massachusetts) have taken advantage of this opportunity, while others (e.g., those in Texas) have maintained the status quo. Still, ESSA continues to promote an economic logic of high standards and strong accountability systems, even as empirical researchers have documented and continue to document how these systems of reform will not achieve their stated goals (Hemelt & Jacob, 2020).

The failure of policymakers' SBA reforms clearly demonstrates that it is a pivotal time to explore the changed kindergarten. In doing so, this book will make it apparent that "we," as members of or participants within the early childhood and elementary school communities, are at a point where the process of schooling must fundamentally change. For me, kindergarten has always represented the canary in the coalmine of public education in the United States. I and many others believe that canary is gasping for oxygen (e.g., Hatch, 2015). The current structure of public schooling is fundamentally flawed and requires what Larry Cuban (1988) referred to as "second-order" changes. Second-order reforms seek to alter the fundamental way schooling is done in the nation—or what Majone (1989) refers to as the core of an education policy (Brown, Englehardt, Barry, & Ku, 2019a). For Cuban, such reforms differ from first-order changes, which focus on improving either the effectiveness or efficiency of how things are done, which Majone refers to as the periphery. Second-order reforms are needed to alter public school systems across the nation at their core so that these systems can live up to and produce the next generation of educated and engaged democratic citizens.

THE PURPOSE OF THIS BOOK

The purpose of my examination into how kindergarten has changed into a program that is conceptualized and enacted through economic rather than democratic conceptions of schooling is threefold: (1) to provide a historical outline of this change; (2) to share what I've learned from studying how local, state, and national education stakeholders make sense of the Kinder-Race and policymakers' SBA reforms; and (3) to put forward practical and achievable ideas for changing the day-to-day practices in kindergarten and public education in general.

I begin this book by examining how we, as a nation, arrived at a place where many folks call kindergarten the new 1st grade (Graue, 2011), which is not a positive statement (e.g., Strauss, 2016). Education stakeholders are worried that children are being turned off from learning and school as soon as they pass through the kindergarten classroom door (e.g., Miller & Almon, 2009). I conclude this history by providing a detailed explanation of what I mean by the Kinder-Race.

Next, to help think through what my work uncovered and to highlight how local, state, and national education stakeholders make sense of the Kinder-Race specifically and of policymakers' SBA reforms in general, I employ four theoretical lenses. As Thomas (2016) noted, theory is simply a thinking tool; it helps researchers make sense of the data they have collected and should not be seen as anything more than that; and, accordingly, no one should be scared of or turned off by the word *theory*.

The Four Theoretical Lenses

Sensemaking. Making sense of the purpose and processes of kindergarten is dynamic and interactive (Coburn, 2001; Spillane et al., 2002). Education stakeholders cognitively and emotionally make meaning of the world around them through their prior knowledge and experiences, their social relations with others, and the context in which they operate (Allen & Penuel, 2015; Brown, Englehardt, Barry, & Ku, 2019a). Making sense of kindergarten is a process in which participants' "mental models act as filters through which the data are understood, a process that may (re)form or reify the models" they have about how children should be taught in school, what they should be taught, and how success in school should be determined (Bertrand & Marsh, 2015, p. 866).

Culturally Sustaining Pedagogy. I position my understanding of the schooling process in culturally sustaining pedagogy (Ladson-Billings, 2014; Paris & Alim, 2014). Culturally sustaining pedagogy (CSP) frames children and their families as subjects, rather than objects, which means who children are and the skills, talents, and sociocultural knowledge they bring to the kindergarten classroom are to be viewed as "something to be enacted or expressed, something that is dynamic and agentic" within the curriculum of the classroom (Goodwin et al., 2008, p. 6). So rather than think of schooling simply as a process in which teachers are to fill students with specific sets of knowledge and skills that they can restate/reproduce on academic achievement tests, which Freire (1970/2006) referred to as a "banking conception" of schooling, the work of Ladson-Billings, Paris (2012), and others (e.g., Gay, 2000) demonstrates how and why school should be a place that empowers "students intellectually, socially, emotionally, and politically by using cultural referents to impart knowledge, skills, and attitudes" (Ladson-Billings, 1994, pp. 17–18). Creating such a learning environment requires teachers and other school personnel to know the experiences, practices, and expertise that children and their families bring to the classroom, which Moll and colleagues (1992) termed their funds of knowledge. Such a vision of schooling is very different and much more complex than simply defining success as students attaining high scores on academic achievement tests.

Figured Worlds. I employ Holland and colleagues' (1998) conception of figured worlds to assist me in the process of investigating how these stakeholders made sense of what kindergarten is and should be. Holland et al. defined a figured world as "a socially and culturally constructed realm of interpretation in which particular characters and actors are recognized, significance is assigned to certain acts, and particular outcomes are valued over others" (p. 52). Figured worlds represent the theoretical entwining of Vygotsky's social constructivism, Bakhtin's dialogism, and Bourdieu's framing of the role of culture in development; that is, knowledge is socially constructed through the interaction of teachers and students as a community that is impacted by the cultural makeup of the students and the larger community in which they live (Brown & Feger, 2010). Figured worlds are context-specific, and therefore one's role—what is valued, accepted, and discussed—depends on the participants who are engaged within that figured world (Holland et al., 1998). Figured worlds do not act in isolation from one another. Rather, they are in constant interaction, and within these interactions, particular worlds carry more value and influence (Brown & Feger, 2010; Urrieta, 2007).

These multiple worlds represent the ideas, histories, and experiences stakeholders bring into their understanding of what is occurring in the changed kindergarten and how they want to alter it so that it aligns with their conceptions of kindergarten. For Holland et al. (1998), such change can occur in individuals (Urrieta, 2007), in the classroom (Graue et al., 2015), or potentially within policy (Pennington, 2007) through acts of improvisation that are "openings by which change comes about from generation to generation" (Holland et al., 1998, pp. 17–18).

Neoliberalism. Lastly, I draw from the political orientation of neoliberalism. As I noted with my colleagues (Brown, Englehardt, Barry, & Ku, 2019b), neoliberalism "is a political rationality" that renders "the social domain economic and . . . link[s] a reduction in (welfare) state services and security systems to the increasing call for 'personal responsibility' and 'self-care'" (Lemke, 2001, p. 203). Foucault (2008) noted that neoliberalism frames the market as the "truth" and "power of society" (p. 148). That is, the governance of society occurs "through the regulated choices of individual citizens" who identify themselves as consumers. The goal for individuals within this system of governance is to make choices that attain "self-actualization and self-fulfillment" (Rose, 1996, p. 41).

Under neoliberalism, attaining an education becomes an individual rather than a societal good (Brown, 2009a), which repurposes the role of the state in the education process as a "regulator and auditor of the 'learning market'" (Biesta, 2006, p. 175). As such, public education systems are now a vehicle that provides citizens with the credentials needed to participate in the market. In kindergarten, this is done through teachers providing kindergartners with the necessary "inputs" of knowledge and skills so that they can attain the required "outputs" on specific standardized achievement tests (Ball, 2007, p. 28). Kindergarten teachers and their public school colleagues are being asked by state and district policymakers to apply what Moss (2014) termed "the correct human technologies" in order to produce "high returns" that lead to the "improved education, employment and earnings and reduced social problems" of their students (p. 3).

My final purpose in writing this book centers on reframing the current neoliberal focus on learning, earning, and consuming through more democratic principles of schooling (Ailwood, 2008). To this end, I utilize George Lakoff's (2002, 2004) cognitive theory of the moral construction of current political discourse in the United States to provide frames that education stakeholders at all levels of governance can employ to redefine the purpose, practice, and potential of kindergarten (Brown, 2006). For Lakoff (2004), frames are mental structures in our cognitive unconscious that shape the way we see the world. To assist our framing of the world, we use metaphors to help us conceptualize our experiences and make sense of our world. Moreover, much of our moral reasoning is rooted in metaphors, specifically the metaphors of moral accounting (Lakoff, 2002).

Metaphorically, we strive to achieve a moral balance in our lives. For example, we use the moral scheme of reciprocation to frame many of the interactions we have with others—for example, if you do me this favor, I will owe you one (Lakoff, 2002). Lakoff links this structure of moral reasoning with our political reasoning. Thus, Lakoff's work offers an understanding of how kindergarten is framed through different forms of moral and political reasoning, and the chance to name how kindergarten currently is being politically conceptualized by a range of stakeholder groups. It also provides the opportunity to consider how this moral and political logic that continues to define schooling through standardization and accountability can be reframed so that those who want to change kindergarten can provide a new logic for such transformation that speaks to a range of stakeholders.

Employing These Theories to Reroute the Kinder-Race

In brief, by employing these varied conceptual frameworks to investigate and understand how stakeholders across different levels of public education in the United States make sense of the Kinder-Race, I begin to illuminate the complexity of what is occurring in kindergarten. I bring together what are often siloed conversations among stakeholder groups around the changed kindergarten specifically and the impact of policymakers' SBA reforms on education in general (Brown, Englehardt, Barry, & Ku, 2019a). This isolation among stakeholder groups often makes it difficult to understand what is driving these academic and instructional changes (Russell, 2011), and whether they reflect the desires of those who legislate, implement, or participate in kindergarten, either directly or indirectly (e.g., Hustedt et al., 2018). Moreover, these fundamental changes in pre-K–12 schooling have settled into the fabric of what school is and what school stakeholders do on a daily basis. Thus, as generations of teachers who have the institutional, pedagogical, and practical knowledge of what kindergarten was prior to policymakers' SBA reforms (and still could be) leave the classroom, the question becomes whether education stakeholders, whether families or classroom teachers, will be able to conceive of a different type of education (Lewis & Holloway, 2019).

To assist in this process of conceiving change, I shine a light on a range of opportunities that can move the conversations around how best to educate U.S. children in new directions. I do so because, as noted above by the Texas representative, rerouting the Kinder-Race requires "intentional and strategic" ideas for change that stakeholders can employ to begin to push policymakers across all levels of governance to pay attention to the day-to-day practices of kindergarten and the larger public education system. I want to change it so that all students can and do succeed in school and are prepared to become active citizens in our nation's democracy (Dewey, 1938/1998). In laying out my arguments, I highlight an untapped awareness by many education stakeholders in my studies who are troubled about the current framing of public education as simply a system that provides children with particular inputs so that they attain specific outcomes. However, when asked how to change the Kinder-Race, almost all of the participants in my studies struggled with providing ideas for achievable change (Brown, Englehardt, Barry, & Ku, 2019a); additionally, when they were able to make substantive suggestions, they questioned whether such change was even possible. Thus, I am intentionally putting forward ideas for change that I believe are practical and achievable—either in the day-to-day practices of the kindergarten classroom or in terms of the policies that currently define pre-K–12 education in the United States.

MY OWN SENSE OF REALITY

Before outlining the remainder of the book, I want to emphasize two points. First, I am not claiming that kindergarten should return to the "good old days." That's ridiculous, for a number of reasons. For instance, we, as a society, know the good old days did a disservice to a large number of children and their families who participated in public schools across the United States (Ladson-Billings, 2006a). Historically, school failure was put on the child and/or the family and ignored the impact/responsibility of institutional and cultural barriers that either hindered or eliminated the opportunity for many children and families to succeed in school (e.g., Varenne & McDermott, 1998). The increased variability of the sociocultural backgrounds and linguistic talents of children now entering kindergarten and their families requires new opportunities for learning that reflect, respect, and extend those backgrounds and talents (Paris, 2016). Additionally, the children who are entering kindergarten more than likely have experienced some form of preschool classroom or have been exposed to a range of academic and social skills and knowledge by their families and/or community members. Accordingly, they need to be provided with learning experiences that extend their knowledge (e.g., Engel et al., 2016). Finally, the early childhood community has a better idea of the types of learning experiences children should be exposed to in kindergarten, and those experiences differ from the traditional visions of kindergarten that center only on play, rest, and snack (e.g., Weisberg et al., 2013).

Second, I also recognize that this book is one of many over the years that has advocated for change in kindergarten/early childhood education (e.g., Miller & Almon, 2009). What I propose in this text is not the "silver bullet" that will solve all that ails kindergarten specifically or public education in general. Rather, this text provides an in-depth look at what kindergarten currently is; how it "got" to this point; how kindergartners, public schoolteachers, school and district/county administrators, researchers, state education workers, policymakers, lobbyists, and public education advocates at the state and national levels make sense of the changed kindergarten; whether they agree with what it has become; and how they might like to see it change so that it reflects their understandings of public schooling. By analyzing all these constructs and perspectives using a range of theoretical frameworks, I provide several actionable ways forward for local, state, and national education stakeholders.

However, educational research consistently has shown that what works in one community may not work in another, or what is valued in one community may not be valued in another; that is, context matters within a democratic society, and it impacts education reform in numerous ways. Nevertheless, after reading this book, you will see the current flaws in how we as a nation do kindergarten and why change—whether second-order or first-order—is necessary. To achieve such change requires collective action by an engaged citizenry (e.g., Erickson, 2014), and by revealing the similarities and differences among these collective actors as they make sense of the changed kindergarten, I do provide ways forward—but not "The Way."

OUTLINING THE REST OF THE BOOK

In Chapter 2, I provide a brief history of kindergarten that highlights how the debates evolved over what kindergarten "is" and "should be." Much of the history that led to the Kinder-Race reflects policymakers narrowing their focus on public schooling to the issues of standardization, academic performance, and accountability, while limiting the resources teachers and students need in order to achieve these goals. Embedded within this conversation about the history of kindergarten in the United States, I discuss why kindergarten matters and how the significance of this program for children's academic performance has led to a range of conversations around the issue of school readiness as well as access to early childhood programs, such as pre-K, which I also examine briefly in this chapter. I then explain the impact of policymakers' reforms on what kindergarten teachers are expected to teach and how they are expected to do so.

I begin Chapter 3 by highlighting how researchers have documented the changes in kindergarten outlined in Chapter 2. Then I provide a detailed look into what the Kinder-Race means for the day-to-day practices of kindergartners. Specifically, I discuss what the students in the study I conducted "do" on a daily basis in literacy and mathematics as they race through kindergarten. As I lay out this detailed description of the Kinder-Race, I discuss how this learning environment does and does not reflect what is known about the best practices of teaching kindergartners, and I examine how those experiences do and do not align with what is known about how children develop and learn as sociocultural beings (Goodwin et al., 2008).

Chapter 4 provides an in-depth look at how those at what Lipsky (1980) termed the "street-level" of reform are making sense of what I term the *figured world* of the changed kindergarten (Goldstein, 2008; Holland et al., 1998). Specifically, I examine how students, teachers, family members, and school administrators make sense of the Kinder-Race described in Chapter 3. Examining what is revealed in this complex analysis of sense-making by those who engage in as well as enact the changed kindergarten provides insight into not only the complexity of the day-to-day experiences in kindergarten but also the possible ways forward in reforming the changed kindergarten at a practical level.

In Chapter 5, I turn to stakeholders that exist outside the figured world of the kindergarten classroom—district/county, state, and national education stakeholders. At this level of enactment, I employ a neoliberal lens to highlight how these stakeholders tend to advocate for a public school system that is designed to produce lifelong learners, earners, and consumers rather than the next generation of democratic citizens (Ailwood, 2008). This neoliberal narrative about investing in children so that they produce high returns in both test scores and the job market, as De Lissovoy (2014) noted, almost becomes insurmountable in considering alternative visions of kindergarten. By unpacking this neoliberal logic in these stakeholders' conceptions of kindergarten, schooling, and education in general, I begin to illuminate what opportunities exist for change/alternative visions of kindergarten and schooling in general.

Lastly, in Chapter 6, I employ the work George Lakoff and others (e.g., Cohen & Mehta, 2017) to consider how to take advantage of the opportunities for change that exist from the classroom to the statehouse. For Lakoff (2004), changing kindergarten requires reformers to provide a compelling alternative or series of changes that offer "others" a yet-to-be realized image of kindergarten that attends to their hopes for children. To be clear, Lakoff (2004) noted that this alternative vision must be grounded in concrete examples that can attain specific solutions to policy problems. Finally, Lakoff (2004) recognized that change is often evolutionary (Majone, 1989), and any change to reframe the conversations around what kindergarten should be is complex and requires a sustained effort to maintain it, which must be acknowledged from the outset by those who want to reform kindergarten.

Thus, to move forward beyond the dominant narratives of school readiness, standardization, testing, and accountability that shape kindergarten requires both Holland et al.'s (1998) notion of improvisation as well as logic that counters the framing of schooling through economic principles (De Lissovoy, 2014). By identifying practical routes for a way forward, as Lakoff (2004) pointed out, my goal is to identify sources of oxygen that can restore the potential of kindergarten, and public education in general, practically, personally, and politically for children, families, and teachers, so that the process of schooling can educate, foster, and sustain the next generation of democratic citizens.

CHAPTER 2

How Kindergarten Transitioned From a Garden to a Race

> For in every human being . . . there lies and lives humanity as a whole; but in each one it is realized and expressed in a wholly particular, peculiar, personal, unique manner; and it should be exhibited in each individual human being in this wholly peculiar, unique manner.
>
> —Friedrich Froebel (1902, p. 18)

This statement by Friedrich Froebel, who implemented the first kindergarten in Blankenburg, Germany, in 1837, demonstrates how this program emerged out of a line of thinking in which the process of educating young children (as well as adults) is more individualized than standardized, and it is this tension that is at the heart of the current debate over the Kinder-Race. To understand how kindergarten has changed, it is first important to know what it was.

FROEBEL'S KINDERGARTEN

At the heart of Froebel's (1902) kindergarten program was his belief that young children were not ready for the academics of what was defined as elementary school at the time. Still, he saw these early years in children's lives to be crucial to their moral and academic development (Brosterman, 1997). As such, Froebel created his kindergarten program to instruct children morally as well as to prepare them for school through three core sets of practices. The program was led by a nurturing teacher who sought to encourage children to develop a thirst for knowledge while also trying to help them become loving, kind, and conscientious enough to use that knowledge for the good of humanity (Brosterman, 1997; Froebel, 1902).

The first core set of principles centered around "songs, games, stories, and gardening" (Ross, 1976, p. 5), which the teacher typically employed to begin as well as guide children throughout the day around a particular focus or theme. Next, the children would work at their communal worktables for 30 to 45 minutes to engage in their daily gift play, which was the second essential instructional component of Froebel's kindergarten. The gifts, which included 3-D and 2-D materials, such as blocks, were used to create pictures or structures that fit into what Froebel termed three fundamental categories: forms of nature, forms of knowledge, and forms of beauty. Exercises with the gifts typically entailed the creation of nature forms (including things from everyday life). Froebel believed that by participating in a creating activity, children grew in their knowledge of God. Moreover, engaging with these gifts opened up opportunities for, as well as connected to, songs, stories, and play activities. For example, as the children would make a bird with shapes, the teacher would move into songs and stories about birds. After introducing children to stories and activities based on the nature forms, the teacher moved into knowledge, which included arithmetic, geometry, and reading. The gifts were designed to represent a logical progression from the whole (unity) into parts (complexity) and a return to the whole.

After gift play, the children would have 45 minutes of active games or simple gymnastics. Then they would do occupation work, the final essential component of Froebel's kindergarten (Ross, 1976). Occupation work, which included such things as materials for drawing or embroidering, can be thought of as complementary crafts such as sewing, origami, and modeling clay. The term *occupation* for these crafts was meant to emphasize the connection between abstract play (art/knowledge) and the useful work of everyday life (Brosterman, 1997). Finally, the class would end the day with a song.

For Froebel, no two days were to be the same, and the gifts, themes, and activities changed on a regular basis (Brosterman, 1997; Ross, 1976). Moreover, while many of these essential components, such as the gifts and occupations, typically are not found in kindergarten today, the structure, the role of the teacher, and the focus on children engaging in hands-on learning experiences that foster a cohesive learning community are still very much a part of the conversation around what kindergarten is and should be (e.g., Copple & Bredekamp, 2009).

THE EXPANSION OF KINDERGARTEN IN THE UNITED STATES

The first kindergarten program in the United States was imported by Margarethe Schurz to Watertown, WI, in 1856. As a German immigrant, she strove to emulate Friedrich Froebel's vision of the program, including teaching children in German (Mackenzie, 1886). As Schurz developed her kindergarten program, Elizabeth Peabody visited her to see how she was implementing Froebel's ideas in the United States. Peabody returned to Boston and opened the first American English-language kindergarten in 1860 (Mackenzie, 1886). As the publisher of the *Kindergarten Messenger* and by putting out several books promoting the program, she advocated for the importance and expansion of kindergarten. She convinced Milton Bradley, whose daughters attended kindergarten in Springfield, MA, to commercially produce Froebel's gifts and occupations (Ross, 1976). She also assisted in the establishment of the Froebel Society in Boston, which eventually became the national American Froebel Union (Ross, 1976). Furthermore, the National Education Association started a kindergarten department within its organization in 1874, and kindergarten teachers founded the International Kindergarten Union in 1892 (Mackenzie, 1886).

Kindergarten advocates, such as Peabody, Lucy Wheelock, and Susan Blow, who opened the first public kindergarten in St. Louis, pushed for the expansion of this program to become a part of children's schooling. They and others argued for kindergarten as a form of preparation for elementary school; others saw it as a form of "child rescue," and some advocates saw kindergarten as means to Americanize the influx of immigrants that were arriving in the United States (Beatty, 1995).

As these programs expanded and became part of public education systems across the nation, kindergarten teachers in the public schools at the beginning of the 20th century "(backed by kindergarten advocacy organizations) took on the mission of trying to influence their primary-grades colleagues in order to correct the shortcomings and abuses they saw in traditional, teacher-centered primary education" (Dombkowski, 2001, p. 529). Moreover, there were conceptual debates between scholars, such as between Dewey's ideas around progressivism and Thorndike's behaviorism (Beatty, 1995).

One such advocate who sought to find common ground between these debates was Lucy Wheelock. She began teaching kindergarten in Boston in 1879 (DuCharme, 2000) and established Wheelock Kindergarten Training School in 1888, which became Wheelock College in 1939[1] (Weber, 1969). She also served as president of the International Kindergarten Union (IKU) from 1895 to 1899 and of the Committee of 19 in 1903, which the IKU established to reconcile the varied debates over "what" should be occurring in kindergarten (DuCharme, 2000). Throughout her life, she advocated for a Froebelian vision of kindergarten that sought to create a learning environment that responded to and expanded children's learning (DuCharme, 2000).

However, pressure from school administrators, primary schoolteachers, and families themselves to ensure children were ready for elementary school created a tension that still exists today in kindergarten. It is a tension between beliefs about what types of learning experiences children should have, such as reading, and how different those experiences and curricula should be from what occurs in the elementary grades (Beatty, 1995; Weber, 1969).

Nevertheless, the Great Depression in the 1930s stalled the expansion of kindergarten, and in some instances, these programs were completely eliminated from local communities (e.g., Austin, TX) and did not reemerge until the post-World War II baby boom (Brewer et al., 2011).

KINDERGARTEN POST-WWII

As kindergarten began to reemerge across the United States for baby boomers, it became the entry point into the nation's public schools. However, it and the public education system in general were drastically changed by the launch of Sputnik in 1957 and Johnson's War on Poverty policies in 1965. Sputnik created a mental competitiveness scare that led to national, state, and local policies calling for the provision of hard content to nurture the academic elite in order to ensure the success of the United States (Archbald & Porter, 1990; Roeber, 1999). The Johnson administration's War on Poverty led to the federal government implementing both the Elementary and Secondary Education Act (ESEA) and the Head Start program, which was part of the Economic Opportunity Act.

Until this point, local school district and county agencies formulated and implemented almost all education policy. However, Sputnik and the implementation of ESEA shifted the role of the federal government in developing K–12 education policy within the United States in four primary ways. First, the federal government began a series of attempts to influence local education policy through inducements; that is, it tied educational changes to increased funding and the provision of particular resources for schools and classrooms.

Second, ESEA made improving student performance a primary concern when developing education policy. Such an emphasis is exemplified in ESEA's requirements for evaluating program effectiveness through the development of the Title I Evaluation and Reporting System (TIERS). Essentially, TIERS makes a clear connection between the effectiveness of education reform and student performance—if student test scores were not improving, it was an issue of either the policy itself or those who were charged with implementing it.

Third, the entirety of Johnson's policies placed the root cause of academic failure, which leads to economic failure, in the child and their home environment; Johnson's reforms saw access to high-quality education both prior to kindergarten and once in K–12 education systems as the vehicle that could lift children and their families out of poverty. Furthermore, the implementation of ESEA began a wave of education reforms that led to the current standards-based accountability movement, which emphasizes standardization, academic achievement, and accountability (Cibulka, 1999).

Lastly, the increased role of the federal government, not only in the education of children but in the everyday lives of citizens across the United

States, that emerged out of the Johnson administration's policies sparked a countermovement in and out of government that sought to stem the tide of policies that expanded what was referred to as the "welfare" state and the increased rights of varied communities (e.g., MacLean, 2017). Specifically, a neoliberal vision of governance began to gain hold among politicians, business organizations (e.g., the Business Roundtable), and political think tanks (e.g., the Heritage Foundation) in the 1970s that have worked collectively through a range of political and symbolic acts to alter the public's core conception of the role of government (Apple, 2001; Brown, 2009b; Harvey, 2005; Smith et al., 2004). Under neoliberalism, democracy is no longer a political concept. It is an "economic one" (Apple, 2007, p. 114). Public agencies are to be defunded and privatized, and "free markets, unfettered by government regulation, [are to] solve social, economic, and political problems" (Weiner, 2007, p. 275). This idea of government/governing does not seek to govern in the traditional sense, but rather through the regulated choices of individual citizens that allow them to accrue the credentials and capital needed to participate successfully in the markets that define society (Apple, 2007; Rose, 1996). Furthermore, for the public at large to "buy into" such a framing requires them to doubt the role of government in providing public services, such as schooling, and, in turn, to view the market as the most effective and efficient means of providing such services as education, health care, and so on (Harvey, 2005). In sum, neoliberalism strives for a "market-based populist culture of differentiated consumerism and individual libertarianism" (Harvey, 2005, p. 42).

A NATIONAL FOCUS ON THE ACADEMIC PERFORMANCE OF CHILDREN

The first wave of reform (Goertz, 2001) was the publication by the National Commission on Excellence in Education (NCEE) of *A Nation at Risk* (1983). The NCEE's report expanded the concern over student performance from low-income families to the entire K–12 public education system. As a result, the Reagan administration began to sow the seeds of doubt as to whether government should be "managing" public education systems (Ansary, 2007). The document's authors proclaimed that the American education system was in disarray and was crippling the nation's economic competitiveness. Its authors proposed reforms that would change the content, expectations, schedules, and teaching of the American school system (Ansary, 2007). Their expectations for all students to meet high standards in order "to secure gainful employment" were rooted in economic rather than democratic principles (NCEE, 1984, p. 11). *A Nation at Risk* (ANR) not only altered the focus of education policy, but in many ways fractured it so that reforms could be introduced that attempted to change it entirely (Apple, 2001).

Following the publication of ANR,[2] a second wave emerged from the nation's governors' pursuit of education reforms[3] that sought to respond to this risk of academic decline by promoting a commitment to educational excellence through such actions as raising high school graduation requirements (e.g., National Governors Association [NGA], 1988). Although ANR called for higher standards, the NGA brought the idea of developing national goals and standards to prominence within the national education dialogue. For example, the NGA's 1989 publication, *Results in Education*, called for the establishment of education goals as well as for instituting performance-oriented accountability systems (Finn, 1990). The political salience of standards was increasing, and the influence of Governors Alexander in Tennessee and Clinton in Arkansas boosted many of the recommendations to the national stage (Vinovskis, 1999). These shifts in education policy escalated the curricular expectations for students in the early grades (Hatch & Freeman, 1988) and led to the increased use of readiness tests for kindergarten and 1st-grade entry (Meisels, 1989).

THE EARLY CHILDHOOD COMMUNITY RESPONDS TO THE PUSH FOR INCREASED ACADEMICS

Professional organizations, such as the National Association for the Education of Young Children (NAEYC) and the Association for Childhood Education International, responded to this emphasis on formal academic instruction and accountability in the early years of schooling, including kindergarten, by publishing organizational responses for what they termed appropriate practices for children ages zero to 8 (Brown & Lan, 2013). Documents such as NAEYC's *Developmentally Appropriate Practice in Early Childhood Programs Serving Children Birth Through Age 8* (Bredekamp, 1987) sparked a series of research-based organizational responses for selecting appropriate types of curricula and assessments to use with children prior to 3rd grade (e.g., Bredekamp & Rosegrant, 1995), and empirically based studies began to identify the negative effects of inappropriate assessments and curricula on children in kindergarten and 1st grade (e.g., Bryant et al., 1991).

A NEW FOCUS ON KINDERGARTEN READINESS

The third wave of reform emerged from the Clinton administration's Goals 2000 legislation,[4] which made its first goal that every child in the United States would start kindergarten ready to learn (National Education Goals Panel, 1991). This push toward improved school readiness for kindergarten and increased academic performance in kindergarten led many to question whether kindergarten itself was changing and becoming more like 1st grade (e.g., Cuban, 1992). For example, Freeman and Hatch (1989) analyzed a stratified random sample of report cards in Ohio to assess whether what Uphoff and Gilmore (1986) termed "curriculum shovedown" from 1st grade into kindergarten was occurring. Freeman and Hatch found that "kindergartners are expected to master specific skills, especially in the areas of work habits, reading readiness, and math readiness" (p. 602).

At the heart of this debate were stakeholder concerns over what was being emphasized when teaching young children; should kindergarten teachers focus on (Brown, Englehardt, Barry, & Ku, 2019a) (1) the development of the whole child across all of the developmental domains, or (2) teaching children specific academic skills and knowledge (Beatty, 1995; Russell, 2011)? When kindergarten teachers take on a developmental focus toward teaching the whole child, which means providing learning opportunities that foster children's social, emotional, physical, cognitive, and sociocultural growth, the children's developmental needs become the pivot upon which all instructional decisions are made (Brown, 2009c). This means that teachers use their knowledge about "child development and learning," the individual learning needs of children, and "the social and cultural contexts" in which their students live to make instructional and curricular decisions (Copple & Bredekamp, 2009, pp. 9–10). When kindergarten teachers focus on teaching young children specific academic skills and knowledge, that becomes the pivot upon which instructional decisions are made (Brown, 2009c). This means teachers focus on creating a set of learning experiences across the school year that teach all children the same set of knowledge and skills.

Many within the field of ECE (e.g., Meisels, 1989) worried that this increasing focus on ensuring that children entered kindergarten ready to learn would promote such inappropriate practices as the use of assessments to determine kindergarten entry (e.g., Gnezda & Bolig, 1988). These gateway exams, if used to deny children entry to kindergarten programs, would exclude "children from participating in the school curriculum" necessary to succeed in elementary school (Shepard, 1994, p. 207).

IMPROVING AMERICA'S SCHOOLS ACT

In 1994, shortly after the Goals 2000 legislation, the federal government reauthorized ESEA, titled Improving America's Schools Act, which ushered in the current era of standards-based accountability reform. Under this reform process (O'Day, 2002), the goal for each of the stakeholders in the education system is to ensure that all students are taught the mandated knowledge and skills (content standards), are tested on their mastery of the content (performance standards), and reach the specified level of achievement they must attain on the tests (proficiency standards). If students do not meet the proficiency standards, consequences, or what commonly is referred to as "high stakes," can be put in place to hold students, teachers, schools, and/or districts accountable. While these high-stakes assessments typically do not begin until 3rd grade, many U.S. states and school districts began to put in place instructional expectations for ECE teachers and a series of assessment measures across the early grades to ensure that children are on a trajectory for success by the time they take their state's high-stakes assessments (Brown, 2007b).

NO CHILD LEFT BEHIND

The implementation of NCLB in 2002 by the federal government increased demands for SBA reform in the United States. Under NCLB, if school personnel failed to improve the adequate yearly progress (AYP) of their students on their state's tests, the consequences were an opening for market-based interventions (Brown & Barry, 2019). Families had the opportunity to transfer out of failing schools or access tutorial services, which could be run by private companies. Persistent failure by schools could result in their reconstitution. This focus on the AYP of students in reading, math, and science led to stakeholders paying further attention to what types of learning experiences children had prior to the mandatory 3rd-grade tests (Brown, 2007c)—that is, did they possess the skills the state assessments demanded they have? For instance, Part B, Subpart 1, under Title 1 of NCLB, known as the Reading First initiative, funded state-grant reading programs and mandated the use of scientifically research-based kindergarten through 3rd-grade reading curricula.

The Solidification of Neoliberalism Within Education Reform

NCLB "solidified neoliberalism as the dominant approach to policy making" (Hursh, 2007, p. 495). By requiring states and local K–12 school districts to set clear goals for students to attain in regard to academic content in reading, math, and science, the Bush administration avoided such costly solutions as teacher training or class-size reduction (Smith et al., 2004). Instead, NCLB created an "auditing" system (Power, 1997, p. 67) that designated students' test scores as the key indicator of quality. Moreover, persistent failure by schools and school personnel to meet unattainable achievement requirements (Linn, 2005) allowed for market-based solutions to be implemented, which "reflect[ed] the long-range plan for the federal government to replace public schools with private" entities (Hursh, 2005, p. 10).

Accountability Shovedown

Not only did NCLB solidify neoliberalism as the dominant approach to education reform, but the focus under NCLB on what students were learning and how they were being taught in order to improve AYP led to what Hatch (2002) termed "accountability shovedown" (p. 462)—the shoving down by administrators and others of content and performance expectations, as well as the didactic instructional practices of higher grades, into lower-grade classrooms, including kindergarten. While worries over academic shovedown have existed for generations (e.g., Katz, 1987), Hatch made clear that the vision of shovedown emanating from NCLB framed learning as a lock-step process where student outcomes demonstrate the effectiveness of teachers. Therefore, teaching practices that emphasize teaching to children's cognitive, emotional, social, and physical domains through a range of instructional strategies are being, or have been, eliminated from early elementary classrooms (e.g., Lynch, 2015). Rather, what has become prevalent is the learning environment in which teachers must meet "prescribed curricular mandates and uniform standards" that focus on teaching children discrete skills in literacy and mathematics to prepare them for achievement tests that await in the later grades (Minicozzi, 2016, p. 308).

ACCOUNTABILITY SHOVEDOWN MOVES INTO PREKINDERGARTEN CLASSROOMS

While the focus of this book is on kindergarten, it is important to point out that policymakers continued to push their reforms into programs serving younger and younger children (Brown & Gasko, 2012; Heimer & Ramminger, 2019). Examples of this include the Bush administration's Good Start, Grow Smart (GSGS) initiative (Office of the White House, 2002), which called for improved student performance and increased accountability in early childhood programs that targeted students ages 3–5. GSGS had three components: strengthening Head Start, collaborating with states to improve early childhood education, and providing information to teachers, caregivers, and parents to assist them in developing partnerships in early education.

Shortly after the implementation of NCLB and GSGS, states across the nation began to expand access to publicly supported prekindergarten programs (Friedman-Krauss et al., 2020; Sherfinski, 2019). The theory of action (Argyris & Schon, 1974) behind the expansion of pre-K is evidence showing that these programs "enhance children's capacity to learn, which might improve their later elementary school performance" (Burger, 2010, p. 160). As such, these programs were now to prepare children for kindergarten (Brown, 2011).

Lastly, the Obama administration's Race to the Top–Early Learning Challenge Grant (RTT-ELC) in 2013 continued to frame education reform through a neoliberal understanding of schooling that required states to attend to the issues of school readiness, academic performance, and accountability.

This grant required applicants to demonstrate that any federal dollars they received for early education offered children access to high-quality integrated early learning programs that used assessments to document improved student achievement, while holding these programs and personnel accountable (Brown & Barry, 2019).

READYING CHILDREN FOR KINDERGARTEN

As you can see, these reforms that sought to improve the academic performance of children as they transitioned from preschool to kindergarten and into elementary school, including the more recent Common Core initiative[5] and the passage of the Every Student Succeeds Act in 2015, which replaced NCLB, defined the public schooling process through an economic model in which students are taught a specific set of knowledge and skills that they must attain so that they can perform at a high level on a series of academic achievement tests. These tests grow in importance as students advance through school, by ultimately being tied to students attaining the credential of a high school diploma. As such, kindergarten becomes a key moment in children's academic careers, and the significance of this moment in children's schooling, in both the short and the long term, has been well documented by researchers. For example, children entering kindergarten at age 5 who are perceived to be lagging behind their peers in cognitive and social measures appear less likely to be successful in grade school, more likely to drop out of high school, and likely to earn less as adults (Dagli & Jones, 2013; Duncan et al., 2007; Halle et al., 2012). Additionally, once in kindergarten, how children perform on reading, math, and social–emotional assessments provides insight into their later school achievement and chances for success in adult life (Claessens et al., 2009; Quirk et al., 2017). Unfortunately, these gaps in children's academic and social achievement that first are noted in kindergarten tend to increase across their time in school (Alexander et al., 2001; Campbell et al., 2002).

THE ACHIEVEMENT GAP

To be clear, the idea of the achievement gap is controversial (Heimer & Ramminger, 2019; Nxumalo & Adair, 2019; Nxumalo & Brown, 2019), and it is not a part of the terminology I use in this book to examine the changed kindergarten. As Delpit (2012) noted, there is no achievement gap when children are born, and as Nxumalo (2019) and others (Valencia, 1997) have pointed out, the very idea of the achievement gap ignores the systemic sources of inequality and racism that persist throughout the United States. Nxumalo (2019), employing the work of Tuck (2009) and others

(Ladson-Billings, 2006a), contends that to move forward "we" must question "the material and discursive *effects* of recirculating deficit discourses," and in doing so, we need to bring "attention to different kinds of stories" (Nxumalo, 2019, p. 165, emphasis in original) that disrupt this taken-for-granted logic so that "radically different ways of relating as humans" can emerge (p. 175).

The difficulty in putting forward these new narratives is that policymakers and empirical researchers often employ the idea of "gaps" to justify education reform or the need for specific instructional interventions (Brown, 2008a; Heimer & Ramminger, 2019). For example, policymakers justified the implementation of high-stakes reforms under NCLB to close what they termed as the achievement gap between White middle-class children and those who were not White middle-class, or for whom English was not their first language (e.g., George H. W. Bush's statement about the soft bigotry of low expectations[6]).

Yet it has been almost 20 years since the implementation of NCLB, and this gap has barely improved. Furthermore, there is a growing body of literature showing that the policies designed to improve children's academic performance have led to early learning environments that do not reflect what is known about how children develop and learn (Alfieri et al., 2011). These policies also deny children and their families who are not White middle-class, or for whom English is not their first language, the same learning experiences as their White, English-speaking, and more affluent peers (Adair et al., 2018; Souto-Manning, 2018). Such learning experiences also have been shown to inflict long-term social (Cho, 2017), emotional (Goff et al., 2014), and academic (Tavassolie & Winsler, 2019) damage on many children (Brown, 2019). This is particularly disconcerting because not only has kindergarten changed, but so have the children entering kindergarten; they are increasingly diverse in their cultural and linguistic talents (National Center for Education Statistics [NCES], 2019).

The intersection of all these issues highlights why having children enter kindergarten ready to learn so that they can succeed in kindergarten and beyond has become a key issue for early childhood stakeholders across the United States and the globe (Brown, Barry, & Ku, 2021; Fletcher & Kim, 2016; Landers, 2013). Thus, I want to spend a moment examining the issue of school readiness.

THE CONSTRUCT OF SCHOOL READINESS

While school readiness has been a key policy issue since the Johnson administration's War on Poverty, what it means to be ready for school is a contentious and often confusing issue because, as Graue (2006) noted, "readiness is the answer to many different kinds of questions" (p. 47). For instance, when thinking about the skills and knowledge children need to possess to be considered ready for kindergarten, Kagan and colleagues (1995), through their work with the National Education Goals Panel in the 1990s, framed children's school readiness through five dimensions: (1) physical well-being and development, (2) social and emotional development, (3) approaches to learning, (4) language development, and (5) cognition and general development.

While Kagan et al.'s (1995) constructs define school readiness through the learning and development of the whole child, the developmental perspective still leaves out the importance of the sociocultural contexts in which children develop and learn. This omission is significant for multiple reasons. First, various cultures view the role of the child and the learning process differently (Brown & Lan, 2015a; Rogoff, 2003), which can affect how children view the world and approach new problems, and has a significant impact on their long-term memory, which shapes how they think about and interact with learning opportunities in the here and now. Second, the sociohistorical positioning of the learning experience in the here and now—such issues as gender, class, sexual orientation, or the physical location of the learning environment—plays a significant role in children's learning. Third, while developmental theory and psychology may seem to indicate that there is a natural course of development (Bloch, 1991; Burman, 1994), there is not. Finally, when thinking about the learning process, it is important to recognize that learning leads development; that is, learning is a social process in which children's sociocultural interactions with peers and adults—including their teachers—assist them in making sense of the world around them, hence leading to further development (Vygotsky, 1980).

Beyond these issues surrounding the dimensions of learning that define school readiness, there is also the issue of how education stakeholders make sense of school readiness (e.g., Brown & Lan, 2018). In much of my research (e.g., Brown, 2013), I draw from Samuel Meisels' (1999) four conceptions of readiness to make sense of this construct: the nativist, the empiricist, the social constructionist, and the interactionist. A nativist views school readiness as being "a within-the-child phenomenon," which means that children are ready to succeed in school based on their level of maturation (Meisels, 1999). An empiricist understanding of school readiness defines school readiness as "something that lies outside the child" (Meisels, 1999, p. 52). Thus, the school, or in this case, kindergarten, is to provide children with a specific set of learning experiences that will teach them the skills and knowledge needed to be ready for elementary school. A social constructionist frames readiness as a fluid construct that is defined by the social setting in which the child resides. As such, "the setting" determines what it means to be ready (Meisels, 1999, p. 49). For example, Graue (1993) demonstrated through studying three different U.S. communities that conceptions of school readiness and the purpose of kindergarten often are determined by the local actors, such as teachers and families, within each social context. Lastly, an interactionist frames readiness as a "bidirectional concept," meaning that readiness is co-constructed "from the child's contributions to schooling and the school's contribution to the child" (Meisels, 1999, p. 49). In my work (e.g., Brown, 2011), I employ three of those four conceptions: empiricist, social constructionist, and interactionist.

Many within the ECE community in the United States frame school readiness through an interactionist lens (e.g., NAEYC, 1995). However, policymakers and other researchers often adopt an empiricist conception of school readiness (Brown, 2008c; Brown, Barry, & Ku, 2021). They do so to both examine as well as direct how teachers (Bustamante & Hindman, 2019), programs (Douglass et al., 2017), or classrooms (Mashburn et al., 2008) ready children and their families for school. As such, the empiricist conception of school readiness dominates policymakers' focus on improving children's academic achievement through the use of standardized instructional policies and practices (Brown & Weber, 2016b).

THE IMPACT OF POLICY ON KINDERGARTEN TEACHERS' CURRICULAR DECISIONMAKING

As policymakers have prioritized readying children for kindergarten and elementary school through the use of standards, assessments, and accountability, a growing body of empirical studies have demonstrated that these reforms are dissuading kindergarten teachers from teaching to what often is referred to as the whole child through a range of instructional strategies (Brown & Weber, 2016a; Lynch, 2015). For example, Bassok and colleagues (2016) analyzed data from two kindergarten cohorts that participated in the Early Childhood Longitudinal Study (ECLS-K:1998 and ECLS-K:2011) and found a large increase from 1998 to 2010 in the time kindergarten teachers spent on academic skills instruction as well as "a concerning drop in time spent on art, music, science, and child-selected activities, as well as much more frequent use of standardized testing" (p. 15). Also, Alford et al. (2016) investigated a total of 91 prekindergarten, kindergarten, 1st-grade, and 2nd-grade classrooms across 21 elementary schools in a large south-central U.S. city and found that, regardless of grade level, teachers "consistently utilized whole class, didactic, teacher-centered instructional practices in their classrooms" (p. 629). Lastly, Christopher and Farran (2020) conducted day-long observations in 98 kindergarten classrooms in a large urban southeastern city and found that the instruction of kindergarten teachers was "almost exclusively focused on basic skills and right answers," and that teachers were three times more likely to make comments that disapproved of children's behavior than approved of it, which matters because the use of positive praise can be predictive of cognitive gains in children (p. 647).

Additionally, as part of the Obama administration's Race to the Top–Early Learning Challenge (RTT-ELC) and the Enhanced Assessment Grants (Weisenfeld et al., 2020) the Kindergarten Readiness Tests were established, which are standardized achievement tests designed to provide insight into the skills and knowledge children bring with them into kindergarten. Weisenfeld et al. (2020) noted that currently, 35 states and the District of Columbia implement some type of entry assessment; four states had an entry exam at one point and phased it out, and nine states do not implement such an assessment. Moreover, these exams were originally quite comprehensive and focused on children's physical, social, language, and cognitive development as well as their approaches to learning (see National Education Goals Panel, 1991), but they now assess primarily children's literacy skills (Weisenfeld et al., 2020).

Combined, the focus of these studies and policies on the academic achievement of individual children demonstrates that kindergartners are more likely to be learning about and tested on literacy and math skills (Brown & Barry, 2019). They are also less likely to be engaged in learning centers that encompass a variety of disciplines (e.g., art, music, science, etc.) and sensory experiences (e.g., sand and water tables) than they were before NCLB.

Essentially, policymakers' SBA policies create learning environments for children in which "learning becomes nothing more than a means to an end"; the inherent value of learning is lost, and children never get "the chance to experience the exhilaration of learning as an inherently valuable human activity" (Hatch, 2015, p. 115). Furthermore, policymakers' focus on standardization, academic achievement, and accountability privileges certain types of knowledge and silences others (Brown & Brown, 2010; Pérez & Saavedra, 2017), while suggesting "that a small group of students are educationally and economically vulnerable" and need "to be isolated and fixed" (Fine, 1988, p. 16).

In sum, policymakers' reforms are shaping kindergarten teachers' conceptions of their students and how to instruct them (Pérez & Cahill, 2016), particularly those students who may possess varying cultural, linguistic, and socioeconomic resources that go unnoticed by policymakers' reforms, through practices based on a "banking conception" of schooling (Freire, 1970/2006). That is, teachers are to simply fill their students with specific sets of knowledge and skills that the students can restate/reproduce on academic achievement tests (Lewis & Holloway, 2019). As I noted with my colleague (Brown & Lan, 2015b), the past 5 decades of SBA reform in the United States have fortified "a White, middle-class conception of school readiness" that has pushed out space within the kindergarten classroom, whether curriculum or instructional practices, that considers what Yosso (2005) termed the "cultural wealth" of children and their families. As a result, these reforms have "the potential to further disengage and/or disempower children and their families as they progress through school" (p. 10).

NOT JUST STANDARDS-BASED ACCOUNTABILITY REFORM

Beyond policymakers' SBA reforms, there are other drivers that are changing kindergarten. These include (Brown, Englehardt, Barry, & Ku, 2019a): empirical studies revealing substantial cognitive development in children (Fox et al., 2010); the expansion of publicly funded preschool (Friedman-Krauss et al., 2020); parents making significant investments in their children's learning prior to kindergarten entry (Kornrich & Furstenberg, 2013); and research documenting the immediate and long-term effects of high-quality preschool and kindergarten programs on children's academic and economic careers (Claessens et al., 2014; Heckman et al., 2010; Quirk et al., 2013). Combined, these factors are significant because they show not only how a range of factors are shaping the landscape of the Kinder-Race, but that kindergarten itself can't go back to what it once was.

Instead, to move forward, I believe that a new understanding of kindergarten needs to emerge that moves beyond the economic principles of standards, academic achievement, and accountability, and considers the larger political and sociocultural realities that children and their families are living in, as well as what is known about how best to support kindergartners as learners within a democratic schooling community. To begin to consider what such a vision might entail, it is important to first understand what the Kinder-Race "is" for children, their families, and kindergarten teachers on a daily basis, and how such a learning environment does and does not align with what is known about the best practices of teaching kindergartners, as well as how children develop and learn as sociocultural beings (Goodwin et al., 2008). I examine this in the next chapter.

CHAPTER 3

Experiencing the Kinder-Race

Depending on your age, the school you went to, and the state/country you lived in when you were about 5 years old, your response to the question, "What was kindergarten like for you?" will differ. For some, kindergarten was a half-day experience, others went just 2 or 3 days a week, and an increasing number attended full-day kindergarten.

What you learned and did with your teacher(s) and classmates also will vary—possibly lots of play, multiple recesses, nap time, snack(s), and singing. Notions of fun, nurturing, and socialization occur across most examples of what kindergarten was like. Yet, as children embark on their journey through elementary school, the Kinder-Race no longer reflects the traditional metaphor of a garden that is to nurture the whole child by cultivating children's social, emotional, physical, and cognitive development (Miller & Smith, 2011). Rather, children are taught more advanced academic content through "teacher-directed whole-class activities" and take more standardized tests (Bassok et al., 2016, p. 4).

What's interesting is that even though there is an increased focus on academic instruction through didactic (teacher-direct-to-child) instruction (e.g., Christopher & Farran, 2020), research has emerged that suggests that kindergartners are being taught many skills they already know (Cohen-Vogel et al., 2021; Engel et al., 2016), which demonstrates that the pressure of policymakers' SBA reforms have led to teachers focusing on *what* they are to teach rather than *whom* they are teaching. However, this focus on academics is worrisome because researchers also have found that limiting teachers' instructional practices to a specific set of learning experiences negatively impacts not only the teachers themselves (e.g., Penttinen et al., 2020) but also the students' conceptions of themselves as learners. This change in conceptions can decrease young children's motivation for school and limit their understanding of how to attend to or manage novel learning experiences (Bonawitz et al., 2011; Pakarinen et al., 2011).

THE SIGNIFICANCE OF THE KINDERGARTEN YEAR FOR STUDENT LEARNING

Concerns about how policymakers' SBA reforms are impacting the instructional practices of kindergarten teachers are important because the learning experiences children have upon entering and once in kindergarten matter (Brown, 2008c; Brown, Barry, Ku, & Englehardt, 2021). Researchers have shown consistently that where children begin their academic careers as kindergartners affects their short- and long-term success in and out of school (Lee & Burkham, 2002; Quirk et al., 2013). Furthermore, how children perform on reading, math, and social–emotional assessments in kindergarten also provides insight into their later school achievement and chances for success in adult life (Burchinal et al., 2020; Claessens et al., 2009). These two sets of findings show that many children who enter school not yet meeting their teachers' and/or policymakers' achievement expectations are seen as unprepared and are treated as such. This makes it extremely difficult for children to be seen as ready, which reinforces the misplaced belief that how old you are defines your academic and developmental abilities.

I am not saying that kindergartners who might be lagging behind their peers in academic skills cannot catch up to their classmates. Pan et al. (2019) found that children who might not yet have the cognitive/academic skills required of them when entering kindergarten were able to catch up to their higher-performing peers in reading and mathematics by 2nd grade if they possessed strong personal and social skills, which the authors defined as self-regulation, social and emotional development, and approaches to learning. However, if children also scored low in personal and social skills and cognitive skills, they were not able to catch up, which is troubling from an educational perspective.[1] This means that children have to perform in a particular way to be seen as ready for being taught academics. In making these statements, I by no means am condemning kindergarten teachers for their instruction. The reality is that most kindergarten teachers are responsible for educating 20 or more children without any assistance, so they probably are putting a lot of effort into ensuring that their classroom runs smoothly. Thus, their focus with some students simply may be on making sure they can engage in the routines of school, while those who already do so might be pushed further academically.

No matter what is happening in kindergarten classrooms, this research clearly demonstrates that kindergarten matters, and the fact that the skills children leave this program with appear to have short- and long-term consequences only reinforces the significance of kindergarten.

THE DAY-TO-DAY IN KINDERGARTEN

To document and study the day-to-day in kindergarten, I conducted a video-cued multivocal ethnographic (VCME) research study (Adair et al., 2018; Tobin et al., 2009).[2] This method of research required me to spend a significant amount of time in Ms. Cutler's kindergarten classroom in central Texas (all names and references to students, teachers, school personnel, and the school itself are pseudonyms). Ms. Cutler has taught kindergarten in the same school for more than 18 years. She had 22 kindergartners and no aide.

Throughout this chapter, I use Ms. Cutler's insight and guidance as well as statements from her students to help portray the image of the changed kindergarten. However, before outlining what a typical day "looks like" in literacy and mathematics, I outline how I framed this work conceptually. Then I detail Ms. Cutler's teaching environment, which is shaped by state, school district, and school policies, to help readers make sense of what is and is not occurring in this kindergarten classroom.

MAKING SENSE OF KINDERGARTEN

I framed my investigation into kindergarten through the conceptual framework of sensemaking (Brown & Weber, 2016a; Coburn, 2001; Erickson, 2014). Sensemaking is "generally understood to be the cognitive act of taking in information, framing it, and using it to determine actions and behaviors in a way that manages meaning for individuals" (Evans, 2007, p. 161). Sensemaking is a dynamic and interactive process (Weick, 1995). How we make sense of the world now "may influence [our] beliefs and how [we] understand the past" (Bertrand & Marsh, 2015, p. 865); for instance, how we make sense of kindergarten now influences how we understand our own experiences with kindergarten as 5-year-olds (Brown, Englehardt, Barry, & Ku, 2019a).

As we create these mental models about such things as kindergarten and are presented with new information, we often "assimilate the new knowledge into [our] existing frameworks of understanding," and this frequently requires us to "be persuaded to abandon [our] commitments in terms of [our] past experiences in order to move forward" (Schmidt & Datnow, 2005, p. 951). However, this does not mean that an argument will persuade you to change your mind. According to research, "we" are all more likely to change our beliefs (and/or practices) and sustain such transformations when we are working in a community that collectively supports us as we negotiate our new understandings and/or practices within our given context (Coburn, 2001). We are also more likely to reject change when it conflicts with our current beliefs (Coburn, 2004) or appears too difficult to do (Penuel et al., 2007). Lastly, how we make sense of such things as kindergarten may vary significantly among individuals (Brown & Weber, 2016a; Erickson, 2014) and/or from the intentions of the local, state, and national policymakers who sanctioned the reforms that led to the current cultural enactments of the Kinder-Race in the United States (Hall & McGinty, 1997).

CULTURALLY SUSTAINING PEDAGOGY

As I discuss how Ms. Cutler enacted and made sense of the Kinder-Race, I position my understanding of schooling in culturally sustaining pedagogy (CSP) (Ladson-Billings, 2014; Paris & Alim, 2014). Such pedagogy emerged out of Ladson-Billings's (1994) conception of culturally relevant teaching (CRT), which is a theory of instruction that puts forward the idea that teachers must foster the academic success, cultural competence, and sociopolitical consciousness of all their students (Ladson-Billings, 1994).

CRT

Briefly, fostering academic success requires teachers to no longer view teaching and learning as an act of transmitting knowledge but as one in which they work "with students so that they can reflect, theorize, and create knowledge" (Nieto, 2002, p. 7). To build children's cultural competence, teachers must help students "recognize and honor their own cultural beliefs and practices" and provide them with the knowledge and skills needed to access "the wider culture, where they are likely to have a chance of improving their socioeconomic status and making informed decisions about the lives they wish to lead" (Ladson-Billings, 2006b, p. 36). By doing this, teachers help students use cultural knowledge and experiences outside of their formal schooling to succeed academically.

Lastly, Ladson-Billings (2014) contended and others have documented (Morrison et al., 2008) that teachers have difficulty taking up the sociopolitical dimensions of CRT, which requires them to engage with children in ways that go beyond the mandated curriculum and "have a direct impact on their lives and communities" (Ladson-Billings, 2014, p. 78). Parson and Wall (2011) noted that understanding how the sociopolitical context creates inequities among different populations of students is an important first step for teachers and makes "the implementation of culturally relevant pedagogy . . . less daunting" (p. 22). To build children's sociopolitical consciousness necessitates that teachers interact with students as subjects (Brown & Weber, 2016a), rather than objects, and include them as active participants in the curriculum development process (Ladson-Billings, 2014). In this way, teachers view children's sociocultural backgrounds as "something to be enacted or expressed, something that is dynamic and agentic" within the curriculum of the classroom (Goodwin et al., 2008, p. 6).

CRT 2.0 = CSP[3]

Paris (2012) and others (e.g., Doucet & Adair, 2013) worry that the term CRT has been co-opted by many within the education system to justify goals and reforms that focus solely on improving children's academic achievement while ignoring the process of fostering children's cultural competence and developing their sociopolitical consciousness. Having this sociopolitical consciousness allows children to develop the skills and knowledge needed to work toward illuminating and eliminating the political and structural inequities (whether policy, access to capital, etc.) that have discriminated against non-White and low-income individuals for generations. Thus, all three components of CRT are essential, and when I discuss CSP and supporting children's cultural competence, I agree with Paris and his colleagues that this includes sustaining and supporting the cultural and linguistic multiplicities children bring into the classroom (Brown et al., 2018).

To engage in CSP requires educators to help their students be aware of not only how the process of schooling works, but also how success in that system aligns with, as well as possibly contradicts, their home, cultural, and linguistic experiences (Brown & Weber, 2016b). Children's culture plays an "active process [in their] meaning making" that they employ to make sense of their world (Street, 1993, p. 25), and this means that they live their lives through their culture. As such, their cultures influence such social-emotional traits as their persistence, attentiveness to work, conversations within their learning community, and self-regulation.

For teachers to employ CSP in their classrooms, they cannot expect all children to approach or demonstrate their learning the same way (Brown & Weber, 2016b), and they must respond to these cultural differences in a positive, humanizing manner and strive to establish warm and personal relationships with their students while still having high expectations (Paris & Alim, 2014). By humanizing, I mean building reciprocal relationships with students and families that are rooted in dignity and care (Brown et al., 2018). To do this successfully, kindergarten teachers, the students in their classrooms, and their families must share their interests, goals, thoughts about schooling, and other issues to foster humane interactions that seek to value and incorporate understanding and voice within the early childhood classroom (Paris, 2012). Such a vision of schooling is very different and much more complex than simply defining success as students attaining high scores on academic achievement tests. Yet the state, school district, and school policies that shape the kindergarten classroom examined in this chapter often ignore such complexity.

KINDERGARTEN IN TEXAS

Kindergarten in Texas, as in the majority of states in the nation,[4] is not compulsory (Kelley et al., 2020). Children in Texas do not have to be enrolled in school until age 6. While the state requires only half-day kindergarten to be offered, it fully funds districts that offer full-day kindergarten. The cutoff for entering kindergarten in Texas is age 5 by September 1 of the current academic year.

Governing Policies

Texas was the birthplace of the NCLB, which became federal law in 2001 under President George W. Bush (McNeil & Valenzuela, 2001). The policy was based on the education reforms that had been evolving in Texas since the 1980s under Ross Perot. If you're interested in that history, I would suggest reading the work of Cruse and Twing (2000), McNeil (2000), and Valenzuela (2005).

This history matters because state policymakers in Texas over the past 4 decades have implemented a range of high-stakes SBA reforms to which school personnel must adhere (Brown, Englehardt, Barry, & Ku, 2019a). For example, state-mandated assessments of students' academic achievement begin in pre-K, requiring assessment of pre-K through 1st-grade students' emergent literacy skills three times a year using a state-approved standardized assessment measure (Brown, 2013). Furthermore, school districts in Texas must assess their students' school readiness at the beginning of the school year. In the school district in which this study is located, school personnel use students' test scores to evaluate teacher and school administrator effectiveness. Furthermore, students who perform poorly across the school year on these assessments typically are provided with a range of literacy interventions to support their growth and development.

State Elementary and Secondary School Policies. State policymakers also implemented reforms that measure public school students' attainment of the mandated K–12 content standards, known as Texas Essential Knowledge and Skills[5] (TEKS), by requiring those in grades 3–11 to take a series of high-stakes exams, known as the State of Texas Assessments of Academic Readiness[6] (STAAR) exams. The high-stakes exams for students, which use their achievement scores to determine grade promotion or high school completion, begin in grade 5 and appear again in grades 8 and 11. In addition, district personnel use students' scores on the state tests to evaluate teacher and school administrator effectiveness, and poor student performance can lead to reassignment or loss of job (Brown & Weber, 2016b).

The stakes for schools and school districts occur under a statewide ranking system that determines whether the schools and districts attained an acceptable level of progress in improving students' academic achievement. If not, a series of mandated interventions and sanctions are triggered, which eventually can lead to schools being closed or reconstituted and district administrators replaced.

An Example of Increased Academic Expectations for Kindergarten in Texas. One way to document the changes that have occurred over the years in academic expectations for children in Texas kindergartens is to look at how the TEKS for kindergarten have evolved. The first set of TEKS was approved in 1997 and first implemented across the state during the 1998–99 school year. They were revised most recently in 2020.[7] Examining these two sets of policy documents reveals a range of examples of how the academic expectations for kindergartners have increased.

For instance, under the 1997 TEKS, by the end of kindergarten, students were expected to name and identify each letter of the alphabet, understand that written words comprise letters that represent sounds, and learn and apply letter–sound correspondences of sets of consonants and vowels in order to begin to read. Under the 2020 TEKS, kindergartners are expected to attain those same skills plus decode to VC, CVC, CCVC, and CVCC words (V = Vowel; C = Consonant); recognize that new words are created when letters are changed, added, or deleted; and identify and read at least 25 high-frequency words from a commonly used list (Texas Education Agency [TEA], 2020, p. 3). When discussing such changes to kindergarten, Ms. Cutler stated:

> Kindergarten has become more like 1st grade. It's really shifted down. The expectations are higher. The kids, sadly, do need to grow up a little faster. With academics, it's not so much play-based learning or exploration learning—that kindergarten is gone. It's, "Sit, focus, learn, get it done, and maybe, you can have time to play later" learning.

Ms. Cutler's statement provides insight into not only how kindergarten has changed as a result of policymakers' SBA reforms but also the ways in which the "contextual constraints" generated by these policies have "affect[ed] the ways in which" she is making sense of her own instruction (Castro, 2010, p. 101). Still, it's not just state policymakers' demands for increased academic achievement that have led to these changes; it is also a result of policies and procedures put in place by district and school administrators (Brown & Weber, 2016a).

District Requirements for Teaching Kindergarten

School districts throughout the state of Texas have responded to federal and state policymakers' reforms by implementing a series of district policies and procedures (Brown, 2015). For example, Ms. Cutler and her pre-K through grade 12 colleagues were expected to follow the district's learning progression documents and pacing guides. These documents provide teachers with daily, weekly, and monthly guidelines for instruction that link instructional materials, including the district's grade-level curriculum, with particular state-mandated pre-K–12 content standards in each of the core subject areas. Furthermore, district administrators required pre-K–12 teachers to use a standardized report card to document students' academic performance and personal development four times throughout the year. District administrators put these measures in place to ensure that every teacher across the district is teaching all students the same content and skills through a similar set of practices for an appropriate amount of time to ready them for the state's high-stakes tests beginning in grade 3.

These changes have occurred since the implementation of NCLB and other SBA reforms (Brown, 2004). As Ms. Cutler noted, when she started teaching kindergarten in the late 1990s, "we didn't have any curriculum. We had nothing. We had no math curriculum, no language arts curriculum, no books, no word wall, no teacher table, no carpet, nothing." Such a statement reflects the shift that has occurred over the past 2 decades. She noted that over the years, "we got a math curriculum. Then the next year or two we got a language curriculum. We just got a science curriculum, and we still don't have a social studies curriculum."

While it might seem like standardizing such things as curricula or report cards at the district level would be beneficial for teachers and students, Ms. Cutler felt it cut up her day into a series of disjointed learning experiences. She noted:

> When I first started, everything was completely integrated. For example, if we decided to spend a week investigating apples, that meant everything we did was focused on learning about apples—literacy, math, science, writing, and so on. Now, everything is disconnected. We have a math block [of time] that does this, and a science block that does that. I miss having an integrated curriculum. An integrated curriculum works better for the kids. It flows. If you're talking about coins and then you immediately shift to leaves and then you immediately shift back to coins, where's the connection? They don't understand the flow and continuity of it all.

Ms. Cutler's concern about the lack of connection in the mandated curricula across content areas is not unique (Brown et al., 2020a; Drake & Savage, 2016), but it demonstrates some of the unintended consequences of standardization and high academic achievement on measures of discrete academic skills and knowledge (Brown, Englehardt, Barry, & Ku., 2019b).

School Requirements

The year prior to conducting my study, Ms. Cutler's school implemented Pearson's AIMSweb academic achievement monitoring system. Each teacher assesses their students every 6 weeks, or six times a year, in literacy and mathematics. AIMSweb is used to ensure that students are on track to attain grade-level expectations; if not, intervention services are provided. As Ms. Cutler noted, "Everything we do is based off of that data." Classroom and students' scores are posted in a room used for professional development and teacher meetings so that everyone can see how the school, teachers, and students are performing in reading and math. Moreover, this focus on data and the "datafication" of teaching (Roberts-Holmes, 2015, p. 313) disciplines teachers and "limits the terms of engagement" they have with their students within their own classrooms and the larger schooling context (Lipman, 2013, p. 569), which in turn restricts the space in which teachers may be able to engage in CSP.

The School That Houses Ms. Cutler's Kindergarten

Ms. Cutler's kindergarten classroom is in a school that is identified by the U.S. federal government as a Title I school—a school in which at least 40% of the children in the attendance area of the school or at least 40% of students enrolled in the school come from low-income families. The most common measure of low-income status is the percentage of children who are eligible to participate in the federal government's free and reduced-price lunch program. Being identified as a Title I school entitles the school to additional federal funding to be used to improve the academic achievement of children from the low-income households.

The kindergarten population at the school level (comprising eight kindergarten classrooms) was 77% low SES, 22% English language learners (ELLs), 18% African American, 60% Hispanic, and 22% White.[8] The student population of the classroom in which I conducted my study was 77% low SES, 18% African American, 60% Hispanic, and 22% White. For some perspective on the demographic makeup of this classroom in relation to the state at the time of the study, of all children in Texas in kindergarten, 60.4% were economically disadvantaged, 17.1% were ELLs, 12.4% were African American, 3.6% were Asian, 51.3% were Hispanic, and 30% were White.

WHAT DO KINDERGARTNERS "DO" ON A DAILY BASIS?

What occurred in Ms. Cutler's kindergarten reflected much of what Bassok et al. (2016) found in their analysis of the Early Childhood Longitudinal Study (ECLS-K:1998 and ECLS-K:2011) data (see Figure 3.1 on pp. 38–39 for the weekly academic goals and daily schedule, both of which were posted in the classroom). The students were spending a significant amount of time in whole-group, teacher-led instruction. Such instructional strategies as play, center time, and art-based activities were replaced with academic learning experiences. Below is an outline of a typical day in this kindergarten classroom.[9]

This schedule outlines an enormous amount of work for Ms. Cutler and her students. When talking about this, Ms. Cutler stated:

> The purpose of kindergarten is getting them ready for 1st grade, obviously, which means the students need to know their letters, sounds, and numbers. All the basic skills outlined in the TEKS for reading, writing, following directions, following the basic rules, learning how to get along, and social skills.

Much of what Ms. Cutler defines as school readiness is a specific set of academic skills and knowledge as well as a particular set of socially acceptable behaviors (Brown & Lan, 2015b). Absent from this statement is the belief that she should assist children in "learning beyond the confines of the classroom" so that they can use "school knowledge and skills to identify, analyze, and solve real-world problems" (Ladson-Billings, 2014, p. 75).

WHAT HAPPENS IN LITERACY AND MATHEMATICS DURING A TYPICAL DAY?

Instruction in Ms. Cutler's classroom begins as soon as the morning announcements end and will continue until the children leave at 2:35 P.M. Below is a glimpse into their morning activities, which focus on literacy and mathematics instruction. Instruction in these two academic areas begins with the daily calendar activity and ends when they go to their specials, which for this day is library.

8:05–8:10: Morning Meeting/Calendar

After morning announcements, Ms. Cutler has the students leave their tables and gather on the carpet in assigned spots for morning meeting and calendar. The meeting is teacher-centered. It entails Ms. Cutler going over the daily schedule as well as giving the children a heads-up about any special or different events planned for the day.

Then, Ms. Cutler first has the students count the days in the month on the calendar to figure out what date it is. The markers she uses to identify each day of the month are cutouts of particular items typically found in that month among White, middle-class families, and these markers typically follow a pattern. For instance, in September, Ms. Cutler employs yellow and orange leaves to mark each day. The leaves follow a typical A-B pattern: yellow, orange, yellow, orange. As the year progresses, the patterns among the monthly images become more complex: AA-BB, A-B-C, and so on.

Next, Ms. Cutler slides her finger up from today's date to the top of the calendar to figure out what day of the week it is. To help the students, Ms.

Figure 3.1. Weekly Academic Goals and Daily Schedule in the Video

Academic Goals for the Second Week of March

Phonics

- We will read she, all, and—etc.
- I will read she, all, and—etc.

Reading

- We will identify different ways the author groups information using text and graphic features.
- I will show by myself where the author used a text or graphic feature to show that something is important.

Writing

- We will share the sequence of steps to plant a seed.
- I will write the sequence to plant a seed.

Math

- We will identify coins.
- I will name coins and their attributes.

Schedule as It Unfolds Over the Day

7:35–8:05	**Arrival, breakfast, and Pledges** (in Texas, there is also a state pledge[10]
8:05–8:10	**Morning meeting/Calendar**
8:10–8:30	**Phonics, sight words, and phonological awareness**
8:30–8:35	**Poetry**
8:35–8:45	**Morning Message**
8:45–9:00	**Small-Group Word Work: blue table**: Consonant-Vowel-Consonant (CVC) bingo sheet; **red table**: Lakeshore sentence writing (noun, verb, object); **orange table:** Word Family Ladder Sheet; **green table**: Raz Kids on iPads; **Ms. Cutler table**: CVC dice-write word.
9:00–9:45	**Shared Reading and Journal Writing at Tables**
9:30–9:50	**Read to Self and Buddy Reading**
10:00–10:15	**Snack and Bathroom Break** (tables of children are sent to a restroom down the hall from the classroom)
10:15–10:45	**Whole-Group Math**: counting (days in school, backwards from 20), dot cards, number identification, number comparison, missing number, dimes
10:45–11:00	**Math Stations**: **blue table**: roll dice, Cat in the Hat counting hats activity; **red table**: Pop Addition/Subtraction game; **orange table:** Shape Pictures: sphere, cylinders, cones, and cubes; **green table**: iPads; **Ms. Cutler table**: graph coins.
11:05–11:50	**Library**: Lesson on Plants and Seeds[11]
11:55–12:25	**Lunch**

Figure 3.1. Weekly Academic Goals and Daily Schedule in the Video *(continued)*

12:25–12:35	**Restroom Break** (whole class)
12:40–1:15	**Science Lab**: Lesson on Plants and Seeds
1:15–1:35	**Writing**: write in Science Journal
1:45–2:00	**Outdoor Recess**
2:05–2:20	**Centers**: free choice, finish unfinished work with Ms. Cutler
2:20–2:35	**Review and put papers and folders in backpacks**
2:35–2:45	**Dismissal**

Note: I've used a version of this figure across several of my peer-reviewed publications, such as Brown, Englehardt, Barry, & Ku (2019a).

Cutler, on a daily basis throughout the year, leads them in the days-of-the-week song, which mimics the *Addams Family* song:

> Days of the week—clap, clap,
> Days of the week, clap, clap,
> Days of the week,
> Days of the week,
> Days of the week, clap, clap.
>
> There's Sunday and there's Monday,
> There's Tuesday and there's Wednesday,
> There's Thursday and there's Friday,
> And then there's Saturday.
>
> Days of the week—clap, clap,
> Days of the week, clap, clap,
> Days of the week,
> Days of the week,
> Days of the week, clap, clap.

As the year progresses and the students learn the song, Ms. Cutler stops on whatever day it is, and the students sing, "Today is Wednesday, today is Wednesday . . . " After the song, she has them identify the month through another song, and finally they say the date together. For example, "Today is Wednesday, March 14." Ms. Cutler then asks, "If today is the 14th, what number comes before 14, '13,' and what number comes after 14, '15.'"

8:10–8:30: Phonics, Sight Words, and Phonological Awareness

Ms. Cutler then transitions to phonics instruction. This involves engaging the students in such activities as beginning sound identification, which progresses from single letters, such as, "What is the first sound of bat?" [the class responds with the "b" sound]; into diagraphs, "What's the first part of chest?" "Ch"; and blends, "What is the first sound of shed?" "Sh."

Next, they engage in an activity that asks them to blend sounds and/or syllables into words. For example, what is "c" "a" "t" or "th" "i" "ck," including made-up words, "wh" "o" "p." From there, she moves into an onset-rime activity (the onset is the initial phonological unit of a word and the rime is the string of letters that follow). To do this, Ms. Cutler will state, "What is "thick" without the "th"? The students respond, "ick," and Ms. Cutler continues, "shock" without the "sh," and they reply, "ock."

Ms. Cutler transitions into sight word identification. Sight words are words that are difficult to decode and do not follow typical rules for spelling. If they know sight words, students will not get tripped up by these words as they read a text or write in a literacy activity. Every morning, Ms. Cutler and the students recite about 30 sight words; the words themselves change over the course of the year, progressing from simple (e.g., I, me) to more complex (e.g., behind, like). During this activity, Ms. Cutler holds up a white laminated 3 x 5 card that has the sight word on the bottom half and a picture related to that sight word on the top half. Once Ms. Cutler holds up the card, the children say the word, spell it, and then engage in a bodily movement accompanied by a short phrase that the teacher created to help remind the children what the word is. For example, she shows a card with the word *good*, they spell it, "g-o-o-d," and then say the word, "good," and then say the phrase, "good job" (Ms. Cutler pats her own shoulder as they say "good job"). Then they spell it again, "g-o-o-d" and add "spells good." They do this for anywhere from eight to 15 words.

When I asked Ms. Cutler about this activity, she told me:

> The TEKS says we only have to teach 25 sight words in kindergarten.[12] But if the kids only know 25 words, they're not going to read Level 3 on their DRA assessment,[13] so all of the kindergarten teachers have upped the number of words to about 50 so that the children know what they need to know to read on a DRA Level 6, which is what the district expects. Those are the words that the Harcourt [reading curriculum] says we teach this week, but we've moved some of the words to be earlier in the year so that the children know the words they need to know for the DRA tests.

Therefore, Ms. Cutler created the scenario I described above to help the children with this activity. She did so because

> Most kids are visual and hands-on, kinesthetic learners. Some make connections through music. One year, I had a student who still didn't know his colors by February, so every morning, I had him jump on the

> carpet and name the color of each square he was jumping on and that helped him. It provided him with an anchor. Originally, we were just showing the students the cards and asking, "What's this word? What's that word?" Until I figured out, "We have anchors for the letters and sounds but we don't have anchors for the words." I tried that with a couple of my classes over the years, and it seemed to really help them. I'll also ask the students to help create the cards. That's another thing. If I get them to give me ideas, participate, take ownership of it, then they remember it better. Like, we were doing the word, "do." I was like, "What kind of thing or picture goes with the word 'Do'?" and a student 2 years ago came up with, "Do you like green eggs and ham?"

Ladson-Billings (2014) noted that "the secret" behind engaging in CSP is "the ability to link principles of learning with deep understanding of (and appreciation for) culture" (p. 77). In the statement above, Ms. Cutler is beginning to make connections between her students' sociocultural learning processes and her teaching, but her focus seems to be on producing outcomes rather than making deep cultural connections.

Still, sight word recognition, as outlined above, is not only a skill that the state kindergarten content standards mandate teachers teach and students learn. It is also a skill that is measured under the school-based assessment system that is used to determine whether kindergartners are on a trajectory to succeed on the high-stakes exam in 3rd grade (Brown, Englehardt, Barry, & Ku, 2019b). When discussing this and other instructional practices she employs in her classroom, Ms. Cutler stated:

> Everything I am expected to do as a teacher focuses back on the data, and my administrators want to see progression. Are we meeting the goals? Do we have 85% mastery of the expectations?

So much of what is covered in the morning routines is Ms. Cutler helping the students gain the knowledge and skills they need to attain so that they can meet the expected levels of academic proficiency. Her statement demonstrates how policymakers' reforms "have led to standardized teaching practices which ignore and silence the rich cultural and linguistic practices of these children and their communities" (Cheruvu, 2019, pp. 103–104).

When I asked the students in Ms. Cutler's class about these sight word and/or reading assessments, Javier noted, "It was easy." Luis added, "Yeah, we had to read, and when we were done answering questions, we got to go play on the computer." When asked what type of questions they were asked on the test, Javier stated, "We read a book and then tell the teacher what happened." Drakar added, "Yeah, then we left the room, and went to the computers to see who has done it, then that next person goes and does the test with the teacher." When asked what they thought about the test, Mariana said, "It was easy," and Luke chimed in, "Yeah, it was super easy." They then were asked why they had to take the test, and Camila stated, "So that the teacher can see we're ready to go to the 1st grade." Angela agreed with Camila, stating, "Yeah, you have to show our teacher we know what we need to know for 1st grade." Across these statements, it appears that the test was a part of how they made sense of kindergarten. By taking the test, they were demonstrating to their teacher that they not only knew what they were being tested on but also were ready to move on to 1st grade (Brown & Barry, 2021). Their sensemaking of this process appears to demonstrate how they view testing as "a prerequisite to later learning," which in many ways challenges traditional conceptions of "what" kindergarten should teach young children (Graue, 2009, p. 12).

After working on sight words, Ms. Cutler then goes to the class ELMO document camera to project a worksheet on a large screen in the front of the classroom that has a random list of lowercase and uppercase letters divided into rows that a student volunteer points to. As the student does this, the class is to recite the letter. The volunteer starts the activity by saying, "Ready, set, go," and starts to point at each letter across the first row and the class states, "j, S, c, i, T," and so on.

Next, at the ELMO, another student volunteer helps the class work on letter–sound recognition by creating the sound each letter makes. After saying, "Ready, set, go," the student points to the first row of letters, which includes the lower- and uppercase letters "w, b, T, r, M," and the children on the carpet state the sound for each letter.

Then another student volunteer takes over and the class works on what is termed fluency words at the top of the worksheet. In March, the students are reading the words "down," "have," and "where." They are in a 4 x 4 grid on the worksheet, as shown in Figure 3.2:

Figure 3.2. Fluency Worksheet

Down	Have	Where	Down
Where	Down	Have	Have
Where	Down	Have	Where
Have	Where	Down	Down

After this worksheet, they do another that has the following four words: "have," "help," "down," and "where." When they are finished with these two sets of words, Ms. Cutler asks the class, "Next time you see these words, are you going to have to sound them out?" And then she sounds out "h-e-l-p" and adds, "To figure it out?" Most of the class replies, "No." She then asks, "Will you have to skip them?" Again, most of the class replies, "No." She then repeats, "No, because you already know it. You don't have to sound it or skip it because you already know it. You'll simply read it as 'help' and move on."

Ms. Cutler then calls another volunteer to the ELMO. For this activity, the class is expected to pronounce a series of C-V-C words that the volunteer will point to. In March, these are the words the kindergartners are sounding out:

pov	fad	vin	hum	jeb
zud	sez	mog	kot	sid
naj	hok	buz	pek	kim
zod	lub	sed	vab	six

When I asked Ms. Cutler about all the "reading" activities she and the students were working on every day during the phonics, sight words, and phonological awareness time, she noted:

> We work on these words every day because of what they're expected to read. For their reading assessments, they can't sound out all the words because not all words can be sounded out. We do those activities every morning so that they become more fluent with their writing, more fluent with their reading so they can pass the next level on the assessment. I will say I've noticed since we've started doing this that the kids are reading at a much higher level. When I first started teaching kindergarten, I don't think the kids would have read past a DRA Level 2. Now, I'd say a majority of the kids are at a DRA Level 4 or higher.

Ms. Cutler's statement illuminates a tension that exists within the Kinder-Race. Because she is teaching the children in a very direct and repetitive manner the skills that will be on the test, it appears that the students are gaining the literacy skills needed to score higher on the DRA. Therefore, higher scores feed into the belief that these repetitive, teacher-directed activities "work." Yet, such logic runs counter to the work of researchers, such as Lerkkanen and her colleagues (2012, 2016); they found that in kindergarten and 1st-grade classrooms in which the teachers placed greater emphasis on child-centered teaching, the children not only were more interested in reading and mathematics but also improved their academic achievement in these content areas at a greater rate than children in teacher-directed classrooms. Furthermore, researchers have shown consistently how instructional approaches that consider the developmental needs of children, while teaching them the academic content they need in order to succeed in elementary school, improve the academic achievement of all kindergartners (Pyle & DeLuca, 2017; Weisberg et al., 2013).

8:30–8:35: Poetry

After completing these phonics and phonological awareness activities, the class stays on the carpet in front of the chalkboard and transitions into a group read-aloud of a poem that Ms. Cutler has now displayed on the ELMO. At the top righthand corner of the worksheet, she shows the class the word they are focusing in on—that word is "she," and "she" is circled. Ms. Cutler points to the word, says it, and then begins to read the poem to the class. She expects the students to read with her. The poem is called "My Bird," and there are underlined blank spaces throughout the poem where students are to fill in the word "she" as they read it. When Ms. Cutler comes to a blank, she fills in the word on the worksheet. Here is the poem:

> This is my bird
> And ____ lives in a nest.
> And _____ thinks her home is
> The very best.
> When ___ is hungry
> And ___ needs to eat
> _____ looks for some worms

8:35–8:45: Morning Message

After this shared poetry activity, Ms. Cutler tells the class she has a riddle for them, and proceeds to write it on the board. As she writes, she asks the students to help her spell the words and asks for predictions as she finishes each line. The riddle begins like this:

> I go high. I go low.
> You sit on me.

Before providing the class with the last line, which has the answer for the riddle, she asks the students for their thoughts. The students provide a range of ideas, such as a swing, a roller coaster, and a Ferris wheel, and then Ms. Cutler writes the final line: I start with "sw." As she does so, several students guess it: "swing."

8:45–9:00: Small-Group Word Work

Ms. Cutler then asks the center helpers to get out the materials for the literacy centers, which are at the class tables or at a kidney-shaped table where Ms. Cutler sits and works with students. Across the week, each child will have a chance to work at each center. Ms. Cutler sends specific children to one of the five centers.

At one center, the children read stories on iPads from a series called Raz-Kids.[14] At another, they write out sentences in their reading-center journals from a game where they pull a subject, verb, and object. At a third center, they are given a bingo card that has a 3 x 3 frame with consonants and vowels in it. They are to make CVC words as if they are playing bingo—up, down, or across. They write the words in their reading-center journals. At the fourth center, they are provided with a sheet of paper that has a picture of three-letter short-o words with lines for the letters they are to write next to the picture. For instance, there is a picture of a mop with _ _ _ next to it, and the children are to sound out and spell "m-o-p." Lastly, a group of students work with Ms. Cutler playing a game where they roll three dice. Two are consonants, and one is a vowel. They sound out their dice to make a word, and then they write the words in their reading-center journals.

As centers come to an end, the students who were not working with Ms. Cutler come to the kidney-shaped table she is working at, and she checks their work. If they did not do their work or did not finish what was asked of them, they have to complete their work at center time, which is the activity they do at the end of the day. Since that is the only time during the day when students actively get to choose their play activity, it seems to be a highly motivating reason to complete their work in their literacy centers. After she checks the students' work, they take a seat on the carpet for a shared reading activity and then journal writing at their tables.

9:00–9:45: Shared Reading and Journal Writing at Tables

During the shared reading activity, Ms. Cutler typically focuses on a reading strategy she wants the students to know as she shares the text with them. Today, Ms. Cutler and the students are working on picture clues to help them decode words. Ms. Cutler reads the class a book titled *Oscar and the Frog: A Book About Growing* (Waring, 2008). The story is about a kitten named Oscar who learns about how animals and plants grow, and how each living thing grows at its own rate. Oscar also learns that some things come from seeds, some come from eggs, and others are born. Each living thing requires some type of nourishment. There is a page about how different animals lay eggs around the pond. In this scene, Oscar is talking to a frog, and as Ms. Cutler reads the sentence, "Dragonflies often lay their . . . ?" she directs the children to look at the picture and asks, "What is the dragonfly laying?" The students respond, "Eggs," and Ms. Cutler says, "Yes." As she does this, she points to the word "eggs" and completes the sentence.

Throughout her reading of the story, Ms. Cutler continues to show the students how to use picture clues in the text to help them read the book. When she finishes the book, she tells the students to get their yellow journals from their cubbies and write about something they learned in the story. She begins to call names and tells the students to grab their yellow journals and start writing.

Ms. Cutler has set a timer for 15 minutes to let the students know much time they have to complete their writing at their seats. Ms. Cutler circulates around the room and supports students as needed: reminding them about how to use capital letters at the beginning of a sentence, how to sound out words, and so on. A popular topic the students have decided to write about is the fact that a coconut can float, which was a part of the story. A majority of the students appear to write about this topic.

As the students complete their writing, Ms. Cutler comes to each student who has a hand up and the students read what they have written. As the students finish reading their sentences, Ms. Cutler sometimes has them edit or add a word. She then gives them a "Falcon Buck" (a green piece of paper similar to a dollar bill with the head of the school mascot in the middle with "1"s in the corner like a dollar bill). A Falcon Buck, in this case, is a reward for engaging in a positive behavior or completing work. Each Friday, a "Falcon Cart" comes to each classroom in the school, and the students can purchase different trinkets from the cart. The Falcon Cart has items like pencils, stickers, a cape that students can rent for the day, and so on. A student must have 10 Falcon Bucks to purchase something, and in some instances items cost more.

When I asked Ms. Cutler about the Falcon Bucks, what often is termed a positive behavior intervention support system (PBIS), she stated:

> Falcon Bucks started 3 years ago. Somebody from the state regional education service center came in and introduced us to this system. It's a schoolwide behavior management system—the bucks are to incentivize positive behavior. You know, "You're doing a good job reading today. Falcon Buck for you." "You were walking nicely in the hall. Falcon Buck for you." It's like stickers. Some kids work for stickers. The kids have responded well to it. They get excited. It's like money, and it actually helps them with math. Because they have to work for 10 bucks, they seem to understand subtraction more. So if I ask a student, "You have seven, how many more do you need?" It's almost automatic for them to say, "I need three more."

When I asked Ms. Cutler how they can earn Falcon Bucks, she said:

> They can earn them in a number of ways across the day. They might get a Falcon Buck for being quiet in the hall or for completing their work. They also receive Falcon Bucks for completing their jobs during the week. Jobs include cleaning the tables after breakfast or snack, watering the plants, handing out folders at the end of the day, cleaning up tables between centers, getting out materials for centers, being the

line leader, being in charge of turning off the lights when the class leaves the classroom, and so on.

On a wall in the classroom to the right of the morning carpet area, there is a chart posting all the classroom jobs. Each job has a pocket, and in it, is an index card with a student's name letting them know what job they have to do that week. There's also another chart, a "bank," that has individual pockets with a child's name on each one. This is where the children "save" their Falcon Bucks to spend at the Falcon Cart. As the week progresses, students see how many bucks they are accumulating in relation to their classmates.

This PBIS model extends the neoliberal "input–output system" framing of education as "an economic production function" (Olssen & Peters, 2005, p. 324), and it equates being a "responsible and moral individual" and/or student to being "an economic-rational actor" (Lemke, 2001, p. 201). Thus, much of what these students are learning about education in general and what it means to be a "good student" is no longer tied to such ideas as the intrinsic value of learning, or learning how to participate in the larger democratic society; instead, being a good learner is about earning the capital required to purchase and consume products that bring them individual joy (Ailwood, 2008).

9:30–9:50: Read to Self and Buddy Reading

Returning to the typical day, as the shared reading and journal-writing activity ends, Ms. Cutler tells the students to grab their book boxes and find a seat to read quietly by themselves. The books in their boxes are ones Ms. Cutler has selected based on the student's reading level. The books are color coded so the students know which books they should be reading. For instance, when talking with Andre, he told me, "The red books let you know that you are ready for 1st grade." While students are to be focused on their own reading, they know what level each of their classmates is on. Also, the students' poetry folders are in their book boxes, so as they complete poems, like "My Bird," they can read those during this time.

As the students read quietly, they are all over the room, some at the tables, others on the carpet, and still others against the wall (all spots are selected on a first-come basis). Ms. Cutler has two students currently performing below grade-level expectations; they go to Ms. Cutler's table and read out loud to her. As they do this, she helps scaffold their decoding of words in the text. Most of the books are pattern books. For example, the book might go, "I can be a doctor. I can be a teacher. I can be a clown," and so on, and the last page might have a phrase like, "I can be anything I want to be."

After 10 minutes of students reading to themselves, Ms. Cutler says, "Ding, ding, ding (as if her voice were a bell). Go with your partner to buddy read." She assigns these buddies based on their reading levels. Each student is to take a turn reading a book softly to a partner, switching back and forth until time is up. Because a student is absent this day, one of the students comes to read with Ms. Cutler at her table.

When I talked with the students about learning to read, Celeste noted that she did not like reading because "it's hard." When asked to explain what she meant, Angela interjected, "It just is," and Celeste nodded her head in agreement. Still, for many of their classmates, reading is enjoyable. Gretchen stated, "I like reading," and Andre added, "I like reading too." Mariana stated, "I like reading because you get smart." Claudia added, "We learn to read words so that when we are looking at words on a paper, and if that's the same word that we learned, we know we can say it. That makes us smarter." When asked why they need to learn to read to get smarter, Ruby commented, "So that we can go on to 1st grade." Across these statements, it's apparent the students have learned the importance of learning to read in kindergarten and view it as a skill they need to possess to be able to go on to 1st grade (Brown & Barry, 2021).

As the students are reading to each other, Ms. Cutler states, "Remember, boys and girls, you are looking for picture clues to help you read your book. Share with your partner where you used a picture clue to help you read your book." After about 10 minutes, Ms. Cutler again says, "Ding, ding, ding, come to the carpet with your book boxes," and the students do so.

As the students come to the carpet, Ms. Cutler wants to have some students share their work as well as provide some insight into what she witnessed during the reading activities to help the students think about their decoding process. She begins by having an eager student, Gretchen, come up and share her story about a little boy with a loose tooth; Gretchen also has a loose tooth. As Ms. Cutler asks her to come up, she asks Gretchen, "You found picture clues in there?" Gretchen nods her head, and Ms. Cutler says, "Well alright, come on up."

Once Gretchen comes to the front, she shows different examples of picture clues. She talks about how she used the picture clues to help her read the sentence, "The boy wiggles his tooth." Ms. Cutler then asks, "Do you like this book because of what you told me this morning?" Gretchen turns her head to the side, smiles, and nods yes. Ms. Cutler says, "You told me you have a loose tooth, right? Is that why you like this book?" and Gretchen continues to nod.

After having another student come up and share, Ms. Cutler says, "Before we go to snack, I have something I want to share. I want to share Celeste's work she did in her writing journal after we did *Oscar and the Frog*, and I said write about something you learned. A lot of you wrote about one fact, like, you said, 'A coconut can float.' Celeste extended her writing. She wrote, "Tadpoles come from eggs. Frogs come from tadpoles."

So she just didn't say, 'Tadpoles come from eggs' or 'Frogs come from tadpoles.' She said two different things and made her story even longer. So she earned a Falcon Buck for that." Ms. Cutler then transitions the students to a 15-minute snack and bathroom break.

10:15–10:45: Whole-Group Math

After snack, the students transition back to the carpet to work on mathematics. They begin each day counting how many days they've been in school with Ms. Cutler using a 100s chart—a chart that has 10 rows, and the first row starts with 1 and goes to 10, then 11 to 20, and so on. Once the class surpasses 100, they sometimes start with 100 and count from there. It depends on the mood of the students and of Ms. Cutler. For example, one day I witnessed them count from 1 to 131, and as they did this, Ms. Cutler added a little incentive to motivate the students by stating, "Let's see who's going to do it because, you know, that's what they do in 1st grade."

After counting to 100 by 1s, they count by 10s, and to help them with this, they sing a little song.

> I can count by 10s
> Up to 100
> I can count by 10s
> Ready here we go.

Next, they count backward from 20 to 0. Ms. Cutler asks the students to use their fingers to help with the process. They start with having all 10 fingers/thumbs up and count backward—20, 19, 18, and so on. At 10, they again put up their fingers and thumbs.

From there, they transition into "DOT cards," an activity that teaches children the skill of conceptual subitizing (Clements, 1999). In this activity, Ms. Cutler shows the students an index card that is divided into two parts like a domino with dots in each part. The students are given only a few seconds to identify the number of dots. Conceptual subitizing helps children develop their ability to recognize patterns as well as estimation. For example, seeing a domino with four dots on one side and two on the other helps them see how these two sets of dots are combined to make six. Moreover, it helps children begin to recognize how to compose (two 10s and one 1 make 21) and decompose (breaking 21 into two 10s and one 1) a number, which also helps children develop their ideas about addition and subtraction (Clements, 1999).

Ms. Cutler starts the activity by asking, "Are you going to count the dots?" Most students reply, "No," but a few say, "Yes." Ms. Cutler replies, "No, what are you going to do? You're going to look for . . . ?" Several students say, "The number," and Ms. Cutler replies, "The big group."

The first card she shows has three dots on one side and six on the other. Ms. Cutler shows it quickly, and then hides it while putting her finger to her mouth in a hushing gesture so that the students will be quiet. Some students state out loud, "six" and another, "three."

Ms. Cutler calls on Celeste, who states, "Ummm, seven." Ms. Cutler repeats her answer and then calls on Lucinda, and she says, "nine." Ms. Cutler repeats, "nine," and asks, "What big number did you see, Lucinda?" She says, "There was six and three." Ms. Cutler says, "There were six in the big group," and then shows the card. She then says, "There are six over here, and this is the bigger group. So I am going to go with the bigger group, six, and then counting the three other dots and pointing to them, 7, 8, 9."

While this activity does appear to support students' development in estimating and recognizing mathematical patterns, it also reflects the never-ending pressure to perform within the Kinder-Race. When I talked with Ms. Cutler about this, she noted, "There's more pressure to have the kids perform at a higher level, academically." I ask whether this pressure is just on her as a teacher or on the students as well, and she replies:

> It's on everyone because if the kids don't meet the goals, and the goals keep getting raised, then they get pulled out for extra this and extra that. Letters are sent home to parents, and so on. So yes, the kids are expected to do more and produce more. They see the pressure. They feel the pressure, "Oh, I got that wrong, everybody else knows it but me." I'm sure they feel it and see it. The kids know, "Well that person knows it . . . that one doesn't." No matter how much you try to hide it, they're going to pick up on it, which is sad.
>
> What bothers me the most is that the district is just looking at the performance data. So by looking at just the end result, they're not seeing the process of learning that's happening. Many of my students started way, way below grade-level expectations, but they've made progress. Yet, they're still behind. Still, I want to celebrate that because not everybody is going to be on the same level. They're human beings.
>
> Still, I understand that they're looking at just the end result because that's the STAAR test; you get just one result. You don't get to look at if you've made progress, if kids have made progress in an area. That's not going to show up on the STAAR results because it's only one test.

Throughout Ms. Cutler's statement, it's apparent that she and her students feel the pressure to perform so that the students do well on the STAAR exam. Because of this, many of the activities they have done and will continue to do are designed to teach the children what they need to know to score well on the STAAR, as well as every other assessment they will take from kindergarten through 3rd grade. While others have documented how teachers like Ms. Cutler have acquiesced to policymakers' demands in their teaching (Brown, 2015; Smagorinsky et al., 2002), her statement also demonstrates how these reforms do not take into "consideration" the "historical, social, or cultural factors that adversely impact people of color in America," which further delimits the space for teachers to engage in CSP (Wynter-Hoyte et al., 2019, p. 430). Rather than seeing the children as "human beings," Ms. Cutler acknowledges she has to frame them as "human becomings" (Qvortrup, 2009) so that they pass the STAAR tests.

Continuing with their mathematics lesson, Ms. Cutler moves over to the ELMO document camera, which has a sheet asking students to identify a random set of numbers in rows. The sheet looks like this:

6	10	14	18	19	0	2	9	4	17	12
12	5	3	6	8	12	14	1	7	18	10
4	9	11	15	6	11	2	16	20	19	3
16	15	4	20	3	12	1	7	0	9	6

Ms. Cutler then has one student point to each number across the row, while having one of the four rows of students seated on the carpet identify the numbers. As this activity begins, Ms. Cutler states, "I am looking for the row who does the best job." As each row takes its turn identifying the numbers, she compliments those students who are participating and stating the numbers correctly by saying, "Good job."

The students then do another activity where two numbers are side by side, and the students in a particular row have to state which number has the greater value. The sheet looks like this:

10	5	6	9	3	0	9	5	0	6
0	3	9	6	5	10	2	4	8	10
7	7	10	4	8	7	0	6	2	5
3	3	6	8	9	5	2	7	9	6

From there, the students do an activity on the ELMO called missing number. The sheet looks like this:

__	4	5	0	__	2	4	5	__
__	2	3	5	__	7	__	6	7
__	4	5	6	__	8	__	1	2
6	7	__	8	__	10	5	6	__

Again, Ms. Cutler has a student come up to the ELMO and point while a row of students states the missing number. To help the students with this activity, she gently holds the volunteer's hand and counts with them as they point. For example, with __ 4 5, she counts backwards, "5, 4," and everyone in the row says, "3." With 0 __ 2, she states, "0 blank 2," and everyone in the row says, "1." From there, the students in each row do it on their own.

After these practice activities, Ms. Cutler moves into the new math content for the day, which is a discussion about dimes. The lesson begins with Ms. Cutler reading to the whole class a book about dimes. Two of the facts provided in the book include, "Dimes are made of copper and nickel," and "Franklin D. Roosevelt is on the front of the dime. Think of rose when you see a dime, and that will help you remember Roosevelt is on the front."

After summarizing some of the key points about dimes—they are worth 10 cents and Roosevelt is on the front—Ms. Cutler returns to the ELMO and places a penny, nickel, and dime on it. She then reviews which presidents are on each of them. She puts an initial under each coin on the ELMO so that the students see each coin with either the letter L, J, or R below it. Luciana says softly, "Little Jessie Rocks," and Ms. Cutler replies, "That's great, Luciana." She then repeats it to the class and writes it under L, J, and R, and says, "If you can remember Little, Jessie, Rock, that will help you remember, Lincoln, Jefferson, and Roosevelt."

Ms. Cutler then moves from the ELMO to a tripod stand on the opposite side of the carpet that has a piece of chart paper on it. Ms. Cutler uses this chart paper to write down facts the students remember about each of the coins the class is studying. The class has already investigated a penny and a nickel. For example, under penny, which is the top left square, are the following facts: Abraham Lincoln, Lincoln Memorial, 1 cent, made of copper and zinc, and brown. For nickel, which is in the top right corner, are the following facts: Thomas Jefferson, 5 cents, gray, made of nickel and copper. Today, Ms. Cutler and the students list facts for the dime, which is in the bottom left corner, and in the coming days, they will move to the quarter. The facts the class lists about the dime include: torch on the back, Roosevelt, oak branch means strength, olive branch means peace, and 10 cents.

10:45–11:00: Math Stations

As they finish the chart, the students transition into math centers. Ms. Cutler has the student helpers get out the materials for the math stations, and then she calls on students sitting in their spots quietly to go to their assigned centers.

At one center, the students take turns rolling two dice, and then everyone places a cube on the number, on a worksheet with little hats that have random numbers inside them, that the two dice add up to. The sheet looks something like this:

7	11	9
10	8	3
4	12	9
9	2	11

At another center, the students do an activity called the Pop Addition/Subtraction game, where they pull out circular cards that look like bubble gum balls that have addition and subtraction equations without the answers. The students are to copy the problem in their math notebooks and write down the answer. For example, they might pull a piece of gum with 8 – 3 = written in it. At yet another center, students are to use a specific set of shapes—spheres, cylinders, cones, and cubes—to draw any picture they want. At the fourth center, students do a matching game on an iPad that has two columns. In one column is a series of numbers (e.g., 7, 5, 10, 8, 9, 11) and in the other column is a series of bead bracelets that have a specific number of beads in each one. The students are to draw a line from the number to the bracelet with that number of beads. Finally, some students are working with Ms. Cutler on graphing coins. They are given a pile of plastic pennies, nickels, and dimes by Ms. Cutler, and then they are to create a 3-column graph based on the type of coin. Once they are done, Ms. Cutler asks them questions about how many pennies, nickels, or dimes they have in each column.

As math centers come to an end and students move to the carpet to prepare to go to the library, Ms. Cutler has the students who were not working with her show her their work. For example, Ms. Cutler asks Mariana, who was at the shape-drawing center, "What shapes did you use to draw your snowman?" Mariana replies, "Spheres," and Ms. Cutler says, "Good. What shapes did you use to draw this part of the gas pump?" Mariana replies, "Cylinders," and again Ms. Cutler says, "Nice work." Students who did little to no work at the math centers, similar to the reading centers, work with Ms. Cutler during center time at the end of the day.

As the students come to the carpet, Ms. Cutler reminds them that they will be going to the library next, and she needs the line leader, door holder, and caboose (who's in charge of turning out the lights and closing the door) to line up. As they prepare to leave, Ms. Cutler has the students recite a chant that follows the tune of "Are You Sleeping Brother John":

Bubbles and Falcon tails,
Bubbles and Falcon tails,
Who has them?
Who has them?
Everybody has them,
Everybody has them,
Let's go now.
Let's go now.

The children leave for the library with a bubble in their mouth, which is to keep them quiet, and their hands behind their back, which is to keep them from touching others. On each side of the hallway, there is a line of red tiles that they are to follow to the end of the hallway, which has a stop sign. The way the students move throughout the building is very similar to a traffic pattern.

SUMMING UP A DAY IN THE KINDER-RACE

In this chapter, I provided a glimpse into the disjointed academic activities this kindergarten teacher and her students engage in each day. When I shared the video with Ms. Cutler, which included the entire school day (see Figure 3.1), to verify that it captured a typical day in her classroom, she noted, "That's a lot. I was getting tired watching it at first because that's a lot of activity, but I guess that's what we do. We do that much each day—wow." I went on to ask her why they "do that much," and she commented:

> To get them ready for 1st grade and beyond. My job is to get them prepared for what public school is—for kindergarten, that's reading and writing. Every teacher wants them knowing all the TEKS for their grade level because each grade builds on the next, and the focus of all grades in on the STAAR.

For Ms. Cutler, and almost every other teacher I've talked with in Texas for this study (e.g., Brown et al., 2020a) and many other investigations (Brown, 2009a, 2015; Brown, Bay-Borelli, & Scott, 2015), the conversation on what is occurring in the classroom eventually becomes connected with the state's high-stakes exam. Preparing her kindergartners for the 3rd-grade tests, as this chapter has demonstrated, has led Ms. Cutler to implement what she terms a "disconnected" curriculum that requires the children to "sit, focus, learn, [and] get it done" so that they can perform at high levels on the range of assessments she must give them throughout the school year.

Ms. Cutler's sensemaking of kindergarten is "based on how [she] notice[s] or select[s] information from the environment, make[s] meaning of that information, and then act[s] on her interpretations" of the Kinder-Race (Coburn, 2001, p. 147). While her interpretation of her context centered on a very limited conception of practice, which appeared to be defined by policymakers' high-stakes SBA reforms, including district and school policies, it did not appear that she made any effort to sustain or even engage children's cultural practices. Researchers such as Ukpokodu (2011) find such inaction troubling because of how long these issues have been at the forefront of conversations surrounding teaching; however, it also demonstrates the need for teachers to be either reminded of, or assisted in recognizing, the need to frame learning through children's sociocultural worlds (Morrison et al., 2008).

As Villegas and Lucas (2002) noted, engaging in CSP "is a lifelong process" (p. 110), and to begin to amend one's teaching requires educators, like Ms. Cutler, to engage with their students as subjects, rather than objects that must obtain particular achievement scores (Brown & Weber, 2016b). By doing so, teachers reposition their students as active participants within the curriculum development and implementation process in their classrooms (Ladson-Billings, 2014). Yet, across the school day, Ms. Cutler positioned her students within the "subjectivities of standardization, containment and obedience," and did not offer her students instructional practices that allowed them to engage in "complex, challenging learning" (Britt & Rudolph, 2013, p. 49).

My concern does not involve Ms. Cutler teaching children the academic skills and knowledge they need in order to succeed in school. As Claessens et al. (2009) found, all children benefit from being taught advanced academic content in literacy, which they identified as "phonics instruction, reading aloud or silently, and working on reading comprehension," and math, which they identified as "addition and subtraction, place value, and ordinality," in kindergarten (p. 426). However, this content should be taught through activities that offer high-quality teacher–child interactions (Bustamante & Hindman, 2019), provide children opportunities to make selections of how and what they want to learn (Brown & Lan, 2013), and offer curricular experiences that represent the children's sociocultural worlds (Brown & Brown, 2010). Furthermore, learning should occur in classroom environments where teachers actively employ culturally sustaining practices that foster prosocial behaviors to engage as well as develop children's temperament (e.g., self-regulation) and motivation to learn within a classroom community, both of which are associated with children's academic achievement (Bryce et al., 2018).

Still, in making these suggestions, I recognize that asking/working with Ms. Cutler or any other teacher to engage in more child-centered and culturally sustaining practices does not guarantee change (Brown & Weber, 2016a). In fact, I worked with district personnel in a large urban school district impacted by policymakers' high-stakes SBA reforms to develop and implement a professional development program with pre-K and kindergarten teachers focused on creating learning opportunities that highlighted issues central to their students' sociocultural worlds in and outside the classroom (Brown & Weber, 2019). We found that these teachers possessed the "disposition" to engage in sociocultural practices in their classrooms that would support students' success in school (Edwards, 2011, p. 506). However, each had difficulty in conceptualizing and enacting CSP in their high-stakes teaching context. Thus, in the end, each teacher relinquished instructional opportunities with their students that explored issues central to the students' lives, and instead engaged in decontextualized content-based learning experiences as defined by district and state policies (Brown & Weber, 2016a; 2016b; Brown, Weber, & Yoon, 2016).

Thus, any lasting change in Ms. Cutler's or any other kindergarten teacher's practice is difficult to achieve (Brown & Englehardt, 2016). Moreover, the instructional activities Ms. Cutler engaged in with her students did not occur in a vacuum and required the support of colleagues, adminstrators, and policymakers for her to shift her practice (Brown & Weber, 2016b). In the next two chapters, I explore how the students, other teachers, families, school and district/county administrators, state administrators, state policymakers, and national stakeholders made sense of the Kinder-Race.

CHAPTER 4

Figuring the Kinder-Race Within the Worlds of Schooling

The Kinder-Race prioritizes children learning a prescribed set of academic skills and knowledge within a compressed period of time so they produce data on achievement tests to demonstrate their possession of the knowledge and skills to succeed in school and, potentially, life (Ball, 2003; Brown et al., 2020b). This datafication of teaching and learning has led to the kindergarten classroom that I outlined in the previous chapter (Roberts-Holmes, 2015): a learning space defined by standards, accountability, and academic achievement, which appears to have restricted how Ms. Cutler made sense of teaching her students a mandated set of competencies. Absent from much of her teaching were the sociocultural worlds of the children in her classroom. This is a theme, along with many others, I pick up on in this chapter to explore how the students in her classroom, kindergarten teachers across Texas and West Virginia, family members in these two states, and school administrators made sense of the Kinder-Race through Holland et al.'s conception of figured worlds. Holland et al. (1998) defined figured worlds as:

> Socially and culturally constructed realms of interpretation in which particular characters and actors are recognized, significance is assigned to certain acts, and particular outcomes are valued over others. Each is a simplified world populated by a set of agents . . . who engage in a limited range of meaningful acts or changes of state . . . as moved by a specific set of forces. (p. 52)

In examining the Kinder-Race, figured worlds are the vehicle by which the education stakeholders co-construct their understandings of kindergarten through their dialogic interactions (Bakhtin, 1981) with themselves and others (peers, colleagues, family, etc.) across the varied contexts in which they operate (classroom, school, home, etc.) in their ever-changing roles within those worlds (parent, teacher, sister, etc.).

This construct of figured worlds often is used to investigate how individuals make sense of themselves (Brown & Feger, 2010; Graue, 2005; Urrieta, 2007). As Holland et al. (1998) pointed out, "People tell others who they are, but even more important, they tell themselves and then they try to act as though they are who they say they are" (p. 3). However, my focus is *not* on how stakeholders figured themselves, but rather on how they figured kindergarten in relation to their role as student, family member, teacher, or school administrator in their given context, and what opportunities for change they believed existed or would want to see so that what was occurring in the Kinder-Race aligned with their conceptions of kindergarten.

Figured worlds provide a permeable but bounded space for the process of sensemaking of a complex "thing"—the Kinder-Race. So rather than simply think about how these stakeholders make sense of one construct, such as school readiness (Brown, Englehardt, Ku, & Barry, 2019), I zero in on how they are figuring the complex dialogic process of the most common "place" where children enter this nation's public schools—kindergarten (National Center for Education Statistics, 2019).

WHY TEXAS AND WEST VIRGINIA?

I studied how stakeholders in Texas and West Virginia figured the Kinder-Race because they differ in terms of region, population, and politics (Brown, Englehardt, Barry, & Ku., 2019a; Sherfinski, 2013). For instance, unlike Texas, West Virginia, at the time of this study, had just exited the Common Core,[1] a nationwide program in which, at its peak, 41 states adopted a common set of academic standards in mathematics and English language arts/literacy. Texas never participated in the Common Core. Furthermore, West Virginia spends about $4,000 more per student per year than Texas, which allows them to offer such educational support as assigning an aide to a kindergarten class if the class enrollment exceeds 10 students. In Texas, the mandated teacher-to-student ratio is one teacher to 22 students.

Additionally, legislators in West Virginia mandated that kindergartners have at least 30 minutes of recess each day, while no such mandate exists in Texas. Finally, in terms of assessment, Texas attached high stakes to its STAAR exams for students, teachers, and schools, which begin in 3rd grade, and West Virginia does not have such high-stakes consequences for its accountability system (see Table 4.1). Combined, these two states offer a nice contrast in how schooling is conceptualized in the United States. However, this by no means captures a "national" perspective. To access such a perspective, I sought national experts, advocates, and researchers to help fill this gap in my work, as I discuss in the next chapter.

THE FIGURED WORLD OF THE KINDERGARTEN CLASSROOM

In the figured world of the kindergarten classroom, the teacher and the students take on different roles, and their acts of engagement with one another carry distinct meanings (e.g., being engaged in a classroom discussion versus spacing out). The world of the kindergarten classroom is influenced by the worlds of a particular school, school district, and the region in which it operates (e.g., rural, suburban, Southeast, West Coast, etc.); the state's policymakers; federal policymakers; and so on (Brown & Feger, 2010).

Figured worlds also consist of the artifacts and the discourses that constitute those worlds. As Holland and her colleagues (1998) pointed out, "Figured worlds are evinced in practice through the artifacts employed by people and their performances" (p. 61). In terms of kindergarten, there are district artifacts, such as the use of the Developmental Reading Assessment (DRA) to assess student reading, the district math curriculum, and the state content standards, known in Texas as the TEKS. Even the documents from national organizations, such as the NAEYC's (Copple & Bredekamp, 2009) guidelines for DAP, mediate how instruction, assessment, child development, and so on are discussed, envisioned, and valued within a kindergarten teacher's classroom (Brown & Feger, 2010).

It is through their dialogic engagement with figured worlds that these stakeholders come to understand kindergarten and the meaning of artifacts, such as the sight word activities Ms. Cutler engaged in on a daily basis with her students. Accordingly, stakeholders' conceptions of the figured world of kindergarten are shaped by their experiences across multiple worlds; depending on how often they come in close contact with the world of kindergarten, their understanding of what is and should be happening in this education space will be impacted by those experiences.

HOW THE KINDERGARTNERS FIGURED THEIR OWN WORLD

In the previous chapter, I provided some insight into how the kindergartners made sense of Ms. Cutler's teaching. When these children were asked how they figured kindergarten in general, they described it, as Luke noted, as "a place where we come to learn so that we get smart," which for Javier meant learning such knowledge and skills as "reading, writing, math, technology, and stuff like that." Tommy responded to Javier by stating, "Don't forget spelling," and Luis added, "The ABCs too." For Luke, Javier, Tommy, and Luis, kindergarten is a world that teaches them the content they need to know to "get smart."

When I asked the children why they need to know in order to be "smart," Luciana stated, "We learn the stuff we need to learn because if we don't learn stuff then that means we don't know anything." Luis also noted, "Because that's what people do all day at school." Claudia commented, "You learn so you get smarter so you can go to 1st grade and then 2nd, 3rd, 5th, and you may go to 10th when you pass 9th and then college." While not all the students talked about getting ready for college,

Table 4.1. A Comparison Between Texas and West Virginia Public Schools

	Texas (Public schools organized at district level)	West Virginia (Public schools organized at county level)
Number of students	5,359,127[1]	273,170[2]
Number of districts[3]/ counties	1,232[4]	55
Per-pupil spending (2016)[5]	$8,485	$12,993
Student to teacher ratio	22 to 1, meaning almost no kindergarten classrooms in Texas have an aide	One aide assigned to a kindergarten class if the class enrollment exceeds 10 students
Sociocultural make-up of student population	12.6% African American 4.2% Asian 52.4% Hispanic 28.1% White 59% economically disadvantaged 18.9% English language learners	4.3% African American 0.7% Asian 1.6% Hispanic 90.4% White 80% economically disadvantaged 1.0% English language learners
Compulsory school age[6]	Age 6 by September 1 of current academic school year	Age 6 by July 1 of current academic school year[7]
Common Core State Standards Initiative (CCSSI)	Did not participate in CCSSI; employs own statewide standards known as Texas Essential Knowledge and Skills	Participant at time of this study; West Virginia formally withdrew from CCSSI in 2017, yet the current statewide College and Career Readiness Standards are modeled on the CCSSI blueprint
State accountability system	STAAR[8] measures students' comprehension of the TEKS. Students in grades 3–8 are tested in mathematics and reading, grades 4 and 7 in writing, grades 5 and 8 in science, and grade 8 in social studies. Grades 5 and 8 are promotion grades and students must pass the 10th-grade test to graduate from high school.[9]	At the time of this study, West Virginia administered the West Virginia General Summative Assessment, which included English language arts/literacy and mathematics in grades 3–11 and science in grades 5, 8, and 10.[10]

Table 4.1. A Comparison Between Texas and West Virginia Public Schools *(continued)*

	Texas (Public schools organized at district level)	West Virginia (Public schools organized at county level)
Kindergarten	Statewide full-day program	Statewide full-day program[11]
Prekindergarten	Half-day intervention program offered to 4-year-old children who qualify based on the following criteria: limited English proficiency, low income, having an active-duty military parent, homelessness, or in foster care	Universal access to part-time program for all 4-year-olds (by July 1), and 3-year-olds with IEPs
Recess	No mandate for recess	30 minutes of mandated recess each day

Notes: I've used a version of this table across several of my peer-reviewed publications, such as Brown, Englehardt, Barry, & Ku (2019b).

1. https://tea.texas.gov/sites/default/files/enroll_2016-17.pdf
2. https://wvde.state.wv.us/zoomwv/
3. West Virginia schools are organized by counties rather than districts.
4. From https://www.nationsreportcard.gov/data_tools.aspx
5. From https://nces.ed.gov/fastfacts/display.asp?id=66
6. From National Center for Education Statistics (https://nces.ed.gov/programs/statereform/tab5_1.asp)
7. West Virginia Policy 2510 (https://wvde.state.wv.us/policies/)
8. From Texas Education Agency (https://tea.texas.gov/WorkArea/DownloadAsset.aspx?id=51539620927)
9. From Texas Education Agency (http://tea.texas.gov/student.assessment/ssi/)
10. From West Virginia Department of Education (https://wvde.us/wp-content/uploads/2018/01/gensummassess_faqs.pdf)
11. From West Virginia Early Learning Readiness: Kindergarten Resource Guide (http://wvde.state.wv.us/oel/docs/workbook2.pdf)

each described kindergarten as a place that readies them for 1st grade, which reflects an empiricist understanding of this construct (Brown & Barry, 2021); "kindergarten" provides a specific set of learning experiences that will teach them the skills and knowledge needed to be ready for 1st grade (Meisels, 1999).

When I asked what they needed to know for 1st grade, the students discussed two primary sets of skills: engaging in good behavior and reading (Brown & Barry, 2021). For these students, being good meant listening to the teacher and showing that you are a good student. Angela stated, "In kindergarten, you have to listen to your teacher, and if your teacher says something like, 'Get your book or write,' you do it." Drakar noted, "You have to do good things. You follow the rules." So, they figured "good" to mean working, following the rules, and being nice to their teachers and classmates. As for reading, Claudia commented, "We read every day so we could get smarter." Ruby added, "We learn to read so that we can go on to 1st grade." Reading was an essential part of how these kindergartners figured how to get smart and be ready for 1st grade.

Much of these students' understanding of kindergarten reflects the Kinder-Race described in Chapter 2—more academics, testing, and so on. However, rather than frame the Kinder-Race negatively, these kindergartners still thought, as Willow noted, "Kindergarten is fun." Davis also stated, "It's fun to learn." Camila added, "I like kindergarten because I like my teacher," and Luke replied, "She makes it fun." Lucinda noted, "She's great because she teaches us, and she's funny because she dances funny." All the students I talked with figured kindergarten through the language of enjoyment, and this enjoyment was tied to their relationship with their teacher—who appeared to be more than simply an instructor who taught them content and behavioral skills. Rather, for these kindergartners, Ms. Cutler has created a figured world with them in which their "understandings" of themselves as students and the "capabilities" they possess "to direct their own behavior" in this world are framed through a positive light (Holland et al., 1998). As researchers, such as Christopher and Farran (2020) and Sonnenschein et al. (2010) have found, these students' interactions within the world of their classroom and their positive relationship with Ms. Cutler are pivotal to their success in school. By having a close relationship with Ms. Cutler, as well as seeing her interactions with them as preparing them for 1st grade, these students felt they were ready to move forward in their academic careers in school (Brown & Barry, 2021).

HOW KINDERGARTNERS WOULD LIKE TO REROUTE THE KINDER-RACE

While these kindergartners figured the world of kindergarten through the language of enjoyment due to their close connection to their teacher, Ms. Cutler, they still wanted to make it, as Luke pointed out, "funner" (Brown & Barry, 2021). Funner includes, as Gretchen stated, "More recess." Willow agreed, "Yeah, I want more recess because I like being outside and playing with my friends." Andre added, "Yeah, I like recess too, and then I like going to centers," which in the daily schedule (see Figure 3.1) occurs right after recess.

Andre said he wanted more centers because "we can play and we can do anything." Davis added, "I can play with so many different centers," and Willow stated, "Yeah, I would like more time to play with my friends in our class." Ruby added, "I would love more center time. We get to play games or play with toys." Claudia added, "Yes, we get to play with the Legos and can build what we want to build." Maria José noted, "And, we get to play with our friends. I love playing with my friends."

These students also would like to refigure kindergarten to include more opportunities to engage in physical education (PE). Angela noted, "I would like to have PE every day" (instead of 3 days a week). When asked why, she said, "Because I love PE." Luke added, "We just love PE because it's so fun. We get to play around with our friends. It's funner than everything." Celeste agreed, "Yeah, we love PE. We love the gym. We get to play so many fun games." While children, like the 1st-graders in Adair et al.'s (2018) study, "really like having the opportunity to move their bodies" (p. 24), these ideas for rerouting the Kinder-Race appear to demonstrate that students are figuring change in two ways.

First, their suggestions reflect their own "history-in-person" within this kindergarten classroom; their proposals for more recess, play, and PE employ their history in kindergarten as well as the "resources" they know are available to them to amend the Kinder-Race (Holland et al., 1998, p. 18). Still, their requests for change reflect a complex understanding of how they figure what kindergarten is and what they would like it to be. Their desire for more "play-based" opportunities is not a denial of academic instruction (Brown & Barry, 2021). Rather, their wishes align with empirical research that consistently has demonstrated that teachers who engage in instructional approaches that simultaneously attend to children's developmental needs, while teaching the academic content children are expected to know, improve kindergartners' academic achievement (Goble & Pianta, 2017; Pyle & DeLuca, 2017). Thus, it may be a matter not of what is taught to children per se, but rather of whether the types of instructional choices (Weisberg et al., 2013) and the interactions kindergartners have with teachers (Bustamante & Hindman, 2019) reflect the children's sociocultural worlds (Paris & Alim, 2017), while fostering positive emotions as well as prosocial/democratic learning behaviors in the students themselves (Bryce et al., 2018).

Second, embedded in these kindergartners' suggestions is a desire to have more "choice and voice" in their learning (Brown & Mowry, 2015, p. 55). Conceptually, Holland et al. (1998) call this *agency*, a term that has been a part of the lexicon of the sociology, anthropology, and economics of childhood for decades (Adair, 2014; Ballet et al., 2011; Gaskins et al., 1992; James et al., 1998; Mayall, 2002; Rogoff, 2003). Holland et al. (1998) employ the work of Inden (1990) to define agency as the ability to act upon one's world as well as to be employed by others to achieve specific goals. These children want to have opportunities to both act upon their learning and know that they are acted upon by their teacher and other school personnel to achieve specific goals.

Embedded in their desires for change is a reflection of the students' *grit*, which is a term developed by Dweck (2006) and extended upon by Duckworth (2016); this means that the students have a sustained interest in the longer-term goal of succeeding in school and getting smarter. Kundu (2020) argued that both agency and grit are "necessary components to every person's success" in and out of school (p. 38). For now, these students appear to possess both grit and limited agency within the figured world of kindergarten. However, the adults who are a part of the everyday worlds of kindergarten question whether policymakers' SBA reforms will support these children in sustaining these two components for their success in school and life (Kundu, 2020).

HOW THE ADULTS WITHIN THE WORLDS OF ELEMENTARY SCHOOL FIGURED THE KINDER-RACE

Unlike the children I talked with above, the figured conceptions of kindergarten held by adults represented a clearer tension "between past histories that have settled in them and the present discourses and images that attract them or somehow impinge upon them" (Holland et al., 1998, p. 4). Even though these histories were different for each adult, there was much consensus among all the stakeholders across Texas and West Virginia as they figured what kindergarten currently is and what they would like it to be (Brown, Barry, Ku, & Englehardt, 2021). Variations did appear among stakeholders in how they related to kindergarten. For example, family members discussed different aspects of kindergarten than kindergarten teachers.

However, a distinctive difference did emerge between the county administrators in West Virginia and all other stakeholder groups (Brown, Englehardt, Barry, & Ku., 2019a). This was because in 2014, policymakers in West Virginia implemented reforms that framed pre-K and kindergarten as "readiness grades" (e.g., West Virginia Board of Education, 2014). This will be discussed in more depth in Chapter 5, but for now, these changes had not materialized in the kindergarten classrooms I visited or into the lexicon of the school stakeholders I talked with for this study. Thus, these policy changes are not part of the discussion in this chapter.

To examine how the adults who operate daily in the figured world of kindergarten made sense of the Kinder-Race, I start with the family members who had kindergartners in two school districts in Texas (Texas School District 1 [TXSD1] and Texas School District 2 [TXSD2]) and two counties in West Virginia (West Virginia County 1 [WVC1] and West Virginia County 2 [WVC2]). Then I discuss this same process of figuring by teachers in those districts and counties, as well teachers in the school in which I made the video, and end with the principals at all five schools (see Table 4.2 for a summary of the districts and counties).

Table 4.2. Demographics for Each Individual School

School	Type of School Community	Total Students in School	White	African American	Hispanic	Asian	Other	Free/ Reduced Lunch	English Language Learner
Video School	Rural/ Suburban	380	23%	12%	64%	1%	0%	73%	20%
TXSD1	Suburban	418	27%	22%	41%	8%	2%	46%	9%
TXSD2	Urban	571	71%	1%	12%	13%	3%	1%	4%
WVC1	Suburban	410	73%	16%	1%	0%	0%	58%	0%
WVC2	Rural	519	97%	0%	2%	0%	1%	100%	0%

HOW FAMILY MEMBERS FIGURED KINDERGARTEN

All the adults in this study had some type of experience with kindergarten in the past. They carried what Holland et al. (1998) termed the "sediment" of past experiences (p. 18); the kindergartners had no such experiences. Even so, the family members I talked with, all of whom were the biological parents of a child enrolled in kindergarten, saw this grade level as a program that prepared children for success in and out of school, which is similar to the statements made by Ms. Cutler and her students. For example, Ms. Knight, a parent of a kindergartner in TXSD1 (see Figure 4.1 for a list of the family members who participated in this study), stated:

> Kindergarten teaches children the social structure of school, the rules and habits. It also teaches them how to build social relationships, learning how to resolve conflicts, which I think is a skill they take all through their lives.

Mr. Pratt in WVC1 also noted, "Kindergarten is the building block for academic learning in school. It provides their foundation." While these adults had different histories with kindergarten than the students I talked with, both of these statements position the world of kindergarten as a place that offers children a particular set of foundational social and academic learning experiences.

Academic Expectations Are Too High

While all the family members figured kindergarten as a foundational experience for their children's academic and social learning, they were worried that the current world of kindergarten was prioritizing academic learning over social–emotional (SEL) development. For example, Ms. Royal in TXSD1 stated, "Kindergarten teaches them reading, but for me, personally, I hope that it teaches children certain social skills, such as being able to learn cooperatively, being patient, empathy because empathy is a very hard thing to teach." Ms. Knight, in the same focus group as Ms. Royal, added, "The most important things children learn in kindergarten are social. It's not reading. That will come with time and practice." Ms. Carter in WVC1 commented, "I wish there was less of an emphasis on academic work in kindergarten and more emphasis on social skills and fine and gross motor development." Similarly, Ms. Dixon in TXSD2 noted, "Kindergarten is the basis for the rest of school. I wish the expectations for academics weren't quite so high, but in general, I think getting everyone ready to start 1st grade is a good thing." Across these statements, families recognized the significance of the kindergarten year in preparing children for the rest of their academic careers (Brown, Barry, & Ku, 2021). Still, they demonstrated a

Figure 4.1. The Family Members

Texas Families

Texas School District 1

Family Member	Mother/ Father	Number of Children	Grade Level of Children
Ms. Royal	Mother	1	Kindergarten (K)
Ms. Knight	Mother	4	2 in K (one is a stepchild), 4th, 8th grade

Texas School District 2

Family Member	Mother/ Father	Number of Children	Grade Level of Children
Ms. Walsh	Mother	3	3-year-old, K, 2nd grade
Ms. Boland	Mother	3	K, 2nd, 3rd grade
Ms. Dixon	Mother	2	K, 3rd grade
Ms. Clements	Mother	4	K, 3rd, 5th, 6th grade

West Virginia Families

West Virginia School District 1

Family Member	Mother/ Father	Number of Children	Grade Level of Children
Ms. Johnson	Mother	2	2-year-old, K
Ms. Carter	Mother	2	K, 3rd grade
Mr. Pratt	Father	1	K

West Virginia School District 2

Family Member	Mother/ Father	Number of Children	Grade Level of Children
Ms. Beetz	Mother	6	From K to age 40
Ms. Hildebrand	Mother	2	3-year-old, K

Note: All family members participated in focus groups.

concern over the emphasis in kindergarten on teaching children academics and, alternatively, they wanted their children to learn what often are termed the "soft skills." Such concerns are important because researchers have demonstrated that teachers who foster children's prosocial behaviors and develop children's temperament positively toward learning also improve children's academic performance (VanSchyndel et al., 2017).

Much of these families' emphasis on providing children with SEL opportunities seemed to be a reaction to the "high" academics they saw their children experiencing. For example, Ms. Clements in TXSD2 commented about this increased emphasis on academics: "Kindergarten is definitely the new 1st grade, maybe even 2nd grade." When asked to elaborate on this framing of kindergarten as the new 1st grade, Ms. Johnson in WVC1 commented, "Kindergartners now have a bigger curriculum to cover. And there's that pressure to perform." Ms. Carter in that same focus group added, "There's pressure in all grades that leads up to the test. My son is in 3rd grade now, and this is the first year of testing. It's really, really a lot of pressure." These family members recognized how the pressure of the test grades has shoved down academic performance expectations into the early grades (Bassok et al., 2016).

Kindergarten Should Not Be 1st Grade

Even though family members recognized this accountability shovedown (Hatch, 2002), which Ms. Cutler also described in the previous chapter, they did not want kindergarten to be the new 1st grade. Ms. Royal in TXSD1 stated, "It shouldn't be 1st grade . . . we don't focus on spreading out the stuff throughout kids' careers." Ms. Carter in WVC1 noted, "Kindergarten is very fast-paced. They move too quickly in all grades, and it's hard on them. It's very hard on them. When you have children that it takes them longer to catch on, they move on without them." Ms. Boland in TXSD2 pointed out, "I want the expectations for kindergarten to be a little less rigorous in general. They're 5-year-olds." Ms. Dixon in that same focus group added, "Where's the joy in the classroom? . . . Something has to give when the standards keep increasing and getting more intense." Ms. Hildebrand in WVC2 commented:

> That's a lot of pressure. I can feel it through the teachers too, and I can tell they are feeling that pressure. The teachers are trying to get all these standards in—you have to teach this, this, and this by the end of the school year because they're tested on it. And it's been difficult on all of us. There's more standards. There's more testing, and there's just more things. They're just racing—racing to the finish line.

Ms. Beetz, who was in the same focus group, added to Ms. Hildebrand's concern about everyone in kindergarten racing to the finish line by stating, "Kindergarten is sometimes too much on the kids. It's nonstop. They do their ABCs, they learn how to tell time, they are writing more, spelling words, and I think it's too much." Ms. Boland in TXSD2 similarly said:

> They expect more out of kindergartners. You need to be reading at the end of kindergarten, and for some kids, it just doesn't click yet. We've also put so much pressure on kindergarten teachers. The kids have to

> be halfway through 1st grade by the end of kindergarten because, as things get further along, you have to keep up—boom, boom, boom, and you've got to keep moving.

Ms. Dixon in TXSD2 worried that if children could not keep up with the "boom, boom, boom, . . . it negatively affects the children because they're going to inevitably feel like they're not meeting the standard somehow—and this starts a negative cycle, which is much more detrimental than whether they could read on grade level." In 2003, Wesley and Buysse, who investigated North Carolinian stakeholders' beliefs about and expectations for children to be ready for school, found similar concerns; a parent in their study stated, "All this pressure that we're going through everywhere is applying to kindergartners now. . . . It's totally ridiculous" (p. 359).

The Negative Impact of "Racing to the Finish Line"

This focus on increased academic achievement, the pressure to perform, and the negative cycle of failure that can emerge if children do not keep up led many of these family members to question the negative impact the Kinder-Race had on their children. Ms. Walsh in TXSD2 commented:

> It's not developmentally or emotionally appropriate to ask children to perform at the level that we are asking them to perform at. Can they do it? Yes. Can they perform higher than we are asking them to? Yes. Is it psychologically hard? Yes.

Ms. Knight, in TXSD1, felt this inappropriateness was going to lead to kindergartners "hit[ting] a point where they don't like learning because they think learning is humiliation and frustration and discouragement and anger rather than curiosity and encouragement and fun and discovery."

Both preceding statements demonstrate how these family members were focused not on the academic abilities of their children, but rather on the lasting impact this academic and accountability shovedown might have on kindergartners (Hatch, 2002).

Ms. Hildebrand in WVC2 provided a statement that summarized these parents' concerns over the detrimental effects high academic expectations might have on children and the parents' struggle to reconcile this tension between high academic achievement expectations for children and the detrimental effects of the Kinder-Race. She commented:

> The school system has such high expectations, which it should have, but it's not set up to help those kids who don't grasp it. There's all these things teachers have to teach, and the children are tested on it at the end of the year. It's a struggle. It's very difficult to teach all those

> kids at the same time, and sometimes kids fall behind. If they don't get it when they're taught it, it's hard for them to keep up, and the teachers don't have that breathing room to go back to help these kids who didn't get it. The system is harsh. Teachers don't have time to go back over it in 1st grade. If students aren't reading when they get there, they're behind. In 2nd grade, you're reading more, and nobody goes back and helps you.

Ms. Hildebrand's naming of the education system as "harsh" symbolizes a recognition of how the current neoliberal figuring of public education has made children appear to be disposable commodities within the market of reform (e.g., Reyes, 2016)—either they attain the required "outputs" or fall to the wayside (Ball, 2007, p. 28). This idea will be considered further in Chapters 5 and 6, but for now, Ms. Hildebrand ultimately is questioning this system of education and what it does to children. Such interrogation symbolizes the abundant concern held by these family members over the current figuring of the world of kindergarten. Such resistance presents an opportunity for change, and when discussing a refiguring of the Kinder-Race, they offered numerous suggestions.

HOW FAMILIES HOPED TO REROUTE THE KINDER-RACE

As Urrietta (2007) noted, the conflicts that are reflected in these family members' figuring of kindergarten offer a powerful learning tool for considering how the Kinder-Race might be rerouted. Similar to the kindergartners and Ms. Cutler, these families wanted to make curricular and instructional changes, which others have documented (e.g., Wesley & Buysse, 2003). However, rather than focus on their desires for children to have such things as more play or recess, which many family members recommended, I focus on how they wanted kindergarten to be a world that assists their children in figuring themselves as competent learners who have the ability to succeed in school and the larger democratic society.

For example, Ms. Boland in TXSD2 stated, "Kindergarten is the start of their school career, so you want them to want to enjoy school. You want it to reinforce their confidence in their ability so they realize they can learn and to go back and learn more." Ms. Boland's statement reflects what Dweck (2006) termed a growth mindset or what Johnston (2004, 2012) framed as a dynamic framing of learning; that is, children's ability to learn is not fixed (e.g., you are either smart or not), but instead children are always learning and should see themselves as learners who are constantly growing in their skills and knowledge. Ms. Walsh in TXSD2 keenly summarized this desire for kindergarten to be a place that helps children grow as people and learners, by stating that it should be a place "where children develop a love of learning and a love for school" so that they see it as "a fun place, it's a safe place, you respect your teachers, you respect your friends." This also would require kindergarten to be refigured in such a way that children are accepted for who they are when they walk in the kindergarten door, which reflects an interactionist conception rather than the empiricist conception of school readiness that these families felt the current kindergarten represented (Meisels, 1999).

Additionally, family members, such as Ms. Carter in WVC1, stated, "There needs to be a balance in instructional opportunities where children take the lead and adults are supporting them, and other experiences where teachers take the lead, but children aren't passive. You should never have passivity on either end." In examining these two "as-if" figured conceptions of what kindergarten should be, Holland et al. (1998) noted that "human agency" can be "frail, especially among those with little power" (p. 5). Moreover, such agency is fraught with tension, not only due to power relations (e.g., Adair et al., 2018), but also as a result of the intermingling of their past histories with the present realities of kindergarten for them, their children, and the schools they interact with on a daily basis (Holland et al., 1998). For these families, it appears that these interactions between their past histories and the current landscape of the Kinder-Race led them to want their children to have, as Ms. Knight in TXSD1 pointed out, a range of learning opportunities throughout the day that offers them choice and voice so they can inject the curriculum with their interests and come to know themselves and their classmates (Brown, 2005a; Graue, 2011).

Moreover, these families wanted what it means to be successful in kindergarten to broaden beyond the standards and assessment measures that appear to dominate the landscape of the Kinder-Race. For example, Ms. Dixon in TXSD2 said:

> I wish there were more opportunities for kids to excel in different ways—just be who you are and explore all kind of aspects of that instead of, "Can you repeat something back to me?" Don't rush it. It's this lost time. If you're not letting them play in kindergarten, that time is gone. They're going to learn to read eventually, but they're not going to get a time to go back and play.

Ms. Clements in TXSD2 added:

> The success of a kindergartner is defined by how much can they read and write at the end of the year. Social skills are no longer a focus, and that's a big problem. You can see it in a lot of classrooms where academics are so pushed. The kids are very book smart, but they don't have a whole lot of problem-solving skills on how to get along and cope, which are things that you really need for your entire life. I

> hope they develop a love of learning and a love for school. That's the one thing I want for my children more than anything else—you love school. It's a fun place, it's a safe place, you respect your teachers, you respect your friends.

These families seemed to figure their "as-if" conceptions of kindergarten as a world that nurtures children's growth mindsets toward themselves and toward others so that they love school (Holland et al., 1998, p. 49).

Such a vision of kindergarten fed into these family members' beliefs that kindergarten, as Mr. Pratt in WVC1 pointed out, is "a public service that is designed to better our children." Ms. Beetz in WVC2 added that kindergarten should be "an introduction to the real world and real people. We have children from different cultures, gay and lesbian families, divorced families, and kindergarten starts them out knowing that this is the real world and how to act in it." Ms. Royal in TXSD1 stated, "I want my kiddo to move on with certain social skills such as being able to learn cooperatively, being patient, being empathetic because empathy is a very hard thing to teach." Combined, these statements reflect how these family members figured kindergarten through their hope that it would foster their children's social–emotional skills as well as offer them the chance to develop the skills and knowledge required to thrive as members of a democratic society (Payne, 2018; Schmidt & Allsup, 2019).

Still, within these figurings of kindergarten as a world that fosters children's SEL, which is required to participate in a democratic society, there were many tensions for these families. They recognized that how they would like to refigure kindergarten might not align with the realities of the world they and their children live in. Ms. Hildebrand in WVC2 spoke directly to this point when she stated:

> It shouldn't go back to the way it was because then you're leaving a huge gap between who is and is not succeeding in school. I don't know how to change it because kids have to come out of kindergarten knowing all these things, but it's hard on them. Especially for the ones developmentally who are just not ready and haven't had those experiences yet. There's not a whole lot you can do about that. I really don't know what the answer is. You want them to be little because they spend their whole life in school, but then you want them to do well and be successful. It's really complex.

Ms. Hildebrand's statement reveals the complexity with which these families struggle in figuring the Kinder-Race. As Holland et al. (1998) pointed out, "Figured worlds take shape within and grant shape to the coproduction of activities, discourses, performances, and artifacts" (p. 51).

For Ms. Hildebrand, the figured world of kindergarten cannot go back to what it once was because she wants to ensure that all children learn what they need in order to succeed in school. Yet, at the same time, she saw what she termed as "the race to the finish line" as denying children the opportunity to be children. In an earlier quote I shared, she labeled this racing through education as "harsh." These families know their children need to succeed but want the process of learning to be altered to help their children progress across their developmental domains, teach them how to become active members of the larger democratic society, and do so in a way in which they come to see themselves as successful learners. Yet, as Ms. Hildebrand pointed out, creating such a system seems "really complex."

HOW KINDERGARTEN TEACHERS FIGURED KINDERGARTEN

Before turning to how the kindergarten teachers figured the Kinder-Race, I want to point out that all 22 of them (see Figure 4.2 for a list of the kindergarten teachers), regardless of their state, district/county, or school, stated that the video I provided for them to watch of Ms. Cutler's kindergarten truthfully reflected what kindergarten is today (Brown et al., 2020a). Examples of this come from Ms. Lyle, a kindergarten teacher in WVC1, who commented, "It's pretty typical, honestly, of what we do," and Ms. New, in TXSD1, who also declared, "It's very similar to what we do here."

Figure 4.2. The Kindergarten Teachers

Texas	West Virginia
Ms. Jefferson Video School (VS)	Ms. Lyle WVC1
Ms. Spade VS	Ms. Willis WVC1
Ms. Thomas VS	Ms. Fletcher WVC1
Ms. Gold VS	Ms. Pfeiffer WVC1
Ms. Ortiz VS	Ms. Fritz WVC2
Ms. Chan TXSD1	Ms. Stoddard WVC2
Ms. Temple TXSD1	Ms. Postles WVC2
Ms. New TXSD1	Ms. Binger WVC2
Mr. Lewis TXSD1	Ms. Enos WVC2
Ms. Johansson TXSD2	
Ms. Barnes TXSD2	
Ms. Patrick TXSD2	
Ms. Walsh TXSD2	

Note: All the teachers participated in focus groups.

An Empiricist Figuring of Kindergarten

Similar to Ms. Cutler, the students in her classroom, and their family members, the kindergarten teachers across Texas and West Virginia held an empiricist understanding of the Kinder-Race: It is a world in which they prepare children for academic success in school (Brown, Barry, & Ku, 2021). For example, Ms. Temple, a kindergarten teacher in TXSD1, noted that "kindergarten teaches them to read. They have to be readers!" Her colleague, Ms. Chan, added, "It's also about math. They have to have numeral automaticity." Ms. Lyle, a kindergarten teacher in WVC1, noted that they are expected to "learn to read between 80 and 100 words by the end of kindergarten." Ms. Walsh, a kindergarten teacher in TXSD2, stated, "I would like them to be at a certain reading level and be able to write a complete sentence," which reflects the Kindergarten English Language Arts and Reading TEK, (b) Knowledge and skills, 10, which states, "The student uses the writing process recursively to compose multiple texts that are legible and uses appropriate conventions" (TEA, 2020, p. 5).

The empiricist figuring of kindergarten, combined with such artifacts as the TEKS or the Houghton Mifflin reading curriculum that Ms. Lyle and her colleagues were expected to use, has created a world in which these teachers are told they can no longer engage in or have available the "landmark features of kindergarten" (Goldstein, 2007, p. 48), for example, blocks, dress-up clothes, a store, a kitchen setup, a doctor's office. Ms. Enos in WVC2 noted, "A woman from the state told us, 'Cute is dead.'" Ms. Fritz, her colleague, added, "They told us not to become event planners for your students, and that was the exact wording used." Ms. Stoddard continued, "We've taken the fun out of it. We've taken the joy away." Ms. Fritz replied, "Isn't that what kindergarten should be? We should be having fun. Learning should be fun." Similarly, Ms. Temple in TXSD1 noted:

> They've took [sic] the fun stuff out of kindergarten, like making a puppet. We get asked, "What is making a puppet going to teach a child?" You have to justify why they are having fun in reenacting a story or even celebrating doing a theme. That's the exciting part about teaching in kindergarten; you get to help make school fun for the children, but we always get asked, "Is that in the curriculum?"

Ms. Pfeiffer in WVC1 made a similar comment: "We do not play in kindergarten." Her colleague, Ms. Lyle, responded, "And kindergarten is not oh so cute," which led Ms. Pfeiffer to reply, "I wish that I could have fun with my students, isn't that so sad?"

"Cute is dead" because of the focus on these academic expectations (Brown et al., 2020a), and as Ms. Walsh in TXSD2 noted, "We focus on academics because I know that when my students get to 1st grade, they need to be at a certain level of performance." Ms. Fletcher in WVC1 stated, "So much of this focus on academics is that if you don't push children in kindergarten, then they're lost in 1st and 2nd grade." Ms. Enos in WVC2 commented:

> If you don't get done what you need to get done in kindergarten, the kids are going to be even further behind academically in 1st grade, and then those academic skills will need to be made up. So, you feel a real need to do as much as you can to get them where they need to be for 1st grade.

When asked for an example of what they meant by this push for increased academics, Ms. Willis in WVC1 responded, "Take sight words, for example; last year, we were told by the county they need to know about 67 sight words before they leave kindergarten. This year, there's probably between 80 and 100 words." In these statements, it becomes apparent that the world of academic achievement seems to be of primary importance, particularly in relation to "what" the students need to be able to know and do when they leave kindergarten.

While planning and teaching to prepare kindergartners for 1st grade and beyond has always been a part of teachers' figuring of kindergarten (e.g., Dombkowski, 2001), all the teachers I talked to were uncomfortable with the current figuring of kindergarten through academic achievement expectations being placed on children—whether from school, district/county, state, or federal policymakers. For example, Ms. Postles in WVC2 commented, "We are doing these children a disservice because we have all these kids who know their letters and their sounds and the numbers, but they don't know how to get along with each other. They can't solve their own problems." Such a statement is quite similar to the concerns raised by the parent Ms. Clements in TXSD2.

Why Kindergarten Isn't Fun

When the teachers were asked why they continue to teach in this manner even if they feel they are doing a disservice to children, two main types of responses emerged. The first focused on assessing the children (Brown et al., 2020a). Ms. Enos in WVC2 noted, "What we do starts with testing because you know this testing is looming out there, and then everything else goes down from that so you have to do this, this, and this to ultimately get ready for the testing." While good teaching requires teachers to pay "attention to students' active knowledge construction or development of higher order thinking skills" through formative assessments that help them plan their instruction (Yin & Buck, 2019, p. 129), the assessments that teachers employ are summative, which are designed to document "how much learning has taken place" for purposes of accountability (p. 129).

An example of the impact of summative assessments on these kindergarten teachers comes from Ms. New in TXSD1: "We are constantly assessing our students." Then she added, "When are we going to have time to teach?" Her colleague, Mr. Lewis, responded to her statement by outlining all the summative assessments he and his colleagues must give:

> We do 16 common assessments that are required by our campus; there are four in each of [the] content areas that we do every 9 weeks. On top of that, we give a state-based early mathematics inventory three times a year, an early basic literacy assessment three times a year, a reading assessment toward the end of the year, and then, progress reports in between the time we assess for the report cards.

Ms. Pfeiffer in WVC1 noted, "We do assessments for report cards four times year, we do a state assessment two times a year, a county assessment four times a year, and then there's just assessments for the school that monitor the progress of students' learning." Ms. Fritz in WVC2 stated, "You get to the point where all this testing makes you feel like you need to teach to the test even though what they're testing may not be developmentally appropriate, or even all that important." Her colleague, Ms. Postles, noted they had a county test in the third quarter with "over 200 questions for a kindergartner." Ms. Binger continued, "It takes about 2 weeks of instructional time away from the students because you have to administer the test one-on-one with the student." This constant process of summative assessment appears to have altered and/or transformed the empiricist conception of how kindergarten is to ready children for later success in school (Meisels, 1999). Instead, what appears to be occurring is a framing of "readiness in the now" (Brown, 2013, p. 570). Teachers are being required to enact a standardized set of instructional and assessment practices that entail the constant deployment of a barrage of assessments beginning as soon as children enter kindergarten. These assessments not only continually measure kindergartners but also require the teachers to enact and maintain a specific set of performance expectations that endlessly expand as children progress from one grade level to the next (Brown & Barry, 2019).

These teachers' focus on readying children for the now also was tied to their preparation of kindergartners for the exams that await them in 3rd grade. For example, Ms. Johansson in TXSD2 noted:

> The paradigm is so different here because even though we've been schooled [to believe] "it's a journey not a race"—that's what we should believe and tout about our teaching. However, because of the 3rd-grade STARR test, everybody has a sense of urgency that you don't want to have, but it's there. You would be a loser teacher

> if you didn't buy in to some of the things that they need to have at least heard of if not mastered for 1st-grade work; so you are in that important line, and you feel pressure to get there. They're going learn it at some point, why can't you take more time to smell the roses and be together? But because of that time frame, we just have to do it now.

Ms. Thomas in the VS in Texas put it more succinctly: "It's literally STAAR prep." Ms. Fritz in WVC2 stated, "It trickles down. There's a lot of emphasis on the 3rd-grade tests. There's a huge amount of pressure on the children and us—we have to get our kids ready to achieve at a certain level." Taken together, these teacher statements demonstrate how the cultural artifact of the 3rd-grade tests in Texas and West Virginia has "shift[ed] the perceptual, cognitive, affective, and practical frame of" teaching kindergartners. Failing to provide children the skills needed to succeed on these tests, no matter the grade level, "positions" these teachers, according to Ms. Johansson, as losers (Holland et al., 1998, p. 63).

The second response, which reflects a more traditional empiricist vision of kindergarten (Meisels, 1999), focused on preparing children for 1st grade. For example, Ms. Enos in WVC2 made a comment similar to the statements made by Ms. Hildebrand, a parent in WVC2. Ms. Enos stated, "We need to get them ready for 1st grade because if you think kindergarten is bad, 1st grade is unbelievable." Ms. Pfeiffer, a kindergarten teacher in WVC1, also noted, "First grade is a huge jump from what they've already been doing in kindergarten." When I asked these teachers (all of whom figured 1st grade in a very negative light) what makes 1st grade different from kindergarten, Ms. Willis added, "As soon as they go into 1st grade, they are taking spelling tests where they have to write their name at the top and number their paper, so we spend the last 9 weeks of school doing spelling tests just to get them ready." What's so powerful about this statement by Ms. Willis is that readying children for success in school goes beyond the traditional 3Rs; it means children must be able to be good at test-taking (Brown et al., 2020a). Developmentally (e.g., Rogoff, 2003), this makes no sense because children are notoriously bad test-takers (Gnezda & Bolig, 1988). Yet, politically, the teachers' framing of students needing to be "good" test-takers as an essential skill for success in school challenges how "we" as a society are conceptualizing what it means to be a learner and a future U.S. citizen (Dewey, 1938/1998).

Why Not Fight for Making Kindergarten Fun Again?

This constant focus on readying students for the later grades, while demonstrating that they, as teachers, are being accountable to policymakers' demands for increased student learning, led many of these teachers to question the type of impact their instruction was having on their students. Ms. Pfeiffer in WVC1 noted, "We push these kids so hard and so fast now; that's why we have a lot of behavior problems. That's why we have a lot of sensory issues, motor development, because nobody gets to play anymore." Ms. Postles in WVC2 added, "I wish they would let us teach," and Ms. Enos replied, "Do policymakers just see kids as test scores? Is that all they want from us? Improved scores?" Ms. Postles answered, "It's so frustrating. We need to make school fun again."

Beyond making kindergarten fun again for students (Brown et al., 2020a), Ms. Johansson in TXSD2 highlighted how these demands for standardization and accountability also have affected the teachers:

> I'm not even Catholic, but I do have some guilt over moving past those teachable moments where you can go broad as a teacher and offer an enriching curriculum to students rather than focusing everything in on reading and writing. I wish I could give myself permission when a beautiful learning moment comes up that allows us, as a class, to go down a different trail but offers wonderful insight and gets everybody charged up about learning. I wish we could let that drive our curriculum more.

Hargreaves and Tucker (1991) long ago called for "the decreasing emphasis on test scores and other . . . forms of accountability" to avoid the "problems of teacher burnout, cynicism, and other negative behaviours" (p. 503), and yet, this issue persists 30 years later. Ms. Johansson knows she is missing important learning opportunities that tap into the interests of her students and show them the "power" of what it means to become a learner who seeks to understand something that they are curious about (e.g., Katz & Chard, 2000).

Still, Ms. Lyle in WVC1 noted, "I'm torn. I love the fact that our kids can read. I love that we are able to push them to do that, but then sometimes, I think that we're pushing them way too hard." Ms. Barnes in TXSD1 commented, "The children can perform at a high level, but I don't think it's appropriate developmentally to push them this hard." There appears to be worry by these teachers that their instructional decisionmaking and academic achievement expectations may turn students off from school (Brown et al., 2020a).

To move in a different direction, Ms. Temple from TXSD1 stated:

> I really wish we could get away from the constant assessment of our kids. I don't mind testing them to see growth and progress—that's important. But there's just no end to it all. We just have a big pile of results that don't all fit together. It's all so fast-paced, and there just isn't enough time in the day to do really meaningful lessons.

Ms. Barnes in TXSD1 summed up these concerns about the impact of testing by stating, "All these academic expectations are getting pushed down. There are so many things that we're trying to keep up with, and it seems like at what cost or the cost–benefit to us, as teachers, and to our students?" Ms. Barnes appears to be arguing that no one benefits from the changed kindergarten, while many may suffer from negative consequences. However, as Holland et al. (1998) pointed out, figured worlds are "formed and re-formed in relation to the everyday activities and events that ordain happenings within" these worlds (p. 53). For these teachers, their activities involve teaching the standards and assessing students' academic achievement, and thus that is how they were seeing the world of kindergarten. Yet, they hoped this world could be altered.

TEACHERS REROUTING THE KINDER-RACE

At the surface level, similar to Ms. Cutler, the kindergartners, and families with kindergartners, the kindergarten teachers who participated in this study would like kindergarten to reinstate many of the practices typically associated with kindergarten (Beatty, 1995). For example, Ms. Jefferson from the VS thought students should have "nap time for at least the beginning of the year to give their bodies a break." Ms. Walsh in TXSD2 noted, "We don't do dramatic play anymore." Her colleague, Ms. Barnes, added, "The district phased that out," and their other colleague, Ms. Johansson, added, "I mean, they kind of make you feel like a loser if you have such things as a kitchen in kindergarten." Such statements reiterate that cute is dead.

Developing Whole Children

Beyond these curricular and instructional changes, these kindergarten teachers, similar to family members I talked with, wanted to develop the children into "whole" beings. For example, Ms. Stoddard in WVC2 noted that children "should learn how to solve their own problems, learn how to be fair, learn how to be responsible, imaginative, and creative." Ms. Barnes in TXSD2 stated, "I want them to develop a love for learning and a pride about their own growth and progress, a proudness in their own personal growth." Ms. Chan in TXSD1 noted, "I wish we had more time across the day for the children to interact with each other so that they could develop an understanding of empathy with others and treat each other with respect." Ms. New, her colleague, continued, "And learn how to be a good friend." Ms. Stoddard in WVC2 suggested, "They need to have more time to socialize. Time to figure out how to solve their problems. Learning how to take turns." Ms. Binger added, "They learn that through playing. They also develop their imagination and creativity. They need more play. I don't think they play enough." The call for more opportunities for socialization and child-directed learning activities, such as play, has been documented by others (e.g., Miller & Almon, 2009). Moreover, these teachers wanted to create a learning environment that is structured but flexible and nurturing, and allows children to pursue individual interests while making connections between school and their own lives; such visions of what kindergarten should be reflect an empirically grounded conception of teaching young children (Ashiabi, 2007; Hamre & Pianta, 2005).

These teachers would like the instructional activities they engage in on a daily basis to make more sense to them and the children (Brown et al., 2020a). For instance, Ms. Fletcher in WVC1 stated:

> I wish we could teach through themes again—something like dinosaurs. Why can't we do a theme about dinosaurs, you might ask? Because we can't stop and do that. We always have something else in math to do. Nothing's connected. You're doing one thing in reading, and then, you're doing something else in another content area and something else in the other content area. It's crazy how all over the place we are.

Ms. Pfeiffer, her colleague, added, "Nothing's integrated." Similar to Ms. Cutler's past experiences in teaching kindergarten, Ms. Lyle added to Ms. Pfeiffer's statement by pointing out, "Many years ago, half of our teaching was thematic, but that was a long time ago." When asked why they wanted to engage in such instruction, Ms. Lyle added, "It goes in more depth." Ms. Pfeiffer stated, "They have more fun too." Ms. Fletcher continued, "They also understand more. Like, 'Now I know why we're doing this because we're going to use it when we go do this subject area.' The students can relate it to other things they are learning." Ms. Lyle responded, "And we can't do this because of the tests." All the teachers I interviewed raised the issue of seeking out a more integrated curriculum. These teachers' pedagogical beliefs about how best to educate children so that they learn with understanding are supported by the work of Drake and Savage (2016), who found that students from across the globe (e.g., Canada, Finland, and Korea) who participated in integrated curricula appeared to do better on large-scale tests of academic achievement (Brown et al., 2020a).

Beyond wanting to return integrated teaching to the kindergarten classroom, these teachers also wanted kindergarten to be a joyful learning experience for children (Fisher, 1991). Ms. New in TXSD1 noted, "I wish sometimes that I could just give them some markers and let them draw. They are 5! Just let them draw." She continued, "But that's not on the test. So, to do anything, you have to tweak it to have an academic purpose." Ms. Chan added, "Doing a craft activity is frowned upon by our district, so if you want to do something like that, it has to relate to the academic expectations, which sucks." Ms. New concurred, "It does suck because playing is frowned upon by the district." Combined, these teachers were concerned that this lack of what they considered to be appropriate learning experiences would negatively impact their students' love of schooling. Ms. Fritz in WVC2 commented:

> I think kindergarten should just be a love of learning. It's a whole new world that they get to explore. I don't think it's important that you look at teaching kindergarten and say that I got to page 552 in the manual. If you go back and ask the kids who are in 3rd or 5th grade, they always remember the fun stuff. They're not going to remember that I did 85 sight words or whatever. I think we've taken a lot of what makes kindergarten memorable away.

Ultimately, these teachers would like to refigure the kindergarten classroom so that both they and their students have more agency in their learning process (Adair, 2014; Holland et al., 1998); essentially, they want to participate in a learning community where they can "equip" children "with the capabilities to pursue opportunities they [both] value" (Walker, 2006, p. 181).

Questioning Whether Such Change Can Be Attained

While the changes these teachers would like to see in kindergarten mirror the suggestions made by Ms. Cutler, her students, and the families of kindergartners, these teachers were skeptical that the Kinder-Race could ever be refigured. For example, Ms. Chan in TXSD1 stated, "People outside of the classroom who make choices about the classroom, like administrators and policymakers, need to see this [the video]." Ms. Temple replied, "I agree," and Ms. Chan continued, "But I am not sure that will change anything." Mr. Lewis replied, "I agree," and he added, "They may think these kids can handle this, so let's extend the finish line and ask them to do more. But when they do that, they don't give you any more time to teach kids to run the race." Ms. Temple stated, "You're right."

This idea of extending the Kinder-Race, which for Mr. Lewis meant "increasing the academic demands placed on children," also was mentioned in a conversation in WVC2. It began with Ms. Fritz stating, "Nobody ever wants to step back from the academic demands we're placing on children and teachers. They never want to go that direction." Ms. Stoddard replied, "You're right, even though they say they want classrooms to be developmentally appropriate." Ms. Fritz responded, "That's exactly right, and nobody ever wants to go there." Ms. Enos added, "But do we really think that policymakers and legislators are going to think that what they are asking us to do is too much, or inappropriate, or do they even know what that means?" Ms. Stoddard replied, "No, they want high academic expectations, which they link to higher test scores." Ms. Lyle in WVC1 also voiced her frustration with policy and policymakers by stating:

> Policymakers have not been in the classroom, and they don't have a clue about what they're asking us to do. And it's frustrating to us because we're sitting here going, "Seriously? You want to teach all of these standards?" They need to walk a day in my shoes and see what needs to be changed.

Ms. Willis, her colleague, added, "But we know that's not going to happen. Those changes are not going to happen." These teachers' statements not only mimic a sense of hopelessness about the future of teaching kindergarten, but also mirror the findings of others (e.g., Lefstein & Perath, 2014). While the teachers had numerous ideas for changing their lived reality, they felt that their concerns over the changed kindergarten and its negative impact on them, future teachers, and their students would go unheard (Brown et al., 2020a).

Failing to Change May Decimate Their Profession

Not only did these kindergarten teachers question whether the Kinder-Race could be altered; they worried that if kindergarten was not refigured, no one would want to teach in such programs in the future. For example, Ms. Fritz in WVC2 commented, "The video shows why the whole system needs to change." This statement led her colleague, Ms. Binger, to respond:

> How are they going to be able to hold on to good, qualified teachers too much longer with the amount of pressure for performance and the expectations, and the amount of time most teachers spend on their jobs? We've got teachers in this building who work huge amounts of hours trying to ready children for the next grade, but I don't know how much longer they can do it.

The pressure to surrender their own conceptions of good practice, and instead "teach to the test" (Menken, 2006), makes Ms. Binger (and the other kindergarten teachers) question how much longer those who are committed to the profession will remain in it (Brown et al., 2020a). Ms. Fletcher in WVC1 also noted, "The job is getting worse each year. Honestly, teaching sucks. I'm just being serious. If I had to do it over again, I would not be a teacher, as sad as that sounds." Ms. Lyle, her colleague, replied, "I don't think I would either." Ms. Pfeiffer replied, "I can go on about this for days, but the pay is crap, the extra work is crap, and I don't get paid for that. When they started shortening my summers, I thought about being a greeter at Walmart, honestly." Many others have documented how policymakers' SBA reforms negatively impacted teachers (Dunn, 2018; Ryan et al., 2017), and this is important because teachers who are stressed are less likely to offer quality emotional and instructional support to their students (Penttinen et al., 2020). Furthermore, this job dissatisfaction speaks back to Kundu's (2020) argument that both agency and grit are necessary for people to succeed. In Ms. Pfeiffer's statement, it appears the grit of these teachers—by that, I mean "pursuing specific objectives over the course of an extended period of time, persisting towards goals despite challenging obstacles" (Kundu, 2020, p. 37)—may be squeezed out of them by the constant and increasing pressure from policymakers to teach the test so that they improve students' academic achievement.

Research also has shown that up to half of all new teachers leave the classroom within the first 5 years (Fantilli & McDougall, 2009), and in schools with large populations of diverse and/or low-performing students, the turnover rate is even greater (Aud et al., 2010). Such turnover not only impacts children, their families, and schools, but also negatively impacts school district budgets (Djonko-Moore, 2016). Furthermore, researchers consistently have shown that becoming an effective teacher cannot be microwaved (Brown, 2010b)—it takes years of teaching in classrooms to develop expertise (Ingersoll & Strong, 2011). Thus, the statements by these teachers demonstrate that if the current world of the Kinder-Race goes unchanged, there may be long-term implications for the health of public education in the United States as a whole.

SCHOOL PRINCIPALS

The school principals I spoke with included those who oversaw the five schools I've discussed up to this point in the chapter plus the addition of a focus group of principals in Texas who enrolled in courses to attain their superintendent's license (see Figure 4.3).

Kindergarten Readies Children for School Success

Like previous participants, these principals framed kindergarten through an empiricist conception of school readiness (Meisels, 1999). For instance, Principal Nye in WVC2 framed kindergarten as "giving children a good foundation for learning. It sets the stage for it. It's getting kids used to routines and being able to follow directions. It increases their ability to be seated, build some stamina, and those basic things." Principal Rogers in TXSD2 noted that kindergarten is "school readiness: children learning how to attend to instruction, working within a group, sharing materials, being

Figure 4.3. School Principals (*n* = 12)

Texas	West Virginia
VS Principal Atwell	WVC1 School Principal Anderson
TXSD1 School Principal Wetherton	WVC2 School Principal Nye
TXSD2 School Principal Rogers	
Pre-K–6 Principal Hernandez*	
Pre-K–6 Principal James*	
Pre-K–6 Principal Ruiz*	
Pre-K–6 Principal Jimenez*	
Pre-K–6 Principal Pena*	
Pre-K–6 Principal Green*	
Pre-K–6 Principal Nunez*	

Note: * = participated in a focus group.

cooperative, and being attentive to the teacher for a few minutes." Across both statements, the principals defined kindergarten as a program that readies children for school.

The Reality of the Kinder-Race

However, when turning to their figuring of the kindergartens in the video and in their own schools, their descriptions of this program shifted toward the Kinder-Race. For example, Principal Anderson in WVC1 stated:

> Kindergarten is much more structured. When I started out as a principal, the children took a nap for an hour in the afternoon, or they came for half-a-day kindergarten. Kids learned their basic ABCs and one to 100. Kindergarten was playing. You go in, they'd have Play-Doh and that kind of stuff. Now, it's more oriented to a math and language arts curriculum. Kids are doing that on day one. There's not that much play time. It's much more structured today than it was in the past.

While these principals knew kindergarten had changed, they still questioned whether the Kinder-Race was appropriate for 5-year-olds. For example, Principal Pena in Texas commented after watching the video:

> I kept asking myself, "Are they having fun?" It looks like we're already killing their joy for school in kindergarten, so what are we setting them up for later? But then there is the accountability and expectations that are put on kindergarten teachers now, and I get that.

> But it's a tough balance. It didn't look like they were having any fun at all, and for some of them, that might be their very first experience with school—so what are they going to think the rest of the way?

Principal Pena's statement mirrors those made by families with kindergartners and by kindergarten teachers; all of them questioned whether turning kindergarten into what Gracey (1975) termed academic boot camp is "killing their [kindergartners'] joy" and setting children up to dislike school (Brown, Englehardt, Barry, & Ku, 2019a).

Why Race from Skill to Skill?

Yet, when asked why kindergarten teachers and their students are racing from skill to skill, Principal Ruiz in Texas noted:

> There are a lot of kids that can't read in 5th grade, so you have to ask, "What were they doing in kindergarten? Why isn't there a sense of urgency in that kindergarten classroom?" I think that it's up to the school leader to spin it positively, to make outcomes-driven work "fun," and to let their teachers know you can still have fun teaching. It can still be an enjoyable classroom, even though there's accountability. We're all going to be held accountable.

Principal Pena's statement demonstrates how these principals figured kindergarten through their state's accountability policies. These accountability policies, Holland et al. (1998), using Vygotsky's (1980) notion of a pivot, maintain, "shift" the principals' figuring from what they would like kindergarten to be to a "different world," the Kinder-Race (p. 50). For this principal, the 5th-grade STAAR exam—the pivot—shifted his figuring of kindergarten to a world that must "urgently" prepare children to be readers. Essentially, these exams led to what Principal Wetherton at TXSD1 termed "academic trickle-down," which meant, "We've got to get to this level by the end of kindergarten, so we can get to this level by the end of 1st, this level by the end of 2nd, and reading proficiently by the end of 3rd."

The Importance of Reading

Principals across both states zeroed in on the importance of reading within kindergarten, which is why the trickle-down that Principal Wetherton described is occurring. For example, TXSD2 Principal Rogers commented, "They need to be reading. I don't know philosophically if I believe that's important or not. I think kids can go into 1st grade without knowing how to read and do just fine. But it's an expectation." Principal Anderson from WVC1 noted, "By the time the children leave kindergarten, they should be able to read basic five-word sentences."

While these principals figured children leaving kindergarten to be readers, that is not to say they didn't recognize how difficult a task this is for teachers to achieve. As Principal Ruiz in Texas noted, "Kindergarten is hard. It's a tough business. Not only academically, but also creating a community of learners—it's tough. Not to mention that teaching kids to read, it is a beautiful thing, not to make it romantic, but it's also like a tough thing to do." While the debate over whether kindergartners need to be readers as they transition into 1st grade has never been and may never be settled empirically (Ehri, 2012; Suggate, 2012), these principals felt that reading was a necessary skill for children to have in order to achieve in the later grades. Such a focus on reading echoed in Principal Nunez's statement:

> They have to leave kindergarten reading. They have to read a certain amount of words per minute. In my school district, we get a report on how your school is doing, on how kindergarten is doing at the beginning, middle, and at the end. We have the TPRI [Texas Primary Reading Inventory] data, and we have DRA data. Kindergarten is very focused on student data.

Principal Atwell of the VS also reiterated the importance of data influencing how this principal thought about reading:

> Kindergartners are expected to read when they leave kindergarten, and not just read, but read fluently. We've seen through the data that if we have full-blown readers in 3rd, 4th, and 5th grade, then the sky is the limit for them.

Both principals quoted above are demonstrating how they figured the world of kindergarten through data. Lewis and Holloway (2019) noted that such "data-driven practices and logics" are "reshap[ing] the possibilities by which the teaching profession, and teaching professionals, can be known and valued, and the ways that teachers can ultimately be and associate themselves in relation to their work" (p. 48). For these principals and their teachers, their "worth" as professionals is tied to student data (p. 38).

The Dangers of Data

While these principals are well aware of how student data are driving curriculum, instruction, and their leadership within their schools, this is not to say that they did not recognize the inherent danger in viewing children or teachers as test scores (Booher-Jennings, 2005). Principal Green from Texas stated, "It was almost like we try to make them grow up too fast in kindergarten so that they can meet certain levels of proficiency by the time they get into 3rd grade." Principal Anderson from WVC1 also commented:

> We've put so much stress on kids that they can't enjoy learning. It's just test, test, test constantly. To the point that when the test actually does come, kids get sick. I'm thinking, "This is not what it's about. This is not what it's about."

Principal Atwell of the VS stated:

> You have to remember that they're 5 and 6 years old, so kindergarten is a balance. It's a very fine line. It's a constant struggle for teachers to balance their instruction because of the pressure to perform. There's a lot of pressure on kids. There's a lot of pressure on teachers. There's a lot of pressure on administrators. It's just a lot to have these kids ready for the tests in 3rd grade.

Across these statements, there is a sense of urgency due to the datafication of schooling and the pressure to perform (Roberts-Holmes, 2015), and yet, each of these principals seemed to question whether the current race from skill to skill is appropriate for kindergartners.

PRINCIPALS REROUTING THE KINDER-RACE

Kindergarten Should Focus on the Whole Child

When asked about how they might go about rerouting the Kinder-Race, these principals figured such change through the district/county and state policies that they had to adhere to as the leaders of their schools (Castro, 2010). Such constraints led these principals to think about how change might occur in a manner that lets education stakeholders know that the goal of public education is to create a system that works for everyone. For example, TXSD2 Principal Rogers stated:

> The current emphasis on test scores at the upper grades has had an impact on the beginning of school. Some of that's been good because it's made the curriculum more focused and created alignment across the grade levels. But the anxiety that it places on the whole school system detracts students from learning, particularly from being able to engage in the discovery process.

While Principal Rogers appears to appreciate how focusing on achievement has caused stakeholders to focus on what is being taught (curriculum) and when it is being taught, this principal is worried that it has led to a schooling process (the teaching) that ignores how children learn and develop.

Principal Rogers wants students to engage in discovery, which aligns with the work of Gopnik (2012). Gopnik and her colleagues (e.g., Gopnik et al., 2000) consistently have shown that children are natural-born scientists consumed with the desire to experiment with and explore objects. To facilitate this type of learning, adults/teachers need to engage children in two types of learning experiences: the process of discovery and the process of mastering what we discover. For Gopnik (2012), children, as well as adults, absorb new information through guided discovery, which increases their capacity for learning; then, through routinized learning, children perfect these procedures so that they become a part of children's long-term memory, which frees their minds to make new discoveries (e.g., learning letter–sound correspondences so that they can focus on decoding words). Both types of learning are necessary, but unfortunately, as Principal Rogers pointed out, the current system of education limits the amount of time students can engage in guided discovery. Thus, Principal Green is worried that spending a significant amount of time on routinized learning experiences can "detract students from learning."

Alongside wanting kindergartners to engage in a range of learning experiences, these principals appeared also to hold a growth mindset toward the children in their schools, as they figured this change process (Dweck, 2006). For example, Principal Wetherton in TXSD1 stated, "Every time the expectation gets raised, the kids get there." Even so, the changes they sought seemed to balance academics with how children develop and learn. Principal Anderson in WVC1 commented:

> Kindergarten can't be structured all day—they're too little. We're pushing our children to be universally competitive, and that's creating so much stress on kindergartners that they develop tummy aches. Kindergarten should be a fun time for learning. They can learn and have fun at the same time.

Principal Rogers in TXSD2 also noted, "Kindergarten should have a lot more play than what we do now, and the primary focus should be social skills rather than academics." Principal Nye in WVC2 pointed out, "It needs to be more relaxed, more body movement for them and all that stuff. The kids should be playing, but learning through play." These statements demonstrate not only that these principals held a growth mindset toward learning, but also that they appear to recognize the significance of fostering children's physical and social–emotional well-being through engaging prosocial learning experiences, such as play (Weisberg et al., 2013), so that children can succeed in life as well as in school (Schweinhart, 2005).

Yet, the Data Do Not Disappear

Even though these principals offered a range of suggestions for rerouting the Kinder-Race, they were not willing to rid kindergarten of outcomes. For instance, Principal Green in Texas stated:

> There should be outcomes, but the hard part is we're working in a system that where your schools are graded off your 5th-grade students' achievement. So there's not as much emphasis on the early grades. As principals, we need to shift our focus to the lower grades, to show them how to make those outcomes, that there's a way to get to them that is more fun and engaging. But let's be honest, principals focus on grades 3rd through 5th because of the tests.

While paying attention to outcomes is important to Principal Green, this principal knows he needs to pay more attention to kindergarten because, as Principal Anderson in WVC1 noted, "School systems do not pay enough attention to kindergarten. It's not an area where they're tested." However, there was recognition by Principal Nunez in Texas that

> All these changes in kindergarten and in school in general are an effect of the standards and testing. If you give teachers and principals certain performance expectations or even just give them [content] standards, they're going to do whatever they think they need to do to meet those expectations.

Principal Atwell of the VS also commented:

> Intrinsic pressure is probably number one, and then you just have the lay of the land. You've got your standards. You've got district expectations. What are you doing to get better as a campus and improve how your kiddos perform? We are responsible for submitting data to the state in the order. You are responsible for the state assessments, and so it's finding a way to address kids' needs so that when they are here, they can learn to the very best of their ability.

According to Principal Atwell, this datafication of the education system is always going to focus the system on student achievement (Ball, 2003).

These principals did not want to purge academics from kindergarten. Rather, as Principal Anderson in WVC1 pointed out, "Kindergarten needs to be a combination of learning and of fun; it can be done simultaneously with structure." To do this, they knew the system had to change, but they did not think policymakers would reform kindergarten. Principal Rogers in TXSD2 summed up this point: "The political figures in our government are pretty clueless about what actually goes on in schools. They should spend a day in a classroom to understand what is going on."

In sum, the principals, like all stakeholders in the study, struggled to align their imagined worlds of kindergarten with the Kinder-Race. They offered a range of empirically based ideas about to how to improve kindergarten as well as the types of students they hoped these programs would produce—essentially, what Hyson (2008) refers to as engaged and enthusiastic learners. However, the accountability policies and tests (whether in 3rd grade or in kindergarten) appeared to act as pivots that shifted their "perceptual, cognitive, affective, and practical" frame of kindergarten, which demonstrates the significance of these "cultural artifacts" in the schooling process (Holland et al., 1998, p. 63). Without reducing the impact of these high-stakes artifacts on them, their teachers, and the students, these principals believe the Kinder-Race will continue.

THE FIGURING OF KINDERGARTEN BY THOSE WHOSE ORBITS REVOLVE AROUND THE SCHOOL

These stakeholders' struggles in refiguring the Kinder-Race reflect "the political-economic, and cultural crosscurrents" of debates over public schooling in general (Holland & Lave, 2009, p. 12). Each stakeholder group appeared to be "caught up in the conflict from their different economic, political, and social locations needed and wanted different kinds of preparation" for kindergartners' "futures in the interest of forging both durable and new identities and life-possibilities" for each child (p. 12).

The students' figured conceptions of the Kinder-Race reflected their histories as well as the collective local practices they experienced on a day-to-day basis (Holland et al., 1998; Holland & Lave, 2009). Even though they felt cared for by their teacher and saw the purpose of kindergarten as preparation for future success—whether reading, 1st grade, or, as Claudia pointed out, "college"—they wanted it to be "funner." Their ideas for "funner" reflected much of what is referred to as developmentally appropriate practices in kindergarten (Copple & Bredekamp, 2009).

For the adults, their conceptions of what the Kinder-Race is and should be were "formed and re-forming in relation to historically specific contexts" and their hopes for what kindergarten could be (Holland et al., 1998, p. 284). Many of the families were not so worried about the academic development of their children. Instead, they wanted kindergarten to develop their children's social and emotional skills so they would be able to see themselves as learners and know how to interact in a positive manner with their peers. Still, some, like Ms. Hildebrand, wanted to ensure that children learned what was necessary so that they did not enter 1st grade behind. The teachers felt a similar pressure, but they also knew what was occurring in kindergarten could not continue for their students or for themselves. The principals made very similar comments, but the tests that held them, teachers, and students accountable for high academic achievement pivoted them from these concerns. They struggled to "reorient" themselves away from these tests, which deterred them from the possibility of creating "new figured worlds . . . as part of a collective" form of change in kindergarten (Holland et al., 1998, p. 282).

While the majority of the children in the video were not White or middle-class, these stakeholders' interpretations of and suggestions for altering the Kinder-Race did not speak directly to culturally sustaining practices (Paris & Alim, 2014). Each stakeholder wanted kindergarten to be a place where all children succeeded, but they appeared to figure their actions individually, which represents how policymakers' neoliberal reforms have altered the ways in which these stakeholders interpreted the purpose of schooling—individual success is what matters. Each of these participants knew that reform required collective action, as Ms. Willis, a kindergarten teacher in WVC1, noted, but they all struggled with envisioning what such change might entail and/or how it could be achieved. This represents De Lissovoy's (2014) and others' (e.g., Ball, 2007) argument that the "power" of policymakers' neoliberal reforms is the "im-possibility" of figuring an alternative. While all these stakeholders wanted the Kinder-Race to end, they felt that those in power are, as Principal Rogers noted, "pretty clueless" about what is going on or how to even change the Kinder-Race. In the next chapter, I begin to unpack this cluelessness and illuminate potential pivots for change, which are explored in Chapter 6 (Holland et al., 1998).

CHAPTER 5

The Tension Between Fostering Democratic Students Versus Individualized Performers

To examine how those who operate outside the day-to-day experiences of kindergarten conceptualize the Kinder-Race and how they would like to reroute it, I employ the conceptual tool of neoliberalism alongside my use of sensemaking, CSP, and figured worlds. Neoliberalism applies an economic orientation toward governance to make sense of policy problems and solutions (Davies & Bansel, 2007). As such, the relationship between government and its citizens around education is one of investor/investment; schools are funded to produce successful learners who become earners and consumers that repay the state over their lifetimes for these initial investments (Ailwood, 2008; Heckman, 2000). Framing education as an investment in human capital, an idea developed by Mincer (1958) and Becker (1964, 1975) using the work of Adam Smith, creates what Rose (1999) termed a strange new coupling of power in which the individuals appear to be "responsible for their own well-being through the choices they make" as consumers (Robertson & Dale, 2002, p. 469). Yet, under this theory of consumer-based governance, the "state remains strong despite appearing to dissolve" (Dahlberg & Moss, 2005, p. 133). It does so through restricting the forms of education kindergarten teachers can engage in by requiring them to attend to state as well as district/county-sanctioned curricular documents and assessment practices (Brown, Englehardt, Barry, & Ku, 2019b). It also puts forward an education system defined through the economic principles of performance and efficiency (Apple, 2001), which is made visible through measuring teachers' ability to produce students who are to attain particular levels of performance on their state's standardized assessments that evaluate their mastery of certain sets of knowledge and skills (McNeil, 2000).

COUNTERING NEOLIBERALISM

Many within education advocate for the implementation of democratic practices (e.g., De Lissovoy, 2014) and policies (e.g., Moss, 2017) to counter this neoliberal framing of schooling. Across these arguments, there appears to be a foundational belief that for teachers and children to resist these neoliberal reforms, they must have the space and opportunity to act freely (e.g., Wells, 2016). For instance, Adair (2014) made the case for agentic learning opportunities within the early childhood classroom where children are "able to influence and make decisions about what and how something is learned in order to expand capabilities" (p. 219). Such learning opportunities are to assist children in taking on the identity of a democratic citizen (Brown, Englehardt, Barry, & Ku., 2019b).

However, Clark and Richards (2017) pointed out that such notions of agentic learning must move beyond "the normative individualized concept of agency where self-interest and individual choice are privileged"—both of which are at the foundation of neoliberalism (Brown, Englehardt, Barry, & Ku., 2019b). Instead, advocates must promote a democratic vision of education rooted in a "social or relational model [that] views agency as emerging through relationships with others" (p. 135). In shifting from choice and voice of the individual child (e.g., Brown & Mowry, 2015), advocates for democratic education should emphasize the need for strong social systems, such as classroom community, in which the opportunity for agency for students, teachers, and other school personnel emerges from the relationships formed, supported, and sustained within those communities; a strong collective community creates the space for the choice and voice of students (Brown, Englehardt, Barry, & Ku, 2019b). It is the tension between this idea of developing a strong collective community and racing toward individualized academic and economic success with which many of the stakeholders who operate outside the day-to-day happening of the Kinder-Race struggled to reconcile as they figured and refigured the Kinder-Race.

TEXAS AND WEST VIRGINIA STAKEHOLDERS

As I noted in the previous chapter, in moving away from those who live and breathe in actual schools and toward the school districts/counties and state-level stakeholders, distinctions across the two states began to emerge when figuring what the Kinder-Race is and how to alter it. Much of this was the result of reforms implemented by policymakers in West Virginia that framed prekindergarten and kindergarten as "readiness grades" (e.g., West Virginia Board of Education, 2014). Because of these differences, I examine these stakeholder groups separately in this chapter (Brown, Englehardt, Barry, & Ku, 2019a).[1]

I start by examining how stakeholders in Texas made sense of the Kinder-Race, since they were most familiar with the policies and practices that shaped the kindergarten classroom I filmed. I then turn to West Virginia stakeholders. Then I turn to national stakeholders who research and/or advocate for public education. I do so to: (1) position what I found across Texas and West Virginia in the broader conversation of kindergarten and public schooling in the United States, and (2) introduce an outsider's perspective to consider possibilities for rerouting the Kinder-Race in ways that might not be reflected in the statements of other stakeholders.

TEXAS STAKEHOLDERS

Public education in Texas is guided by a range of high-stakes accountability policies that hold children and school personnel accountable for improving students' academic achievement; Texas was the birthplace of NCLB. While others, including myself, have examined how these policies have affected "education" in the state (Goldstein, 2008; McNeil, 2000; Valenzuela, 2005), none have examined how these stakeholders make sense of a typical day in kindergarten. I begin my examination into their sensemaking by examining district stakeholders first and then transition to state stakeholders (see Figure 5.1 for a list of participants).

District Administrators Figuring the Kinder-Race

District stakeholders echoed many of the same interpretations and concerns about the Kinder-Race as those who interacted with kindergarten classrooms on a daily basis. For example, all framed the purpose of kindergarten through an empiricist lens (Meisels, 1999). Ms. Summers, the assistant superintendent in TXSD1, stated that kindergarten is a place where children develop "the ability to attend to instruction, to work within a group, share materials, and learn to be cooperative with others." Ms. Gordon, the humanities coordinator in TXSD2, also noted, "Kindergarten teaches children to recognize certain sight words, letters and numbers, their symbols, write words, and really be able to sound out words." Both statements define kindergarten as a place where students learn how to be students as well as gain the foundational academic skills required to succeed in school.

Furthermore, these stakeholders were well aware of how kindergarten and the entire education system have changed. For example, Ms. Valdes, the bilingual coordinator for the VS district, said, "The expectations for the various grade levels have changed dramatically." Mr. Berninger, her colleague and the literacy coordinator for the VS, added, "The expectations have been raised a lot!" Ms. Valdes responded, "Yes, they've been raised because kindergarten sets the foundation for the future. It's sad that we have to look at standardized testing and that type of expectation, but truth be told, we're focusing on teaching those tests." Ms. Valdes, in common with many others throughout the book, connected this change in kindergarten to policymakers' implementation of high-stakes testing and accountability

Figure 5.1. District and State Participants in Texas

District Participants	State Participants
Ms. Valdes, Bilingual Coordinator* of VS District	Member of Texas State Board of Education
Mr. Berninger, Literacy Coordinator* of VS District	Texas Education Association ECE Member
Ms. Summers, Assistant Superintendent in TXSD1	Texas Education Association Governance Officer
Dr. Kennedy, Assistant Superintendent* in TXSD2	Texas House Member on Education Committee
Ms. Gordon, Humanities Coordinator* in TXSD2	Lawyer on Texas Senate Education Committee
Mr. Levens, Technology Coordinator* in TXSD2	Policy Analyst for Texas Senator on Education Committee
	Legislative Director for Texas Representative on Education Committee
	Senior Advisor to the Texas Governor
	Director* of Lobbying Group for Children in Texas
	Legislative Lobbyist* for Lobbying Group for Children in Texas
	Intern* for Lobbying Group for Children in Texas
	Representative from State Lobbying Group Supporting Public Education in Texas
	Reading Research Institute (RRI) ELL Specialist
	RRI ELL District Liaison #1
	RRI District Liaison #2
	RRI District Liaison #3
	RRI Teacher Trainer #1
	RRI Teacher Trainer #2
	RRI Teacher Trainer #3

Note: * = participated in a focus group.

shovedown (Hatch, 2002). For instance, Mr. Levens, the technology coordinator in TXSD2, explained:

> The expectations in kindergarten get pushed down from above; 5th-grade teachers push this off to 4th grade, and so on. So there's a lot of pressure for kindergarten teachers to get through content because they're setting up students for the 1st-grade teacher, and the

> kinder teachers want to make sure they're ready—all of that goes all the way to 3rd grade when the big tests come rolling in.

Ms. Summers in TXSD1 made a similar statement: "Kindergarten sets the foundation. They're going to be taking a state assessment by 3rd grade, and I can't imagine a child doing too well on that assessment without learning what they need to learn in kindergarten." Dr. Kennedy, the assistant superintendent in TXSD2, added, "Higher expectations keep getting pushed lower and lower, and when you combine that with the testing and the accountability system, the joy has been taken out of kindergarten." These stakeholders, like the kindergarten teachers in the previous chapter, saw the joy being taken out of kindergarten for not only students but also teachers. However, they understood why teachers were shoving down these academics. Ms. Valdes in the VS district explained, "In kindergarten, you have to think about the foundation that they are building in 1 year, and one bad teacher can ruin it. No kinder teacher wants to be that one teacher." Her statement reflects the sentiments of Ms. Johansson, a kindergarten teacher in TXSD2, who did not want to be that "loser teacher."

Across these statements, the logic of neoliberalism is present. For instance, Ms. Valdes's statement reflects De Lissovoy's (2014) argument that teachers have become "salespeople for their own pedagogical performances" in which they may market themselves to colleagues, families, administrators, and so on, through producing students who attain high scores on achievement tests in 3rd grade (p. 428). However, this is not to say these stakeholders have embraced this neoliberal framing of schooling. For example, Dr. Kennedy in TXSD2 offered this explanation as to why there was academic shovedown: "We're in a society where all students need to learn at a high level so that they can go on to some sort of postsecondary schooling. To make that happen, we have to increase instructional time and resources in kindergarten." Yet his colleague, Mr. Berninger, also replied pointedly:

> It bothers me that we push children too much beyond where they are developmentally and give them too much work. I know this happens because of the high expectations that have been placed upon the teachers and the increased expectations at each grade level on what the children need to learn as they move up in school. All of it has become too much.

This exchange reflects a level of discomfort that appeared to be felt by the majority of education stakeholders I talked with across the study. De Lissovoy (2018) noted that neoliberalism produces a logic in which there appear to be no alternatives, which can be seen in Dr. Kennedy's statement. However, as Foucault (1982) reminds us, "Power is exercised only over free subjects," which means that "individual or collective subjects . . . are faced with a field of possibilities in which several ways of behaving, several reactions and diverse comportments, may be realized" (p. 790). In this case, these district stakeholders offered several suggestions for rerouting the Kinder-Race so that teachers and their students could engage in the learning experiences they felt were appropriate.

District Administrators Rerouting the Kinder-Race

Some of the alternatives these stakeholders proposed to alter the Kinder-Race included the following. As Ms. Summers in TXSD1 suggested, "If you have two adults working in a classroom with kindergarten students, we would be able to truly prepare them for being successful in 1st grade," and such preparedness has been tied to increased success for kindergartners in school and across their lifetimes (Chetty et al., 2011; Christopher & Farran, 2020). These stakeholders also hoped kindergarten would be a place where there was, as Ms. Gordon in TXSD2 stated, "more play, more conversation with and among the kids so that teachers build children's creativity, sense of wonder, their inquiry and interest, and their engagement in learning for themselves." Ms. Gordon's statement appears to advocate for more choice and voice for students and kindergarten teachers within the learning processes that take place in kindergarten (Brown & Mowry, 2015). Her colleague, Mr. Levens, added:

> They need more hands-on learning, asking wondering questions, curiosity, an environment where curiosity is bubbling up and kids are feeling free to ask questions and the teacher is teaching off that. I know there is a set curriculum to get through too, but the students need both. We want to develop their incubator/entrepreneurial mindset that I think that, as a nation, the United States is really good at, so we need to get our kids good at thinking outside the box, solving problems, and figuring out how to learn. It's essential. Those are the skills our kids need to have going on throughout life.

While Mr. Levens is advocating for what often is framed as a "balanced approach" to instruction (e.g., Graue, 2011), he also is illuminating the failed logic of the current neoliberal push toward standardization and accountability. While that logic is rooted in a belief that public goods should be basic services (Apple, 2001), Mr. Levens demonstrates that such logic has the potential to harm a primary engine for the economy, entrepreneurialism. Such a disconnect can illuminate an opportunity for change within the current framing of education, but it also may simply reinforce the framing of schooling through economic rather than democratic principles.

Nevertheless, collectively, these stakeholders' statements demonstrate how they, as administrators, struggled to reconcile the demand for increased academic achievement with their desire to provide children with opportunities to develop their interests, social skills, and motivation to learn through more balanced instructional experiences (Brown, Englehardt, Barry, & Ku, 2019a). De Lissovoy (2014) noted that the neoliberal ideology that this system of standards, academics, and accountability promotes functions "less through the beliefs that it promotes, and more through the procedures that it repeats" (p. 428). It appears that the procedures of teachers teaching the test to improve student performance create a logic of teaching that these stakeholders struggled to unhinge from their sensemaking of the Kinder-Race specifically and schooling in general.

State Stakeholders in Texas

Making Sense of Public Education in General. When I discussed the Kinder-Race and possibilities for reform with stakeholders at the state level in Texas, many within this group framed their interpretations through an understanding of public education as a constitutional right within the state of Texas. For example, the Texas Education Association governance officer stated:

> The mission of the public education system of the state is to ensure that all Texas children have access to quality education that enables them to achieve the potential to fully participate now and in the future in the social, economic, and educational opportunities of the state and nation. That mission is grounded in the conviction that the general diffusion of knowledge is essential for the welfare of this state and for the preservation of the liberties and the rights of citizens.

This officer is linking the "welfare" of Texas and its citizens to being educated, which reflects arguments put forward by such past politicians as Thomas Jefferson and education reformers as Horace Mann. This belief in educating the future citizens of the state of Texas was echoed by the lawyer on the Texas Senate Education Committee, who noted:

> In the Texas constitution, it says that a general diffusion of knowledge is necessary to secure the liberty and rights of the people, and I think one of the things that we really try and do in the committee is really about that.

The policy analyst for the Texas senator on the Education Committee also stated, "We have a constitutional responsibility to provide for public education to the citizens of this state." Again, these stakeholders appear to be advocating for what often is perceived as a foundational principle of democracy.

However, as these stakeholders continued to discuss this constitutional right for Texas citizens, they linked public education to economic principles. For example, the TEA governance officer continued:

> I see all of it as a pipeline that starts with children being born and our collective responsibility to those children culminating once they are well positioned to be effective, productive members of the Texas citizenry. The overall job of public education is to follow a child from their earliest moments through to the point where they're able to do that through the military, through a postsecondary education, through some other career track.
>
> At every step along this conveyor belt, education professionals are interacting with that child and scaffolding them up toward the next level of proficiency. In Texas, we've identified materials and assessments that help attain a certain level a of proficiency. The state statutes are essentially the state's way of saying, "By roughly this age, here's what we think kids ought to know and be able to do."

Within this statement, this officer puts forward many democratic ideals (e.g., "our collective responsibility"). Yet, at the same time, the language of neoliberalism is present: framing education as a "conveyor belt" that helps children attain a "career track."

This neoliberal logic reverberated across the statements of many other state-level stakeholders. For example, the director of lobbying group for children in Texas commented, "Hopefully, we, as a state, are getting more kids on the track to graduate high school, be successful, and be productive as opposed to being a fiscal burden for the state." A representative from a state lobbying group supporting public education also noted:

> The state becomes more productive with a stronger education system; the state has better workers and better parents. Anybody who is better educated is going to be a better citizen. I also think that the state having young children go to kindergarten allows families to work at least for part of the day, and that benefits the state economically to have more productive workers. But that's not really the biggest benefit. The biggest is having really high-functioning citizens.

For these stakeholders, public education is tied closely to economic production, whether "high-functioning citizens" or having children in school so parents can work, which almost everyone I talked to saw as a benefit of offering kindergarten to all children and their families.

While this logic seems benign, a Texas House member on the Education Committee made the case that this was not so. This member stated:

> Every time we tried to lessen the accountability system, the Texas Association of Businesses folks would get up there and say, "We need metrics. If we're going to spend 50 + billion dollars a year on public education, we need to know that our return-on-investment is working." And my struggle is, I get it. Testing, for me, being from a very low-income community, means we want to ensure equity.
>
> Testing really has become the biggest force in terms of an institutionalized culture within the public education system, and that has been problematic. This accountability culture has been informed by outside forces telling legislators what to think and what to do in regards to Texas's public education system.
>
> My concern is that the direction that we're headed right now will lead us not to have a public education system in the future. It will be completely privatized because that's all you see happening in the budget. If we underfund schools, put in a new accountability system and testing structure that labels schools from A through F, and if you're F for so long, turn you over to a charter school, it becomes a cycle. Furthermore, there's a quota because we want so many schools to be failing, and if so many schools are failing every single time, and then you turn them over, eventually, all those schools will be privatized.
>
> I didn't think that public schools were in so much danger until I was on the public education committee, and I could just watch it happen—let's underfund these schools so much, and then, let's implement an accountability system. Let's fail them, let's turn them over, and you could see the puzzle pieces coming together because they'd all come in different pieces of legislation—this strategy has been in place for over a decade. Now, it's coming into fruition, and there is nothing on the other side to counter it.

The point this legislator is making has been made by many others who are critical of neoliberal education reform (e.g., Apple 2001); they are pulling together many of the larger threads of concern as to how public education in states like Texas is being disentangled from state responsibility to a private right for each citizen. According to this legislator, by creating systemic failure through a grading system in which public schools are expected to attain a passing grade that increases each year, the calls for accountability provide the political space for legislators to shift funding toward the private sector.

These two views of public education (state constitutional right vs. neoliberal framing of individual responsibility) appear to contradict each other. Yet they seem to be entwined in the current SBA framing of schooling—access to an education system provided by the state that is governed by and promotes the economic principles of cost, production, and accountability. This contentious logic is present throughout the statements made by Texas stakeholders as they discuss the Kinder-Race.

Figuring the Kinder-Race. State stakeholders were not comfortable with the Kinder-Race. For example, a member of the Texas State Board of Education commented, "Kindergarten has devolved into 1st grade lite, and there's not a lot of excitement and joy in such classrooms." The Reading Research Institute District Liaison #1 also noted, "Kindergarten teachers, like all teachers, are feeling the pressure with the state standards and the achievement expectations." Her colleague, District Liaison #3, responded, "There's a lot of pressure in kindergarten. You are teaching a lot of academic skills. We need to be empathetic to the challenges these teachers face. It's a hard job, and people do this job because they love kids." A representative from a state lobbying group supporting public education in Texas also noted, "I think for all the grades there is a lot of discussion that there are just too many TEKS; that applies to kindergarten as well. It leads to teachers teaching where they're trying to check some of the boxes." Again, these statements reflect an awareness of how accountability and academic shovedown are impacting kindergarten (Hatch, 2002), and none of these stakeholders seemed comfortable with such changes.

At a fundamental level, these stakeholders were worried about how this pressure to perform was impacting teachers and children. For instance, the member of the Texas State Board of Education noted:

> It's fundamental to our human nature to want to learn, but somehow, we beat it out of everybody—through over-testing, boredom, lack of imagination. Kindergarten sets the trajectory, and it's really important to have a successful launch. It sets children's feelings about school. Kindergarten is really the first time they get an opportunity to say, "Here's what I think about school."

Beyond promoting a growth mindset to assist children in developing an identity as learners (e.g., Johnston, 2012), this board member is focusing on how kindergarten "launches" children as learners. For example, the work of Deci and Ryan (2000) demonstrated that to motivate children to learn requires three primary psychological needs to be met. Children need to: (1) have a sense of autonomy in the learning process, (2) feel competent that they can complete the task at hand, and (3) feel a sense of relatedness to those within the learning situation. Deci and Ryan (2000) found that if children feel unsupported in any of these three needs, it negatively impacts their motivation and engagement with the learning experience. Thus, "to have a successful launch," the learning experiences in kindergarten need to move away from teaching the test and begin to reflect the needs and wants of the children in the classroom (Brown et al., 2018).

While advocating for a growth mindset toward learning within kindergarten classrooms across Texas was quite a common theme among the statements made by members of this stakeholder group, many were still hesitant to reduce the academic and achievement expectations for students at this and other grade levels. For example, the TEA ECE person commented:

> The expectations of what children should know and be able to do are appropriate and not my concern. It's the approach to instruction that I would like to see changed. One thing that we, as adults, are uncomfortable with is academics, but the kids in your video were engaged, interested, working, and understood the expectations.

For this ECE person, the issue with the Kinder-Race is not the content children are expected to learn, but rather how the children are being taught. Additionally, the lawyer on the Texas Senate Education Committee worried that the current logic of the education system is framed through passing the test rather than producing excellent students. The lawyer noted:

> All we do in Texas is expect students to pass the STAAR test or to pass some kind of statewide assessment, and we don't ask them to be excellent. And we don't ask them to push boundaries. I would love it if our definition of success in kindergarten wasn't just getting them ready for 1st grade, but was getting them like, 1st grade and halfway through 1st grade.

This focus on holding high expectations and ensuring that students learn the content and skills needed to succeed in school was also present in the comments of the senior advisor to the Texas governor:

> Kindergarten is not play time; this is not a joke. Our students in Texas cannot read on grade level by 3rd grade. The only way we can change that is by focusing on these early education classrooms. Still, I don't think it's all up to a kindergarten teacher to be the one that gets their kids ready for 1st grade. Families and their communities should be a part of this process too.

These state-level stakeholders do not appear to want the academic achievement expectations for kindergartners to be changed. Rather, they would like other education stakeholders to recognize the importance of learning in kindergarten and to think about how changes might be made so that all children can attain these academic expectations. Before turning to their proposals for change, it is important to recognize that these latter statements leave the system intact. Moreover, when linking these ideas to the arguments put forward by the Texas House member on the Education Committee, it becomes more apparent that the logic of neoliberalism impacts how stakeholders conceptualize the Kinder-Race specifically and public education in general.

Texas State Stakeholders Rerouting the Kinder-Race

To reroute the Kinder-Race, many of these stakeholders offered the same first-order changes (Cuban, 1988) that others have made (Brown, Englehardt, Barry, & Ku, 2019a; Goldstein, 2008). For example, the TEA ECE person stated, "I think we need to really focus more on development of the whole child." The representative from a state lobbying group supporting public education suggested, "I would like it to be hands-on, actually interacting with materials and things, and allowing kids to talk to each other more about the answers they're coming up with and defending it." RRI Teacher Trainer #2 commented, "More adults in the room would allow the certified teacher to be more fully there with individual students." Her colleague, RRI District Liaison #1, suggested, "I think there needs to be a bigger push for authentic learning rather teaching the standards." The legislative lobbyist for a lobbying group for children in Texas noted, "As far as what kindergarten teachers are expected to teach, let's pick out a few things that they [kindergartners] really need to know and then give the teacher a little more freedom beyond that." Across these statements, these stakeholders appear to be focused on offering kindergarten teachers and kindergartners more choice and voice in the learning experiences occurring in kindergarten (Brown & Mowry, 2015).

In order to do this, some, such as the legislative director for a Texas representative on the Education Committee, suggested moving away from the teaching the test. This director noted:

> One thing that we're trying to move away from is teaching to a test. We want applicable learning and to make sure that Texas kids are learning in a way that they can apply things in the classroom to the outside world, whether that be college or career readiness. Honestly, I think one of the things that is driving this the most is we have teachers, parents, and students coming up here and saying teachers can't teach. Let the teachers teach.
>
> You've also got kids that are super stressed out about these high-stakes tests. The teachers are also frustrated because essentially their school year ends in April because that's when the tests are over. They've got a whole other month of learning but the kids don't necessarily want to learn because their test was already done.

While this statement appears to be advocating for changing what's occurring in the classroom on a daily basis, this director still linked teacher agency, which is to provide students with "applicable learning," to "a tool of the state for self-regulation and self-governance of its citizens, rather than an exclusive part of the emancipatory project it professes to be" (Clark & Richards, 2017, p. 135). Rather than allow teachers to pursue children's interests so that they can lead the lives they wish to live, many state-level stakeholders wanted students to learn the required academic standards so that they could be productive citizens. To do so, many suggested reforming teacher training.

Improving Teacher Training. The senior advisor to the Texas governor stated that to improve teacher development, "we need better professional development for those teachers in the early years. We need to equip teachers with the resources that they need to be successful." This advisor took this idea a little further and linked development and support to the profession of teaching itself.

> It all comes back to the teachers. I wish the profession of teaching was elevated. Improving schooling is about the teacher and how that teacher feels about the job that they're doing; most teachers do it because they want to change lives. People need to realize how hard it is and how valuable these teachers are. If you could change that, then you can completely change what happens in a classroom.

RRI District Liaison #1 made a similar argument, stating:

> We're going to test these children on these standards, and if your standards test scores come in too low, we are going to start evaluating the teacher. We need to figure out how we take those mediocre teachers and coach them up so they aren't mediocre. I can guarantee you that those mediocre teachers don't want to be mediocre. They just don't know how to improve, and they have been beaten down to think, "I'm never going to be a good teacher, I have all of these things sitting on top of me, I'm not going to improve."

This liaison's colleague, RRI District Liaison #2, added:

> I had a really good teaching friend say to me once, "You're really, really fortunate if your child has one outstanding teacher in the whole K–12 experience, and you are really, really fortunate if you only have one bad teacher. The rest of them are mediocre," and so we really need to think about how we train our teachers.

While all these statements for improving the teacher workforce through training, professional development, and public support have been supported by empirical research as means to improve student learning (e.g., Williford et al., 2017), such proposals keep the current system intact. In doing so, teachers ultimately will be responsible for children attaining policymakers' academic performance expectations.

The Difficulty of Reform. Thus, when talking about actually implementing their first-order (Cuban, 1988) changes, these stakeholders struggled to conceive how such reform might move through the state legislature and change the "system." For example, when looking at issues such as student-to-teacher ratios, the policy analyst for the Texas senator on the Education Committee noted:

> The problem is that if we mandate something like there being a certain student-to-teacher ratio, that is a drain on scant resources, and it's very difficult to get something passed in the legislature that is going to have that large a fiscal impact on the budget.

This analyst's statement demonstrates how education reform in Texas must be framed through a zero-cost perspective. The analyst continued, "As far as legislative things, I'm not really sure how much we can do from here. A lot of that is local initiative." The legislative director for a Texas representative on the Education Committee added:

> Education is expensive, and Texas has 5.2 million school-aged children that they're required to educate, over 1,200 school districts. It's expensive to educate kids, and there's just so much money that goes into it. That's where we run into a problem. We live in a state where we don't have income tax, so we don't have that extra revenue, and funding becomes a huge issue. There's all sorts of ideas floating around to put more funds into the system, reappropriate certain things. But at the end of the day, when you're dealing with a comptroller who's often saying that we have to cut budgets across all agencies, then you have a school finance crisis where you've got these kids that aren't necessarily getting as much money as they need to be educated—what do you do? And nobody wants to raise taxes and nobody wants to pay more money to educate somebody else's kid. That's something that we always hear.

Combined, these statements demonstrate how education reform in Texas is difficult because of funding issues. For example, DeMatthews and Knight (2018) found that between 2008 and 2017, Texas decreased funding per pupil by 12.6%, while the student population increased by 13.7%. Essentially, addressing the cost of public education in Texas still appears to be the foundational issue limiting first-order change.

This is not to say that the only reason education reform in Texas is difficult is funding. Another issue, according to the lawyer on the Texas Senate Education Committee, is nostalgia. The lawyer explained:

> People are impressed by the academics kids can do, but they want change. So there's this tension between their memories of kindergarten—more playing, going out to recess, and that type of stuff—and change. Nostalgia is our number one obstacle for policy change. We have state senators asking [why] kids aren't taught cursive anymore? Beside the fact that kids don't even have to write papers with a computer anymore or just speak into their phones, we don't know what 90% of the jobs in 2030 are, and yet, we have legislators worried about cursive? So I think to tie down education and education policy in nostalgia is not best for kids.

This lawyer's concern over nostalgia connects back to the earlier concern over how education is framed in Texas. For this lawyer, to prepare students to be productive citizens, the conversation has to shift from what was done in the past to the future.

Yet such logic distracts education stakeholders from focusing on the needs of children in the here and now, and frames childhood as a process in which children are always becoming and never being (Qvortrup, 2009). In doing so, state-level education stakeholders appear to disregard how kindergartners "are shaped by the kinds of childhoods they are experiencing today" (Uprichard, 2008, p. 311). Additionally, similar to school stakeholders, some questioned whether policymakers actually knew what happened in schools. For example, the Texas House member on the Education Committee commented, "I think that legislators don't understand kindergarten at all. I think there's a really big disconnect." Combined, such statements demonstrate the complexity and difficulty in pushing change in kindergarten specifically and public education in general.

What Might Be Done? I began this book with a quote from the Texas House member on the Education Committee in which that legislator asked, "Where is the group that is literally just working on changing what's taking place in the classroom on a daily basis—be it kindergarten or any grade?" Answering that question appears to be one possible avenue for change. Remember, the legislative director for a Texas representative on the Education Committee stated that policymakers were interested in moving away from teaching the test because of "teachers, parents, and students coming up here and saying teachers can't teach." When pressed on what might be required to advocate for change in the classroom, the Texas House member on the Education Committee added:

> You have to guide legislators toward making changes that are concrete, which is very difficult. Ratios [teacher to student], that would be an easy build, but it would be an expensive build—you would have to have more facilities, more educators, etc. But that's something concrete that we can fix.
>
> Still, it's not that great ideas aren't out there. It's that there's no vehicle, no strategy, no long-term commitment, no financing, no leadership to bridge the academic ideas and the halls of power. To shift and start to change, policy has to be collective, but without all of that in place, I don't even think you can start. To do that takes a strategic plan. Here are the things that you want to have happen, and here's the research to support it. Then, I would meet with the Speaker of the House's office, then the Lieutenant Governor's office, and then I would go to the Education Committee. I would also work during the interim to get things on the interim agenda (the Texas legislature meets biannually), and then I would have bills drafted for the next session and get them filed when session starts. All along the way, I would strengthen the relationships because the only way anything happens here—the only way anything moves—is through relationships. You need a lobby team who is here, who knows the staff of legislators, and is meeting with that staff during the interim. Then, during the session, you have to get people to testify and then they follow up to make sure that the bill does get drafted.
>
> If your bills get drafted and filed, you have to remember there are almost 10,000 bills filed, and this is a part-time job, supposedly, but it's not. So, if you want something to happen, you not only have to have a legislator who will file the bill, but you have to have someone behind the scenes to talk to 181 legislators about that one bill. You need an institutional support system to get things done. But that doesn't just help legislators with bills; it also helps legislators with working with state agencies, like TEA, so that they have some strategic institutional support to push the bill through.

While this legislator's suggestions for reform may not be surprising, they do provide an outline for how change might occur in a state like Texas. The irony of this statement is that for a state focused on a neoliberal economic conception of public education that emphasizes limited funding, implementing such a strategic plan requires a vast amount of fiscal and human capital, and for those who work in public education, both are scarce.

WEST VIRGINIA STAKEHOLDERS

Unlike in Texas, policymakers in West Virginia appeared to be thinking about how to address the academic shovedown that had been occurring in the early grades across their state. When I met with and/or talked to county- and state-level administrators and policymakers, they were in the process of reverting kindergarten and pre-K to "readiness" grades. Accordingly, the county- and state-level stakeholders framed kindergarten differently from school principals, teachers, and families in West Virginia (see Figure 5.2 for a list of West Virginia county and state participants).

This change was the result of legislation implemented in 2014 that was to alter the instructional practices that take place in pre-K and kindergarten, both of which were to be "readiness grades" (e.g., West Virginia Board of Education, 2014). Still, enacting policies that framed kindergarten and pre-K differently did not decrease the academic expectations on children once they entered 1st grade. Furthermore, in 2015, under Senate Bill 524, the West Virginia State Legislature repealed the Common Core standards. Still, as Ms. Holgorsen, the curriculum director in WVC2, noted, "We now say, 'We're not a Common Core state,' but really, the standards are almost exactly the same. They changed a few words here and there, but it's essentially the same thing."

County Stakeholders Figuring the Kinder-Race

When I discussed the Kinder-Race with county-level stakeholders, these policy changes led many to express thoughts similar to those of Mr. Carey, the WVC1 curriculum director, who stated:

> We are getting closer back to where we were 15 years ago. While we were focused solely on academic readiness and increasing the academic rigor of schooling for the past 10 years, the change that occurred in 2014 has us focused on the development of the whole child—ensuring they are ready not just academically, but socially, physically, emotionally. Still, what was expected in 1st grade is now expected in kindergarten, and 6th grade is now what we used to do in 10th grade.

While Mr. Carey noted that state-level reforms had shifted how kindergarten was to be viewed within the context of public schooling, he also pointed out that what was expected for teachers in kindergarten had changed: "What was expected in 1st grade is now expected in kindergarten." When asked what those expectations were, his colleague, Ms. Hastings, the kindergarten liaison for WVC1, commented, "They [kindergartners] need to be achieving what the content standards say they should be doing; that includes knowing up to 100 sight words. Developing an increasing

Figure 5.2. County and State Participants in West Virginia

County Participants	State Participants
Mr. Carey, WVC1 Curriculum Director*	State Coordinator of Elementary Education
Ms. Hastings, WVC1 Kindergarten Liaison*	State Academic Officer
Ms. Holgorsen, WVC2 Curriculum Director	State Director of Early Learning
	Secretary of Education
	Former Assistant State Superintendent
	West Virginia State School Board Member and Former State Legislator
	West Virginia Senator and Member of Senate Education Committee
	West Virginia Representative and Member of House Education Committee
	Representative from West Virginia Business Group That Supports Public Education

Note: * = participated in a focus group.

vocabulary, being ready socially, knowing how to collaborate with each other, and so on." Ms. Hastings's outline of the achievement expectations for kindergarten reflects what the WVC1 kindergarten teachers discussed in Chapter 4.

This shift in the framing of kindergarten as a readiness grade, without decreasing academic achievement expectations, may be why, as Ms. Holgorsen, the curriculum director in WVC2, pointed out, what was occurring in the kindergarten classrooms that were a part of my investigation had not changed. Ms. Holgorsen commented:

> The problem is our kindergarten teachers think that their students need to know every letter of the alphabet going into the 1st grade, and that's not even our standards anymore. So there's this disconnect between kindergarten and 1st grade, and we have to work on bridging that gap with the expectations of kindergarten as a readiness grade with what it means to be prepared for 1st grade.

While the disconnect that exists between policy formulation and its implementation in classrooms has been documented for decades (e.g., Cohen & Spillane, 1993), addressing this gap between the academic achievement expectations of kindergarten and 1st grade was a struggle these stakeholders had yet to resolve. As the kindergarten liaison in WVC1 stated, "The academic expectations are not decreasing, but we are changing the way teachers are to present academic content to students. It's now more discovery-based and guided instruction rather than direct instruction from the teacher." However, as I pointed out in the previous chapter, the kindergarten teachers did not appear to receive this message to decrease academic expectations or possibly believe they could teach their students in the manner this liaison describes because the expectations had not changed (Brown et al., 2020a).

Moreover, the administrators in both counties questioned whether these changes would "work." For example, Ms. Holgorsen in WVC2 stated:

> We're having a hard time reconciling how we are supposed to teach the students against the standards that we're required to teach. I'm having a really hard time figuring out what's the best way to make sure our kids master these standards that we're being held accountable for, at the same time making sure that there is a lot of hands-on, inquiry-based, and student-led instruction. I don't know what to do.

Ms. Holgorsen's struggles also were reflected in the statements of Mr. Carey in WVC1, when he noted:

> I don't think how we are supposed to teach kindergartners will deliver enough direct content to them. I like direct instruction, and I don't think it's wrong for teachers to do a few high-quality worksheets with their students as long as there is a point in doing them. Teachers should not just hand them to them and say, "Here you go, good luck."
>
> I am worried that down the road we are going to see children's test scores go down. For example, we no longer do the 100s chart every day, and we no longer focus so much on children learning up to 100 sight words. I worry that we are not putting in enough academic expectations for our students. I think we need more of a mix of academics and social skills.

Both administrators' statements illuminate the mixed messages occurring around curriculum and instruction between county administrators and classroom teachers (Linn, 2005). For example, Mr. Carey questioned whether teachers were teaching their students 100 sight words, and every teacher I talked with in WVC1 mentioned they were and struggling with that expectation. These administrators' statements also bring to light a central tension within the field of early childhood education specifically and public education in general (Brown, 2011, 2013). There is a lack of "trust," or possibly understanding, about the way in which what is considered student-led instruction as well as instructional strategies like "play" can teach children the academic knowledge they need in order to succeed in school. I revisit this issue in Chapter 6, but for now, researchers consistently have found that instructional approaches that simultaneously attend to children's developmental needs and the academic content they are expected to know may hold the most promise for improving kindergartners' academic achievement (Goble & Pianta, 2017; Weisberg et al., 2013). Nevertheless, these stakeholders will be held accountable if students' academic performance dips, and thus their fears are tied to not only the students they work with but also their own careers.

County Stakeholders Rerouting the Kinder-Race?

Unlike all the other stakeholders I've discussed until this point, these county administrators' understanding of the Kinder-Race was unique. They knew the race had changed course in West Virginia, and instead of asking for more change, they were struggling to make sense of how to put the most recent reforms in place (Brown, Barry, Ku, & Englehardt, 2021). As both Ms. Holgorsen in WVC2 and Mr. Carey in WVC1 remarked, they struggled with wrapping their heads around how to engage in more student-led/play-based instruction while meeting high academic achievement expectations. They both wanted to be reassured that the changes they were implementing would not harm their students, teachers, or themselves. Moreover, they wanted to make sure that the education system in West Virginia was properly aligned. For example, Ms. Holgorsen in WVC2 said:

> I think that whoever is making these decisions at the state level needs to make sure that this is what they want kindergarten to look like. If so, our teachers need to know that. For example, I had just heard for the first time the State Director of Early Learning say that our kindergarten classrooms need to look more like our pre-K classrooms. That's the first time I'd ever heard her say that, and if that's what I'm going to be held accountable for, I need to know that. So a common message needs to get out there that these are the expectations, and then we need to get that to our teachers and support them in that—providing some professional development, additional training, materials, and those kinds of things. We just need to know what the expectations are. We're happy to do whatever, but we just need to know.

Thus, these administrators appear willing to change the practices of kindergarten within their counties, but they want to be sure that (1) they have the support of state policymakers in accomplishing this goal; and (2) the changes they make will continue to improve students' academic achievement. They know that their students' test scores are the currency by which they will be valued by state policymakers (Ball, 2003), and thus the core (Majone, 1989) of "what matters" within their education system has not been altered by these reforms.

State Stakeholders Figuring the Kinder-Race

As I noted when discussing how state stakeholders were making sense of the Kinder-Race in Texas, many of the families, teachers, and principals I talked with (see Chapter 4) wanted state policymakers and administrators to see the video I created because they felt that state stakeholders, particularly policymakers, did not know what was occurring in the changed kindergarten on a daily basis. Interestingly, the secretary of education made a similar statement:

> We need to stop doing policy. If it were up to me, I would burn all the policies! There's too many policies. If you would go to one of our State Board of Education meetings, those board members, who are volunteers and lay members, for the most part, do nothing but look at huge books full of policies and amend them endlessly. Policies just get in the way. They never get out of that building over there. "Go out to a school and see what's happening. Don't sit there and make a policy!"
>
> Kindergarten is a very special time, and I love it if they can learn their letters and learn their colors and learn some discipline and blah-blah-blah, but it should also be a time for outdoor exercise, indoor exercise, lots of snack time, and fun. We need to foster their creativity and desire to learn, and the endless policies are extinguishing that.

The secretary worried that policymakers' reforms were impeding kindergarten teachers and their students from engaging in learning experiences that could foster children's desires to be learners. As noted before, policymakers in West Virginia had altered their policies to begin to address this issue, and as I talked with other stakeholders at the state level, they also wanted to foster children's desire to learn while at the same ensuring that they were learning the knowledge and skills needed to succeed in and out of the classroom.

Creating Lifelong Learners. The tension between supporting teachers and students in the learning process, and ensuring that students learn what is needed to succeed in school and life, was also present at the state level in West Virginia. For instance, the state school board member and former legislator commented:

> When thinking about the level of academic performance we're expecting of these kids, at times, we forget what we're asking of these kids at that age, and how very good they are at those things. Sometimes that sort of surprises you a little bit. But, there's just no way they can come prepared for 1st grade to learn if they don't have these skills when they do that.

While this board member seems a bit taken aback by the academic expectations placed on kindergartners, these stakeholders also see that there is no alternative for children other than attaining these skills so that they are successful in 1st grade. As Lipman (2013) argued, the "strength of accountability discourses" (p. 569) is that they clearly frame what student learning must entail.

Others at the state level were worried that these expectations for kindergartners were too high, which led them to question what these high expectations might be doing to children, teachers, and schools. The state academic officer commented, "There's so much pressure to get these kids ready that they need to spend more and more targeted time and we're losing that sense of an integrated, holistic approach to the whole child." A former assistant state superintendent in West Virginia stated, "Kindergarten has become a race. It's not the journey of childhood. Children are just being pushed from skill to skill to skill." The secretary of education also noted, "The creative part of kindergarten is dying. It's being extinguished and killed. It breaks my heart. I would like to see more creative ways to give them confidence and be a part of a successful endeavor." Both are worried that, as the state director of early learning pointed out, "Every one of them brings to kindergarten the belief they can be anything, but as I said, we see by age 8 research shows us that children already know, 'I'm not going to be successful.'"

What West Virginia State Stakeholders Wanted Their Reroute to Be. With these worries about the pressure being put on kindergartners by the high academic achievement expectations in mind, many of the stakeholders had a range of hopes as to what kindergarten could be. For instance, a representative from a West Virginia business group that supports public education pointed out:

> Kindergarten sets that stage and the expectations for children, so, at a minimum, there has to be a strong foundation in kindergarten in literacy and numeracy. Still, rather than pushing expectations down from college about what learning should be about, we need to stop and really listen to the early learning experts that know about brain development and understand about how to engage children in hands-on opportunities and all those other things.

This idea of having a kindergarten teacher who could engage children in what would be considered developmentally appropriate learning experiences (e.g., Copple & Bredekamp, 2009) also was expressed by the state coordinator of elementary education:

> A high-quality classroom is one where children have the opportunity to be met at their own developmental level. It's the teacher's job to

> meet the children where they are at rather than say, "You come here and you do this for this number of minutes and then do that." I think, obviously, reading is a very important component here in West Virginia, and I suspect in other states around the country too. We do have a significant gap between the number of students that are reading on grade level by the time they enter 4th grade. I think anything we can be doing in kindergarten to prepare students so that they can be as much on track as possible when they enter 4th grade is great.

This coordinator's statement again illuminates the tension between wanting teachers to engage in practices that support children where they are developmentally and ensuring that children are on a trajectory to succeed academically (Brown, 2007b).

As the state academic officer noted, the reforms that had been implemented in previous years were to get at this issue. The officer stated:

> What we're hoping to see is a change in the environment; there's not a lot of sitting or large-group time. We want to see well-rounded, center-based classrooms where these kids are engaged and have a lot of autonomy—but also one in which a routine is established. We want to see a lot more time spent in small groups—we're not seeing the personalized learning right now.

This officer seems to be speaking back to what others are hoping is occurring in kindergarten classrooms and argues the policies that were passed were designed to create such classrooms.

Still, across these statements is the empiricist conception of kindergarten readying children for school success (Meisels, 1999), which was echoed by policymakers in Texas. The West Virginia representative and member of the House Education Committee noted, "There's a recognition that what we do in the early grades is going to have a great impact on a student's future success." The West Virginia senator and member of the Senate Education Committee also stated:

> Kindergarten is the place where children who are behind in their development can get caught up. It provides an opportunity for the families as well as the students to learn what is expected of the student in terms of behavior and basic skills. Kindergarten is the first step in reducing the achievement gap in students from different socioeconomic backgrounds.

Entwined in these legislators' empiricist framing of kindergarten is the neoliberal logic of gaps and investments. This idea of being behind is "entangled with deficit assumptions" about children and their families (Nxumalo & Adair, 2019, p. 665), which this House member framed through the language of the achievement gap. In doing so, these state-level stakeholders frame children and their families as being what Dumas and Nelson (2016) termed "materially vulnerable" (p. 33). Thus, within this neoliberal rhetoric, kindergarten becomes a vehicle that prepares unready children for academic success (Brown, 2008a), and as a result this empiricist conception of school readiness can overlook the promise and brilliance children bring to this process (Pérez & Saavedra, 2017), as well as the practices families engage in to prepare their children for school success (Huber et al., 2018).

This neoliberal framing of kindergarten specifically and education in general as "the ideal mechanism of recovery" for those who "have not" (Slater, 2015, p. 3) was reiterated by others at the state level. For instance, the state academic officer commented:

> A really high-quality kindergarten program personalizes it, really focuses in on where those gaps are for each child—a more balanced approach—less transitions for young kids and bigger chunks of time on learning. Those are going to be the programs that have the most impact and really prepare them for 1st grade and beyond. I think if we can close some of those gaps early, it's going to have the biggest impact.

The West Virginia state school board member and former state legislator also noted:

> As far as kindergarten goes, you want to be sure that children are developing the skills they need to be ready to read, to write, and to do basic math at grade level. There's just no way they can be prepared for 1st grade, 2nd, and particularly 3rd grade if they don't have these skills when they do that, particularly 3rd grade, so that they go from learning to read, to reading to learn sufficiently—that way, they're ready to learn when they hit those later grades.

So while some state stakeholders wanted to ensure that kindergarten was a place that met children where they were and provided them appropriate learning experiences, such practices were to prepare children to read so that they could continue to grow academically as they progressed through school. Such statements reinforce the "prevailing [neoliberal] discourse" that "insists" children become "entrepreneurs" who possess a specific set of "cognitive and symbolic capital" needed to succeed in school and society at large (De Lissovoy, 2018, p. 202). These stakeholders wanted children to be excited about school and learning, but this excitement was tied to a particular type of learning and to becoming a specific type of student.

Continuing to Reroute Kindergarten

While West Virginia had already implemented a series of policies to reroute kindergarten, one area that a few state stakeholders still hoped to improve in their public education system was teacher training and education. For example, the secretary of education noted:

> We need to improve teacher preparation. Our policies can really dictate their pedagogy, to the point where they don't have any fun either as they prepare for the profession. Naturally, they pass that affliction on to the children. We also pay them so poorly that they don't stick around long.

This secretary's statement appears to reflect Ryan et al.'s (2017) argument that there is an "important link between high-stakes testing, accountability policies, and teacher attrition" (p. 8), and in making this statement, the secretary seems to assume that this will not change. The director of early learning also noted that the state needs "teachers who are well versed in child development, know about standards, and are versed in curriculum so that they can create and implement an environment that intentionally supports children's learning." However, as the West Virginia representative and member of the House Education Committee commented, "I think one of the challenges we have in West Virginia currently is that we have a number of individuals in our classrooms that are emergency certified." Combined, these stakeholders, who appear to want all kindergartners to succeed, are revealing the failures of policymakers' neoliberal reforms in achieving this goal. Their reforms frame education as an outcomes-based economic system that projects "an illusion of meritocracy, where all students are perceived to have equal access to a high-quality education" (Brathwaite, 2016, p. 437). Yet this commodification of teaching and teacher education also has led to the expansion of emergency-certified teachers as well as nontraditional certification programs (e.g., Teach for America) that "dismiss the notion that teachers need formal teacher education before stepping in a classroom" (Baltodano, 2012, p. 496). Such policies not only deprofessionalize teaching but also position teachers as disposable commodities who are easily replaced by those who are willing to teach where and how their state or local system dictates (Brown et al., 2016; Einboden et al., 2013).

Why Continue to Reroute Kindergarten?

For these state education stakeholders, kindergarten mattered, and they had made several policy changes to improve it; besides making it a readiness grade, the state also mandated an aide for classrooms with more than 10 students and that every kindergartner have 30 minutes of recess a day. When

I asked why this occurred, much of what I was told was that such changes were a good investment for West Virginia. For example, the West Virginia representative and member of the House Education Committee noted:

> We want to obviously prepare them to either enter the workforce or to pursue a postsecondary education, so just having those skill sets necessary in order to pursue either one of those areas. I think we need to do our very best to provide the students the skills they need to pursue whichever avenue fits their goals. Still, I would hope that parents would advocate for educational choice, so that if they are in a school system that is simply not performing up to the students' and parents' expectations, they have real options regardless of where they live or their income level.

This policymaker's statement appears to be framed through notions of individualism—allowing students to pursue their individual interests, while advocating for parental choice.

The representative from a West Virginia business group that supports public education noted:

> Kindergarten is the first step to ensure that all students are on a path to be college and career ready. By having a high-quality kindergarten, we gain a long-term benefit of maximizing that opportunity, when children's learning is still in really high gear and their brains are still developing. Doing so just makes sense, so it's a matter of recalibrating how we think about our investments as a society.

This representative is focusing on governmental investments, specifically the notion of human capital, that Heckman (2000) and others (e.g., Reynolds et al., 2018) employ to advocate for education. The state director of early learning also discussed this investment as follows:

> We know that even the return on the investment is huge whenever kids have those high-quality learning programs to attend—especially those children that come from poverty.
>
> We know that they may not have those opportunities, resources, and experiences at home that they might have if their children are in a high-quality kindergarten program. This is not to negate what families can provide, and I think that's one of the things we always have to be cognizant of—that family is the child's first teacher. We truly do need to honor that. I know that kindergarten can give all children access to resources, to new knowledge, and the opportunity to interact with their peers—all of which can be very rich and very positive for them.

Across these statements, these education stakeholders position kindergarten as a program that can prepare children for a lifetime of academic and economic success.

The hidden danger within their rhetoric is that they are framing public education through markets, standardization, and accountability (Brown, 2015), and as such, kindergarten becomes an increasingly important aspect of the "neoliberal lifeworld" (Slater, 2015, p. 1). This is a lifeworld in which policymakers' "rhetoric of readiness and risk seduce[s]" teachers, families, and children from notions of "subjecthood into markethood" (Sonu & Benson, 2016, p. 243). In this way, policymakers and their allies create opportunities "to expand sectors of potential profit accumulation" within public education so that they increase their "opportunities to actualize their" neoliberal "visions" of governance (Slater, 2015, p. 4).

What Can Be Learned From West Virginia's Rerouting of Kindergarten?

I began this discussion of how state stakeholders in West Virginia were making sense of the Kinder-Race with a quote from the secretary of education calling for no more policy. Until this point, that idea has not been shared by this secretary's peers across the state. However, the former assistant state superintendent stated that, in fact, it was the elimination of policy that led to West Virginia's rerouting of kindergarten. I end this subsection with this superintendent's statements about how the rerouting occurred, to highlight another possible direction policymakers and advocates may go to end the Kinder-Race—a direction that is quite different from the one proposed by the Texas House member on the Education Committee. The former assistant state superintendent described the rerouting process this way:

> Reforming kindergarten wasn't about what policies we needed in place. It was what policies we needed to remove because over that 20-year journey we had taken away what was wonderful out of kindergarten. We started with kindergarten as getting children to be learning in an environment that was rich with opportunity and rich with literature. Then, we put in a policy where you have to have 20 minutes of this and 30 minutes of that, and then you test them. We piled on and made early learning look like miniature 8th grade.
>
> What we've done over the past couple years is asked, "How can we remove policy so that we are focused on the standards that we want every child to know, understand, and be able to do?" So we started removing policies. The first thing we did was remove time constraints—not just for kindergarten, but for the whole of elementary so that it no longer says that you have to have 90 minutes of reading, 60 minutes of math, 30 minutes of social studies. Instead, our policy

> is that these are your standards and this is how you're going to be accountable for them.
>
> Policy work is not piling on. It's removing restrictions that keep the professionals in the classroom from making decisions about what's best for that child's learning. All policy decisions about children should be made as close to the classroom as possible. It shouldn't be made by a legislature or State Board of Education. What we need to do at the policy level is to set the parameters that keep any harm from happening to children and set what we want all children to know at the end—what a college career and civically ready graduate is at the end.

In West Virginia, there appeared to be a realization that the direction in which the Kinder-Race was headed was not working. To begin to reroute the education process, state-level education administrators and policymakers realized they needed to cut back on the demands being placed on teachers and provide some resources where needed, such as having an aide in classrooms where there are more than 10 kindergartners. Yet state policymakers did not eliminate the academic content standards or assessments for accountability, but they did want to provide teachers with more opportunities to make "decisions about what's best for that child's learning" at the "street level" (Lipsky, 1980). However, as the statements made by county- and school-level personnel, as well as families and kindergarten teachers in West Virginia, demonstrated, these reforms do not appear to be enough to alter what was occurring prior to the implementation of these policy changes in 2014. Still, an alternative was offered, one that left the logic of neoliberal reform intact, which created the Kinder-Race in the first place.

NATIONAL STAKEHOLDERS

To broaden my analysis and discussion of the Kinder-Race, as well as to consider possibilities for rerouting the Kinder-Race in ways that might not be reflected in what is occurring in Texas and West Virginia, I sought out the input of national stakeholders who either research and/or advocate for public education issues (see Figure 5.3 for a list of national participants).

The Kinder-Race Is What "It" Is

When I began to share my work with others across Texas and West Virginia, and at the national level, many stakeholders questioned me, before viewing the video, about whether I could create a video of a typical day of kindergarten. Yet, as I have demonstrated with participants in Texas and West Virginia,

Figure 5.3. National Participants

Policy Expert for National Early Education Advocacy Group*
Senior Advisor for National Early Education Advocacy Group*
Liaison with State Groups That Are Part of the National Early Education Advocacy Group*
Representative from a DC Think Tank Focused on Solutions to Public Problems
Representative from an Organization Committed to Providing Low-Income Children Access to ECE
Representative from a National Early Childhood Grant Organization
Representative from a National Organization Representing State Officials in Education
Representative from an Organization Representing State Officials in ECE
Representative from a National Organization Committed to Closing the Achievement Gap
Representative from a National Principals Organization
Representative from a National School Board Organization
Researcher at a National Early Childhood Research Organization
Early Childhood Expert from National Alternative Teacher Staffing Organization
National Early Childhood Teacher Educator and Early Childhood Advocate
National Early Childhood Researcher Who Studies Kindergarten Teaching
National Advocate for Froebelian Kindergarten Programs

Note: * = participated in a focus group.

those who knew what kindergarten had become stated that the video *is* what occurs in kindergarten classrooms across the United States, even if they disagreed with *what* was occurring in these classrooms. For example, a researcher at a national early childhood research organization stated, "This is a typical kindergarten day; that's exactly what I would expect to see." A national early childhood teacher educator and early childhood advocate added:

> It's kindergarten, and it's overwhelming. My first impression was, "Wow, these kids are really good," given the rigor of the curriculum, the expectations, the lengthy whole-group times, and the lack of opportunities to go outside and have any free-choice time. They go through almost 6 hours before they actually get to breathe fresh air, and then only for 15 minutes.

In this statement, the advocate has identified what kindergarten is and why what it "is" concerns them. A representative from a national school board organization put it bluntly: "Kindergarten has become a little junior high." This led a national early childhood researcher who studies kindergarten teaching to state that in becoming such a learning program, kindergarten "is horrible and boring. Not horrible, it's just what it is. It is in many cases what school looks like for kids. It's boring. It's flat—at least the teacher was nice." A representative from a national principals organization added, "The video was troubling to me, because many of the things that I know are appropriate for children were not happening, and in fact, it was almost an egregious act of pushing down in curriculum and inappropriate practice for kindergarten." Again, these stakeholders, like those in Texas and West Virginia, are troubled by how the accountability shovedown has led to the Kinder-Race (Hatch, 2002). As Christopher and Farran (2020) found in their own investigation into practices that support children's learning in 98 kindergarten classrooms, the majority of which were Title I classrooms, such classrooms do "not seem to be very positive places for children to be." The instructional focus of teachers is on "didactic, primarily whole group instruction, with teachers talking most of the time, and children exhibiting rather low levels of involvement in learning and no time to work with peers" (p. 647).

What Was "Not Happening"?

As the national principals representative pointed out, many of these stakeholders' descriptions of their interpretation of the Kinder-Race centered on what they wanted to see occurring in a kindergarten classroom. For example, the liaison with state groups that are part of a national early education advocacy group contended, "Children had very limited opportunities for physical play, and movement, particularly child-directed movement and play." A senior advisor for that same advocacy group added, "They had very few opportunities for child-directed activities of any kind, very little physical activity, and very few opportunities to interact with their peers." These concerns match those shared by kindergartners, teachers, families, school/district/county administrators, and state stakeholders. All want to ensure children have more opportunities for choice and voice in their learning (Brown & Mowry, 2015). I will return to this idea in Chapter 6, but for now it is important to recognize that these stakeholders were not asking for teachers to engage in more direct instruction in academic skills. Rather, they appeared to be seeking more opportunities in the classroom where children could engage in learning experiences that encompassed all their developmental domains, allowed them to make choices, and offered them chances to engage with their peers (e.g., Pyle & Danniels, 2017).

Getting Ready for the Test

These stakeholders offered a range of explanations for why kindergarten had become a race from skill to skill (Brown, Ku, & Barry, 2020a, 2020b). All mentioned what the representative from a national principals organization framed as "the pushing down." This representative continued, "It was very obvious. It was all about the test. To the sense that the teacher was even using flash-cards to get the kids ready for the tests; telling them, 'The faster you read this, the faster you're going to learn to read and write.' When we know that every child develops differently." As a national advocate for Froebelian kindergarten programs pointed out, "The whole education system is managed by what we measure. We measure what we're, as adults, interested in—literacy essentially, memorization, and all that. That's why kindergarten is focused on skills prep for the 1st grade."

These stakeholders interpreted Ms. Cutler's instruction as being centered on "multiple-choice teaching" practices meant to prepare children for academic achievement tests (Smith, 1991, p. 10). They thought this led to a classroom where, as the national early childhood teacher educator and early childhood advocate commented, "these kids are totally other-regulated. The teacher has regulated every single element of their experience." The representative from a national organization committed to closing the achievement gap also noted, "She was a lovely teacher who works really hard, but those poor children were being worked within an inch of their lives. They didn't look like they were having a lot of fun, and she looked like she needed help." In fact, a policy expert for a national early education advocacy group stated, "What's most disheartening is the fact that she's probably seen as a pretty good teacher within the district and was clearly responding to external pressure from administrators in her school and maybe state." Combined, these statements demonstrate how policymakers' neoliberal reforms have led this teacher to "other-regulate" her students in a manner intended to teach them the academic skills and knowledge to succeed on the test.

Concerns About Kindergartners

These stakeholders worried that Ms. Cutler's teaching the test and other-regulating her students' actions negatively impacted both the children and Ms. Cutler. The national Froebelian advocate noted:

> I felt sad for the kids and the teacher. They were capable of more, but they had this system that they had to navigate. We're telling them that this is what school—"This is your day. This is where you're going to spend most of your time then you're going to have to go home and decompress from that."

This advocate frames the Kinder-Race from a systems-level perspective, a system of education that fails to consider best practices for teaching as well as how children learn (e.g., Moss, 2014). A representative from a national school board organization similarly stated:

> This is why we have students that just continually get burned out because they haven't had the opportunity to be a child. They haven't had the opportunity to love learning and to be curious. They've just been pushed from skill to skill to skill. It's not showing up on these 5-year-olds, but it may show up on the same children when they're 14. We need to take a long view of what schooling is doing. Not that teacher, but what schooling is doing to children.

Like the Froebelian advocate, this representative is making the case that to rethink the Kinder-Race (and schooling in general) requires the lens of school reform to be focused on the system itself—not just the acts of individuals—which counters the neoliberal tendency to fracture and individualize policy problems. If such rethinking is not done, the system will continue to fail students and their families, and cause them as well as kindergarten teachers to burn out (Ryan et al., 2017; Virtanen et al., 2016).

Combined, these stakeholders do not hold a positive view of what kindergarten has become, and their critiques appear to be about the quality of learning experiences children are having and the instruction of the teacher. Yet, in making these critiques, they also recognize that these negative learning experiences are a result of what the system of public education has become—preparing for the tests through didactic learning experiences.

NATIONAL STAKEHOLDERS REROUTING THE KINDER-RACE

The suggestions made by these national stakeholders for rerouting the Kinder-Race reflected many of the ideas put forward by other stakeholders, which demonstrates that there is a consensus among stakeholders for changing kindergarten—a necessary ingredient for reforming education systems (Cohen & Mehta, 2017). One area of focus for change among these stakeholders was to provide a range of learning opportunities for students rather than implementing a banking model of schooling (Freire, 1974, 1970/2006). A representative from a national organization representing state officials in early childhood argued children should be in classrooms where

> The teacher and the children engage in authentic relationships, and the teacher listens to children's stories while incorporating the skills that she wants children to learn in more authentic ways. By authentic, I mean building upon the rich experiences that children already bring to the classroom. I want the teacher to develop children's dispositional skills like conflict resolution, problem solving, higher order thinking by using real stories and real things that happen in life, literature that is diverse, and to help children get a feel for a love of learning.

A representative from a DC think tank focused on solutions to public problems thought that engaging in such activities would develop children's:

> Social–emotional skills. They need to be engaged in experiences that build their approaches to learning. Their executive function skills, as well. They do need to also have background knowledge about the world. That will help to build their reading skills. But without background knowledge, they're not going to comprehend what they're actually reading.

This representative's statement reflects Hyson's (2008) argument that teachers must pay attention to children's feelings (enthusiasm) and actions (engagement) in their instruction. For example, researchers have found that children who have a high motivation to read typically spend more time reading, which leads to their developing better comprehension skills about what they are reading, choosing more complex material to read, and feeling more successful as a reader (Guthrie et al., 2000). Instructionally, Hyson (2008) and others (e.g., Diamond, 2013) have shown that students' emotions serve as the primary motivator of their behavior; they must be motivated by their emotions to engage in positive learning behaviors. Thus, Hyson's (2008) work highlights the importance of recognizing that when "teaching" children anything, instructors need to balance their intentions between the goals of skill acquisition (e.g., learning the short-vowel sounds) and fostering children's dispositions toward such acquisition (e.g., seeing this process of learning to identify phonemes correctly both as beneficial for learning to read and as fun). If teachers fail to pay attention to their students' feelings and emotions, they not only decrease the likelihood that their students will learn the new skill (e.g., identifying short-vowel sounds), but also can diminish children's desire to learn in general (e.g., students learning to "hate" school).

Several national stakeholders also talked about providing children with more opportunities for play. In stating this, the representative from a national principals organization noted, "There's this false dichotomy about play and learning," and the national early childhood teacher educator and early childhood advocate added:

> Play is what we need in kindergarten. The problem with that is unless you have teachers who are sufficiently trained to bring out the serious learning that goes on in play and how to promote that as well as understand how to individualize all these different children's levels and everything, those kids are not going to succeed academically.

This advocate's statement reflects the work of such scholars as Pyle and Danniels (2017) and others (e.g., Van Oers & Duijkers, 2013), who contend that play must be rethought in the kindergarten classroom. Pyle and Daniels (2017) argue that:

> Rather than decreasing the amount of time children spend in play in favor of explicitly teaching prescribed academic skills, perspectives on the role of play in learning can change, with opportunities to support children's social, emotional, and academic development within the context of play-based learning. (pp. 284–285)

This advocate wanted to move beyond the play versus academics debates (e.g., Brown, 2005a; Brown, Barry, Ku, & Englehardt, 2021; Miller & Almon, 2009) and instead think about instruction in kindergarten in a more complex manner (Brown et al., 2018; Goldstein, 2007).

These stakeholders also wanted more opportunities for the teacher to interact with the students. The representative from the national organization representing state officials in education stated:

> What I care about is what kinds of activities are kids doing, and how is the teacher interacting with them, so that they're learning, and creating, and developing habits of positive engagement and learning. You want it to be in tune to the importance of social competence, and executive functioning, and physical development. You want there to be intellectually engaging stuff.

This representative is referring to the importance of supporting children's "executive-level functioning" as they progress through school (Diamond, 2013). Children's executive-level functioning skills develop in their brain's prefrontal cortex—the part that controls our most complex intellectual functions, including our ability to self-regulate both emotionally and cognitively (Miyake et al., 2000). These skills cannot be taught through a simple lesson (e.g., "Let's learn how to self-regulate, children!"), and while developing them is essential for the learning process, it takes time (Brock et al., 2009). These researchers have shown that children's executive functions develop through children having a range of consistent and supportive learning experiences in and outside school and their homes. That is, children learn many of these skills from their interactions with adults, like their teachers (e.g., seeing how adults deal with stress). Thus, to foster children's executive-level functioning, as this representative pointed out, requires that they have consistent and appropriate routines in the classroom, working with teachers who model appropriate behavior, foster a growth mindset toward learning (e.g., see mistakes as learning opportunities and give children the chance to correct such errors), and establish a supportive and caring relationship with the children.

According to the senior advisor for a national early education advocacy group, kindergarten classrooms that offer choice and voice as well as support children's executive-level functioning will materialize only when

> There is a better public understanding of how children learn and what are appropriate expectations for them. There also needs to be a different emphasis in terms of assessment of teachers and children—less reliance on narrowly defined assessment experiences that are frankly easier to measure. There needs to be more meaningful assessment of larger, or higher order, thinking skills; an absolutely greater investment in terms of making sure the teachers who are teaching kindergarten are also prepared in early childhood; and administrators need to understand child development and early education and how to support teachers appropriately.

This senior advisor appears to be asking for second-order, rather than first-order, change that alters the entire system and requires those involved in kindergarten and other early learning programs to understand how children develop and learn (Cuban, 1988). This advisor's suggestions were echoed by the representative from a national organization committed to closing the achievement gap:

> What we need to do as a matter of policy is really incorporate child development into the training we give both to teachers and to principals and other school leaders, including superintendents and people up the food chain. Those folks need to understand what appropriate child development looks like, and that social, emotional development and physical development are just as important as literacy and math skills, which we're not doing right now. So those are policy changes.

This representative's call for improved training not only was mentioned by many other stakeholders in this study (e.g., RRI District Liaison #1 and the West Virginia secretary of education), but such an idea also reflects an empirically based need to improve the learning experiences of children in kindergarten classrooms (e.g., Pyle & Danniels, 2017).

In addition to training in how children develop and learn, access was the other issue these stakeholders were concerned about. For example, the representative from an organization representing state officials in early childhood stated:

> One big thing you could do with policy is level the playing field to a greater degree than we are currently doing based on what we provide for kids at age 5—making sure more kids are able to benefit from a

> high-quality, full-day kindergarten program that has very high-quality teacher preparation. We also need to ensure future kindergarten teachers have solid coursework and clinical experiences. Then, they have an induction process that has them working with more experienced teachers, including having coaching and observation feedback—all that razzmatazz.

Again, there was a consistent call for improved training and support of kindergarten teachers. Some states have tried to implement such systemic support (e.g., North Carolina[2]), but such models require funding, time, and institutional and administrative support (Ritchie et al., 2016)—resources that are not supported by policymakers' neoliberal education reforms.

The Policy Problem(s) That Need to Be Rerouted

Education policies are formulated and implemented to attend to policy problems (Rist, 2000), "and what is seen as a 'problem' depends on both the place and time in which the issue is being studied or addressed" (Brown & Barry, 2019, p. 17). Because these national stakeholders were not speaking in the context of an immediate school, district/county, or state as they talked about rerouting the Kinder-Race, they spent more time than other stakeholders clarifying what the policy problem "was." For example, the liaison with state groups for a national early education advocacy group stated:

> It's clear the teacher is being evaluated for her ability to improve academic achievement, which means her hands are tied. There's a disconnect between what teachers are told by their profession is best practice, and what they're held accountable for in their work environment.

This problem, the tying of teachers' hands, was the result of NCLB. As the representative from a national principals organization stated:

> I blame wholeheartedly for what's in that video on No Child Left Behind, and I worked on No Child Left Behind. What we're seeing in schools is a real consequence of this policy because we have a generation of principals who have grown up, and teachers for that matter, who teach the test.

This representative's statement illuminates how NCLB has led to administrators and teachers, like Ms. Cutler, who make all their decisions, as Ms. Cutler pointed out, "based off . . . data," and how the current generation of school staff are "children of reform" (Brown, 2010a).

In turn, as the representative from an organization committed to providing low-income children access to ECE pointed out:

> NCLB created an accountability system where superintendents are under pressure to improve test scores immediately. They're not going to put money in kindergarten because those kids are too far away from taking the test. Superintendents last an average of 3 years, and you're not even sure those kids are ever going to take tests on your watch. We've essentially created a systemic incentive for kindergarten to be ignored. It's become a dumping ground for the worst teachers, and we have data that shows that in many instances that's what it's become. So we need to start holding people accountable for quality in kindergarten.

The national early childhood researcher who studies kindergarten teaching made a similar point:

> We've created a policy environment where superintendents and principals are constantly moving around, and they constantly bombard teachers with this and that initiative, many of which conflict with each other—it's crazy. Teachers long ago figured out how to fly under the radar. They know they're going to last longer than the principal and the superintendent.
>
> I also think that nobody has any trust in buying into anything because it's going to disappear—that's a huge issue. The superintendent average across the nation is like a year and a half. It's absurd. Principals, there seems to be this trend of, "Oh, well they did a really good job in this school, so we're going pick them up and take them out." Don't do that! It never works because the teachers follow the principal, and then you've got this whole breakup, and whatever it was that was happening for that school stops, and not enough teachers can follow the principal to the next school to make it better. All those family and long-term relationships disappear. I don't know how you make a policy about that, but why there isn't forward thinking, and conversations, and dedication to that going on . . . I just don't see very many people facing the facts—get a plan and stay with it!

This researcher has outlined what numerous empirical studies have documented in terms of administrator and teacher turnover (Grissom & Mitani, 2016; Snodgrass Rangel, 2018), as well as the comments that were made by school principals in Chapter 4.

To fix these policy problems requires, as the senior advisor at a national early education advocacy group stated, "multilevel change—change that involves schools and their principals, families, and policymakers." To garner such change, many of these stakeholders, such as the national early childhood teacher educator and early childhood advocate, noted, requires families demanding change. This advocate stated:

> Parents themselves are starting to get really upset about what's going on in kindergarten. It's the whole democracy thing. Policy is driven by public opinion more than anything, and if public opinion shifts on it to a large degree, then policymakers, including people who are in high positions of decision making in schools, are going to have to respond to that. Now, it's never going to go back. That pendulum is never going to swing back, nor should it. It should never go back to where kindergarten was just "play all day."

This advocate's statement reflects a growing body of empirical work that demonstrates how families have influenced the policymaking process in a manner that has affected their children's learning experiences at school (e.g., Brown, 2008b; Marsh & Wohlstetter, 2013). For example, Mitra et al. (2016) documented how families' decisions to opt their children out of their state's testing system influenced the outcome of a state standardized testing system.

Recognizing the Limits of Policy

When thinking about the impact of policy and its ability to change schools, one has to consider what exactly policymakers can mandate. The representative from an organization committed to providing low-income children access to ECE stated:

> When I think about policy there are certain things you can mandate. You can mandate that you cannot put more than 20 kids in a kindergarten room, and that's incrementally helpful for sure. Still, there are certain things that you can't actually mandate. I can't mandate all kindergarten teachers love their students, but, in fact, a great number do. But ultimately, it's not just about, "Oh we'll pass a law and make it better." It's about how do we build a strategy for what it's going to take to improve kindergarten teaching at scale, and then, over time, implement the policies and provide the funding necessary to make that actually happen. How do you scale creating a learning environment where children want to learn, and learn a ton of information, but also, they are cared for—they are being paid attention to, and they have engagement with each other and with adults?

This representative's statement is similar to the statement made by the former assistant state superintendent in West Virginia. The policy problem appears to be clear, but how and whether policy actually can reroute the Kinder-Race also need to be considered. For this representative, such thinking requires a detailed strategy to be developed, which echoes the suggestions put forward by the Texas House member on the Education Committee. I examine this issue in more detail in the next chapter.

STRUGGLING TO REROUTE A RACE THAT PRIORITIZES ECONOMICS OVER DEMOCRATIC LEARNING

Stakeholders at the district/county, state, and national levels recognized how policymakers' neoliberal high-stakes SBA reforms created the Kinder-Race, and they wanted to reroute it. Yet, for district/county stakeholders, such a reroute seems difficult when they are required to meet state policymakers' accountability expectations. For state stakeholders, the reroute focused on instruction and teacher training. In West Virginia there appeared to be a better understanding of teaching aligned with what experts know about child development and learning. Yet the issues of academic achievement and accountability were ever-present (e.g., Mr. Carey in WVC1 questioning whether these reforms were doing a disservice to children), as a result of their own beliefs as well as the requirements of federal policy. At the national level, there seemed to be many parallels between these stakeholders' interpretations of the Kinder-Race and the statements made by stakeholders at all levels of implementation and governance. However, unlike among state stakeholders, there appeared to be a strong willingness for altering state and federal accountability policies. However, these national stakeholders do not govern or oversee the Kinder-Race, and thus they questioned whether their proposed changes would materialize.

All these stakeholders recognized that if kindergarten does not become a space where children learn how to become members of a collective whole (Clark & Richards, 2017), then they may never develop the skills necessary to actively engage as democratic citizens (Dewey, 1938/1998). Many suggestions to achieve such change were offered, and in the case of West Virginia, some are being implemented. Yet the neoliberal focus on individual success in and out of school, and the accountability policies enacted to ensure such success, appeared to overpower any potential for change (Brown, Weber, & Yoon, 2016), as well as to compress the space to discuss children and their families through more culturally sustaining language (Paris & Alim, 2014). Thus, in the next chapter, I outline strategies to move forward beyond the dominant neoliberal narratives of school readiness, standardization, testing, and accountability that shape the Kinder-Race.

CHAPTER 6

Kindergarten Is the Expansion of Learning

The central tension over the purpose, process, and direction of kindergarten has been (Ross, 1976) and continues to be over "what" children and teachers should be doing on a daily basis (Goldstein, 2007; Graue, 2011). Historically, most education stakeholders have framed kindergarten as a place that nurtures children (Dombkowski, 2001). However, policymakers' recent focus on the issues of school readiness, standardization, testing, and accountability has made kindergarten a place where teachers race their students from skill to skill.

Stakeholders in Texas, in West Virginia, and at the national level, like many educational stakeholders (e.g., Stipek, 2006), worry that this joyless, singular focus on children learning specific sets of academic knowledge and skills limits the instructional practices of educators (e.g., Parker & Neuharth-Pritchett, 2006) as well as demoralizes them as professionals (Dunn, 2018). They also recognize these policies as denying children the opportunity to engage in learning experiences that reflect their sociocultural worlds (Achinstein & Ogawa, 2006), their own interests in learning (Paley, 2009), and their level of learning and development (Jalongo, 2007). Yet these same stakeholders, with their desires for change, struggle to move beyond the hegemony of accountability that girds neoliberal education reform (Lipman, 2013)—often making suggestions (see Table 6.1 for a summary of their suggestions for rerouting the Kinder-Race) about how to do SBA reform better (e.g., Baker et al., 2015). This makes it difficult to find practical routes to move the Kinder-Race past the dominant neoliberal narratives of school readiness, standardization, testing, and accountability.

REROUTING THE KINDER-RACE

At a general level, all the stakeholders discussed in this book would like to reroute the Kinder-Race; they have not accepted "it" as the way kindergarten *should* be (Brown, Englehardt, Barry, & Ku, 2019a). They appear to possess a clear desire for change (e.g., Brown, Barry, & Ku, 2021a).

Table 6.1. How Stakeholders Wanted to Reroute Kindergarten

	Students	Families of kinder-gartners	Kinder-garten Teachers	School Admini-strators	District/ County Admini-strators	State Stakeholders	National Stakeholders
Make K "funner"	X	X	X	X			X
More center-based learning	X	X	X	X	X	X	X
More integrated curriculum		X	X				X
More play and/or physical activity	X	X	X		X		X
More opportunities to socialize	X	X	X	X	X		X
Develop children's love of learning		X	X	X	X	X	X
Develop children's social–emotional skills		X	X		X		X
Offer more "balanced" instruction		X	X	X		X	X
View student success as more than academics		X	X				X
Improve teacher training						X	X
Reform entire education system		X	X	X	X	X	X

Specifically, these stakeholders want kindergarten classrooms to become places where: (1) children engage in meaningful learning activities that foster their desires and competence as learners, (2) teachers listen to their students while fostering positive emotional and social interactions, and (3) children take lead/ownership in their learning while seeing themselves as capable learners—all of which have been shown to improve children's academic learning (e.g., Christopher & Farran, 2020). Sadly, such calls for reform in kindergarten have existed for generations (e.g., Fisher, 1991), and yet nothing has changed (e.g., Bassok et al., 2016).

Still, as Cohen and Mehta (2017) noted, "In our governance system, successful system-wide reforms must mobilize parents, teachers, and others to create and sustain support for major change in the organization of schooling and instruction" (p. 680). Thus, to take advantage of this collective desire for reform so that "we" may move forward in rerouting the Kinder-Race, I turn to the work of George Lakoff (2004), who contends that we, as human beings, make sense of the world through particular frames/frameworks. These mental structures exist in our cognitive unconscious, and we use them to shape the way we make sense of the world.

I am drawn to Lakoff's work (Brown, 2006) because he employs his construct of frames to understand how we, as members of our democratic society, create our political understanding of the world around us—remember, education is a political act (e.g., Apple, 2001). Lakoff (2002, 2004) argues that we frame the world morally through metaphors of moral accounting, and he links this structure of moral reasoning to our political reasoning. Specifically, we base our political framing of the world on our moral construction of the family—the "Nation-as-Family" metaphor. Currently, the political landscape of the United States consists of two *dominant* frameworks, conservative and liberal. These frameworks are not absolutes, and depending on the political issues, we may fluctuate between frameworks. Within the Nation-as-Family metaphor, conservatives use a Strict Father morality to frame their politics, and liberals use a Nurturant Parent model. If individuals are able to recognize how these moral structures (Strict Father or Nurturant Parent) frame policy, they will then be able to understand how those who adhere to a different morality fail to understand the reasoning in their arguments.

THE STRICT FATHER AND NURTURANT PARENT METAPHORS

In brief, conservatives employ a Strict Father morality that assumes human nature is motivated by rewards and punishment. Without such a structure, there would be no morality. Lakoff asserts that this patriarchal perspective frames the father as being in charge and responsible for supporting and protecting his family. His wife's responsibilities include supporting him while running the home and raising the children. Within this model, Lakoff (2002) states that "children must respect and obey their parents; by doing so they build character, that is, self-discipline and self-reliance . . . and the respect for the legitimate authority [that] are the crucial things that children must learn" (p. 33). The Strict Father moral framework defines governmental expenditures for things like social programs as immoral because they "violate the very thing that . . . makes morality possible: rewards for discipline and punishment for lack of it" (Lakoff, 2002, p. 183).

The Nurturant Parent morality, favored by liberals, promotes a family structure that adheres to the principles of love and nurturance rather than strict authority. Parents do not rule over their children, but rather they emphasize a household environment where obedience emerges from love and respect. Moreover, the responsibility for raising the child lies not only in the family but also in the community at large. The child is taught to take on responsibility out of love and respect for the parent and for the community, rather than out of fear of punishment. Thus, for parental authority to be legitimate within this model, parents "must explain why their decisions serve the cause of protection and nurturance. Questioning by children is seen as positive, since children need to learn why their parents do what they do and since children often have good ideas that should be taken seriously" (Lakoff, 2002, p. 34).

These different moral structures demonstrate how when conservative and liberal politicians talk about public education and policy, they are talking about two different things; conservatives see government regulations as a form of interference, which must be abolished, while liberals frame them as a form of protection, which must be supported and maintained (Lakoff, 2002, p. 26). In terms of public education, conservatives see the current structure as promoting values and agendas that attack their Strict Father moral structure. Schools promote multiculturalism, tolerance for gay rights, feminism, histories of Black, Indigenous, people of color (BIPOC), and so on. These ideologies support the Nurturant Parent perspective. Conservatives argue not only that such a perspective has caused public schools to fail because of its inability to promote self-discipline, but that the Nurturant Parent slant found among public institutions has led to a decline in the nation's moral values and an uptick of society's social problems (Lakoff, 2002). Thus, conservatives have no choice but to limit the role of public education and to promote a "back-to-basics" agenda. Without such reforms, the nation's morality will continue to deteriorate.

DEFINING THE KINDER-RACE USING LAKOFF

Generally speaking, conservatives who adhere to the Strict Father morality push for education reforms centered on school choice, standardization, testing, accountability, and limited resources, which creates a neoliberal market-based system grounded on rewards and punishment, for example, retention. These policies, which currently define public education across the United States, frame schooling as a basic service that provides a certain set of skills; that is, public education is "a tool of the state for self-regulation and self-governance of its citizens, rather than an exclusive part of the emancipatory project" that prepares children to participate in and support a democratic society (Clark & Richards, 2017, p. 135).

Those who adhere to the Nurturant Parent morality contend that the conservative commitment to teaching basic skills ignores the empirically based belief that it's best to educate the whole child (e.g., National Research Council, 2000). However, conservatives position such resistance to their neoliberal reform structure of public education as the very reason why students are failing to perform. Furthermore, this Strict Father morality framing of schooling not only has eliminated particular acts of schooling but also denies the Nurturant Parent argument to expand the education process so that the histories of BIPOC children and their families are a part of this process (Grande, 2018). Rather than focus on celebrating the histories of those attending public schools, the current school curriculum, which defines the Kinder-Race, reflects a Strict Father morality centered on issues of school readiness, standardization, testing, and accountability.

REROUTING THE KINDER-RACE: KINDERGARTEN IS THE EXPANSION OF LEARNING

To reroute the dominant neoliberal reforms that define the current context of public education and the Kinder-Race requires more than simply using the metaphor of the Nurturant Parent. It requires imposing new ideas on the framing of kindergarten that go beyond the constructs of school readiness, standardization, testing, and accountability. Lakoff (2004) argues that words do evoke frames, but the ideas have to be in place before the words can make sense. Therefore, Lakoff's work demonstrates that in developing a counterargument or rebuttal to the Kinder-Race, I must offer a new framing of kindergarten. Thus, I contend that the metaphor of kindergarten as a race must be replaced by the metaphor of kindergarten as the expansion of learning—based on Hubble's (1929) law about the expanding universe.

In stating that *kindergarten is the expansion of learning*, I am intentionally avoiding such fixed terms as *journey*, *odyssey*, or *exploration* because I do not want to assume there is an ending to children's (or adults') learning. When an ending or clear destination is attached, systems of assessment and/or accountability easily can be installed and stakes created, and it is a race again (e.g., the 5th-grade STAAR exam pivoting the figuring of kindergarten by principals in Texas back toward the logic of policymakers' high-stakes reforms).

In framing kindergarten as an expansion of learning (see Figure 6.1), I also am moving away from the traditional garden metaphor to decenter the teacher as the gardener who tends to their students. Instead, I am prioritizing learning as a collective act in which teachers, students, and the larger learning community work together to foster the learning of everyone involved (Clark & Richards, 2017). Engaging in such community-based practices supports all students and seeks out alternative ways of knowing (e.g., Fregoso Bailón & De Lissovoy, 2019).

This image creates space for acts of improvisation that can redefine the purpose and process of kindergarten (Holland et al., 1998). It also allows for the teacher's pedagogical practices to be embedded in learning experiences that mirror the sociocultural worlds of all community members within every kindergarten class (Paris, 2016). When framing kindergarten as the expansion of learning, the learning process is collective in nature, always in flux, never static, and does not progress in a lock-step or linear manner from skill to skill—for example, moving from academic skill A, to academic skill B, to academic skill C, and so on. Kindergarten as an expansion of learning

Figure 6.1. Kindergarten as the Expansion of Learning

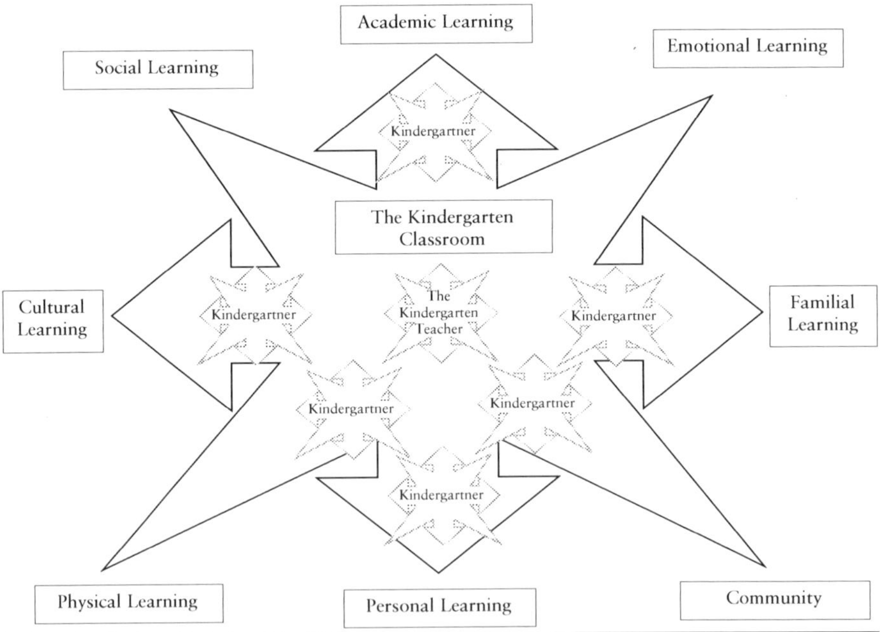

The eight categories of learning in this figure are only suggestions; each classroom community will be different.

recognizes both the current "being and becoming" of students so that they all succeed "in the present and the future" across multiple forms of learning (Uprichard, 2008, p. 311). To replace the Kinder-Race with kindergarten as the expansion of learning metaphor requires both practical and political change.

HOW TO ENGAGE IN THE EXPANSION OF LEARNING

Moving forward practically requires engaging with the stakeholders whose voices have been shared in this book and proposing a new framing of teaching, learning, assessment, and accountability. Thus, I start with the practices that support kindergarten as the expansion of learning and then move to strategies to support and engage the stakeholder groups I discussed in the previous chapters.

Reframing Teaching and Learning

Reframing teaching in the Kinder-Race so that it expands to reach all children and the entire learning community in a positive rather than punitive manner requires teachers to "inject the curriculum with their [students'] interests" (Brown, 2005a, p. 124). It also requires offering children a balance of child-directed and teacher-led learning opportunities that engage the whole child (Graue, 2011), which includes a child's "mind, body, and heart" (Brown et al., 2018, p. 9).

Empirically, there have been several alternative proposals to improve instruction in the kindergarten classroom (e.g., Jones & Nimmo's [1994] emergent curriculum; Katz & Chard's [2000] project approach). For now, I want to focus on two forms of instruction: guided play and RIGOROUS DAP. Both expand the learning of all children through instructional practices that balance the interests of the student and teacher. Guided play is a form of instruction that teachers can employ across the school day or for specific periods of time (Brown, Barry, Ku, & Englehardt, 2021). RIGOROUS DAP is an overarching framework of instruction that seeks to provide teachers direction in structuring their entire curriculum across the school day (Brown et al., 2018).

Guided Play. Guided play seeks to foster children's academic learning through a blend of child-led activities with teacher guidance and scaffolding during those play-based interactions (Wallerstedt & Pramling, 2012; Weisberg et al., 2013). Such learning experiences are "child-directed" activities in which "children lead the play and guide their own learning and discovery within a framework of careful adult guidance," and with that guidance, "adults support and subtly guide children's learning through setting up the learning environment, commenting on the play, [and] asking questions that encourage deeper thinking, discovery, and reflection" (Ilgaz et al., 2018, p. 1251). Teachers must attend simultaneously to children's developmental needs and the academic content they are expected to know; this practice has been shown to improve children's literacy skills (Stone & Christie, 1996), language skills (Tsao, 2008), math skills (Stipek et al., 1995), and socio-emotional skills (Berk & Meyers, 2013). These outcomes align with the professed goals of all the stakeholders interviewed for this study (Brown, Barry, Ku, & Englehardt, 2021).

In practice, this means you would see classrooms where children are active and engaged in learning experiences and where the teacher constrains "the environment just enough to help ensure that the child engages with relevant materials and encounters relevant experience . . . in service of the learning goal" (Toub et al., 2016, p. 122). The goal would be to create a learning environment that balances the needs of each child with the kindergarten teachers' academic instruction in a manner that nurtures and extends each kindergartner's desire and ability to succeed in school individually and as a member of a learning community (Brown et al., 2018; Bryce et al., 2018).

RIGOROUS DAP. RIGOROUS DAP is not a theory of instruction (Brown, Feger & Mowry, 2015). Rather, RIGOROUS DAP (see Figure 6.2) is both a construct and an acronym that offers 11 principles of instruction in which early educators can engage with their students daily (Brown et al., 2018). RIGOROUS DAP comprises two parts: academic rigor and developmentally appropriate practices. Academically rigorous learning environments create the conditions for children to learn at high levels. Academic rigor is not "a checklist of teacher behaviors and a model lesson that covers content standards" (Wagner, 2008, p. 24). Rather, it is the process of working with

Figure 6.2. The Practices of RIGOROUS DAP (Brown et al., 2018)

Reaching all children
Integrating content areas
Growing as a community
Offering choices
Revisiting new content
Offering challenges
Understanding each learner
Seeing the whole child
Differentiating instruction
Assessing constantly
Pushing every child forward

Note: These 11 principles are a modified version of what I originally proposed with Brian Mowry (Brown & Mowry, 2013, 2015).

all students in a manner that addresses the whole child through whole-body learning experiences that "challenge the mind" and "connect learning to real world context[s]" (Washor & Mojkowski, 2007, p. 87).

Developmentally appropriate practices foster instruction focused on the growth of all children in the classroom. This instruction occurs across all developmental domains through children's linguistic and cultural skills in a manner that addresses both the sociocultural worlds in which they live and who they are as individual learners (Copple & Bredekamp, 2009).

By engaging in RIGOROUS DAP, teachers make instructional decisions that address the developmental domains of the children in the classroom, their sociocultural worlds, and what they need to know in order to succeed in their immediate learning community, the grade level itself, and the larger world. To do so requires teachers to provide children with multiple learning opportunities, through a range of instructional strategies, like guided play, to gain the knowledge and skills needed for success. As the school year progresses, teachers build on the content of instruction and increase their performance expectations for children. At the same time, teachers ensure that they provide appropriate levels of support to children through practices that reflect the children's sociocultural worlds, by consistently monitoring their achievement across all developmental domains. The goal is that by the end of the school year, every child has—or is on a trajectory to soon attain—the academic, sociocultural, emotional, and physical knowledge and skills needed for success in and out of school.

CSP and RIGOROUS DAP. In our outlining of RIGOROUS DAP (Brown et al., 2018), my coauthors and I specifically spoke to the issue of ensuring that teachers incorporate culturally sustaining practices within their teaching. Conceptually, RIGOROUS DAP is an essential component in "Reaching" all children through practices that "See" the whole child, and at the same time "Understand" each child as a learner so that teachers can "Push" them forward and ensure the class is "Growing as a community."

In practice, this requires teachers to foster academic success, cultural competence, and sociopolitical consciousness—the three essential components of Ladson-Billings's (1994) CRT—for all their students. Such practices not only impact the actions and lives of children in the kindergarten classroom, but they also require teachers to address the societal (i.e., a high incidence of poverty among culturally and linguistically diverse children) and political (i.e., being told what to teach and when) issues outside of their classrooms (Brown & Lee, 2012).

Fostering academic success requires teachers to view their instruction as a process in which they work "with students so that they can reflect, theorize, and create knowledge" (Nieto, 2002, p. 7). To build children's cultural competence requires teachers to help students "recognize and honor their own cultural beliefs and practices" and provide them with the knowledge and skills needed to attain "access to the wider culture, where they are likely to have a chance of improving their socioeconomic status and making informed decisions about the lives they wish to lead" (Ladson-Billings, 2006b, p. 36). To build children's sociopolitical consciousness requires teachers to view students as subjects, rather than objects, and include them as active participants in the curriculum development process (Ladson-Billings, 2014). In sum, these are the culturally sustaining pedagogical practices that seek to create "humanizing" learning communities and disrupt the "legacies of educational inequities" (Cheruvu, 2019, p. 116).

Morrison et al. (2008) pointed out that engaging in CSP "ultimately clashes with the traditional ways in which education is carried out in our society" because teachers are expected to deliver academic content in a direct manner to all students at the same time (p. 444), which can result in kindergarten teachers viewing the act of engaging in CSP as a "herculean" endeavor (p. 444). To develop a complex repertoire of developmental, cultural, and curricular knowledge in order to engage in humanizing and empowering sociopolitical pedagogy requires teachers to view learning as a process that "trouble[s] social issues and normative perceptions in a critically conscious manner" so that they and their students can position themselves as "agents of change in their classrooms and beyond" (Souto-Manning, 2017, p. 96).

To assist all teachers in engaging in CSP with their students, Paris (2016) contends that teachers must understand:

1. The systemic nature of racialized and intersectional inequalities and their own relative privileged or marginalized position within those systems
2. That education participates in and often perpetuates such inequalities, though it also can disrupt them
3. The ways deficit approaches historically have perpetuated and continue to perpetuate racialized inequalities, and the nature of asset approaches and how to curricularize them
4. That critical asset approaches do improve academic achievement, but that current measures of achievement are narrow and assimilative and thus not the sole goal
5. That humanizing relationships of dignity and care are fundamental to student and teacher learning; that is, those relationships engage teaching in ways that allow teachers and students to foster complex understandings about one another that disrupt damage-centered (Tuck, 2009) deficit views[1] (p. 8)

Paris's suggestions bring the issues of race, class, culture, and community to the forefront of teaching, and require teachers to ask themselves: Am I simply perpetuating the status quo and asking children to assimilate to a system that may not value who they are as learners? Rather than conform to the issues of school readiness, standardization, testing, and accountability within the Kinder-Race, teachers must embrace and sustain the variation that exists within our classrooms so that we are "Reaching all children," "Growing as a community," "Understanding each learner," "Seeing the whole child," and "Pushing every child forward."

To do this work requires teachers to access the funds of knowledge children and their families bring to school so that knowledge can become the foundation of the curriculum being employed in the classroom (Moll et al., 1992). It also requires teachers to seek out practices and the sociocultural histories that often are pushed out of the classroom in the name of standardization and accountability (Adair et al., 2018; Pérez, 2019), which would "be different and unique to each setting and spatial location in relation to the unique power relations embedded within each space" (Eizadirad, 2019, p. 203). This will necessitate classroom teachers to engage in such acts as counterstories, which are stories that reveal how White privilege and other forms of discrimination silence those who are not a part of the dominant cultural group (Delgado, 1989); storytelling from ancestors across generations, such as grandparents or community elders (Grande, 2018); and/or poetry from the children's sociocultural worlds (Fregoso Bailón & De Lissovoy, 2019).

Still, Paris (2016), as well as Ladson-Billings (2014), recognized that the elements he outlines (as well as the ones I am arguing for via RIGOROUS DAP) ask public schoolteachers to work in opposition to the system that employs them—for example, focusing on the needs of the children and their community rather than the academic content policymakers and/or administrators expect them to teach. This is something all the kindergarten teachers I talked with struggled to do in their own classrooms. Moreover, Evans et al. (2020) also remind us that teachers cannot use CSP "as a tool of assimilation" or to simply "gain students' attention" (p. 6). Doing so simply leaves the current neoliberal system of education in place. Thus, to engage in CSP, as Villegas and Lucas (2002) noted, is a lifelong process that requires determination and courage.

Reframing Assessment

When thinking about guided play, RIGOROUS DAP, and CSP as instructional means to expand kindergartners' learning, teachers must be "Assessing constantly," and thus, when rerouting the Kinder-Race, assessment plays a central part in ensuring that all children expand their learning. Not only is *assessment* a term that has several meanings; it is also both practically and politically contentious. Thus, to reframe assessment requires some clarity.

Shepard et al. (1998) pointed out that there are four general purposes of assessment: educational planning, accountability reporting, identification of special needs, and evaluating programs and monitoring trends. Educational planning is rooted primarily in teachers' employing informal and formal assessment measures, but standardized tests can be a part of this process as well. Still, the other three purposes require teachers to use a standardized assessment of some sort.

To expand the learning of all children, assessment should focus on guiding the educational planning of teachers and other school personnel, which requires teachers to assess and monitor children's achievement so that they can adapt their instruction and provide children with learning experiences that develop their individual skills and knowledge in relation to grade-level expectations, the expectations of the learning community in which they all operate, and the expectations of the child's sociocultural worlds. Essentially, in reframing the Kinder-Race as the expansion of learning, teachers are always assessing their students in relation to something—that something can be an immediate, short-, or long-term goal. It can be academic, developmental (physical, social, emotional), cultural, or personal, which includes the needs and wants of children's families.

In reframing assessment, it is important that this construct not be seen simply as marking how much a child knows; rather, it should incorporate evaluating how children see themselves as learners and as members of a learning community, and their ability to tackle new academic and/or developmental challenges with which they are presented on almost a daily basis in kindergarten. One suggestion might be to have a family/parent–teacher conference where the student is asked to complete a novel learning challenge, which often is framed as performance-based assessment (e.g., Meier & Knoester, 2017). Upon the student's completing the task, the teacher, family, and child would discuss the child's learning strengths and growth areas; how the child was thinking about learning, saw themself as a learner, and positioned themself and their learning within the larger classroom community; and where they wanted to go in their learning.

For this framing assessment to take hold, a conceptual shift needs to occur so that the neoliberal technocratic views of teaching, learning, and assessment are altered. These constructs must be replaced with what Moss (2017) termed teaching rooted in "experimentation" to allow teachers and kindergartners to work "on a diversity of projects inspired by [their] different ideas, desires and circumstances" that expand their learning (p. 24). This "social or relational model" of democratic learning emphasizes "relationships with others" and challenges the neoliberal "individualized concept" of learning that promotes "self-interest and individual choice" (Clark & Richards, 2017, p. 135). Doing so not only repositions all children, families, and communities as knowledgeable and capable (Brown & Lan, 2018; Nxumalo & Adair, 2019), but also necessitates rethinking about the assessments used to measure the children's learning so that the neoliberal logic of accountability can be reframed (Eizadirad, 2019).

Reframing Accountability

As De Lissovoy (2014) noted, the framing of accountability converts the teaching and learning "from experiments in democratic relationships and inquiry to performance of rituals aimed not only at inculcating a set disposition in students, but also capturing the intelligence of students for the purposes of the system and its reproduction" (pp. 429–430). Apple (2001) contended that to counter this focus on students' future test scores, incomes, and/or consumption, school stakeholders should replace this currency of test scores with a currency that prioritizes students' ability to participate within a democratic classroom in the here and now. Both De Lissovoy and Apple are speaking back to Lipman's (2013) point that policymakers' systems of accountability create a hegemony that materializes, reproduces, and reinforces the Kinder-Race specifically and public education in general through what Lakoff (2002) termed a Strict Father morality framing of the schooling process.

To reframe this construct requires the repositioning of who is accountable to whom, in two ways. First, at a systems level, policymakers should be held accountable for providing the resources needed to support teachers, students, and their families. I recognize that elections have consequence, but in large states like California, Florida, New York, and Texas such a shift requires more than simply replacing one policymaker with another (e.g., Valenzuela, 2005). It requires a public accounting of the resources, including curriculum, textbooks, teacher training, and compensation, that policymakers and other education administrators (e.g., state school boards) are providing to support all teachers, students, and their families. Second, at the local level, teachers, schools, and districts/counties should be accountable to their local community, which in states like Texas can vary significantly. Such democratic understandings of schooling redefine accountability and the power dynamics within this construct.

Historically, two accountability systems that might provide insight into a way forward include the National Assessment of Educational Progress (NAEP), which has been employed since 1969 to measure what students across the United States know and can do in various subjects, and state and/or school-based, performance-based assessment systems (Brown, 2004).[2] Under NAEP, students in grades 4 and 8 are assessed in reading and mathematics every 2 years and in other subjects periodically. Such a system measures the progress of schooling in general across states, and it provides insight into areas where support can be provided.

In terms of performance-based assessments (e.g., Meier & Knoester, 2017), when SBA reforms were first implemented, states such as Kentucky, New York, Maryland, and Wisconsin either developed or implemented such performance-based assessments as a means to assess student learning. Performance-based assessments ask students to perform an activity or a task that involves a series of steps in order to demonstrate their understanding of the question, rather than simply choosing the right answer (Baker, 2002). However, states either abandoned their plans (e.g., Wisconsin) or stopped employing the assessments due to their cost to implement (Archbald & Porter, 1990; Darling-Hammond, 2003). Still, schools and districts[3] also have developed a range of performance-based assessments to ensure that the learning of all students is being monitored and supported as needed (Meier & Knoester, 2017).

Again, I am not advocating for any system of accountability, particularly one that pivots school stakeholders away from the unique needs of teachers and students in classrooms (Brown, 2009c). Such decisions need to be made in local communities. What I am proposing is that to frame kindergarten as the expansion of learning requires the current system to move away from accountability shovedown (Hatch, 2002) to the promotion, documentation, and expansion of individualized and community-based learning.

SUPPORTING AND ENGAGING STAKEHOLDERS IN EXPANDING THE LEARNING OF KINDERGARTNERS

With these conceptions of teaching, learning, assessment, and accountability reframed through the lens of the expansion of learning, I now turn to strategies to support and engage the stakeholder groups I discussed in the previous chapters—moving from the kindergarten classroom outward.

Supporting Students

To begin, if kindergarten is to be a site where the expansion of learning is taking place, and if children are to be successful as individuals and as community members within this context, several transformations need to occur. First, how students are framed as learners needs to be altered (e.g., Nxumalo & Brown, 2019). Beyond taking on a dynamic framing toward learning (Dweck, 2006; Johnston, 2004, 2012), the brilliance and potential of each child must be the central point of contact upon which each school actor builds their relations with each child (Cannella, 1997; Pérez & Saavedra, 2017; Swadener & Lubeck, 1995). As Qvortrup (2009) argued, children must be seen as human beings and not "human becomings," and have a right "to be taken seriously as claim-makers and right-holders, economically, socially and politically" (p. 647).

Therefore, the construct of school readiness must be rethought. Currently, both the focus on children's future academic performance (Uprichard, 2008) and the fixation on their "readiness in the now" (Brown, 2013) reify the narratives of school readiness, standardization, testing, and accountability. Instead, a multifaceted conception of school readiness should be employed (Brown, Barry, & Ku, 2021). That is, children's readiness for school should be seen as something that is continuously reshaped by the contextual, cultural, and personal expectations of those involved in educating each and every child—such as the family, kindergarten teacher, other school personnel, and so on. Such a shift would ensure that families and school stakeholders avoid the trappings of the empiricist framing of school readiness (e.g., Brown, 2021). Furthermore, as I argue along with my colleagues (Brown, Barry, & Ku, 2021), replacing the empiricist notion of school readiness that currently defines the Kinder-Race with a multifaceted conception of this construct also might depathologize the ways in which minoritized children and their families are currently "blame[d] . . . for perceived gaps or problems" that need fixing, "as if they were broken or behind" their White middle-class peers (Souto-Manning & Rabadi-Raol, 2018, p. 209).

To rethink children/students and the construct of school readiness also requires reconsidering how adults engage with children/students on a daily basis. Beyond engaging in the practices of guided play, RIGOROUS DAP, CSP, and other expansive forms of instruction (e.g., Helm, 2015), as many of the stakeholders in this study point out, the learning environment must become a place that empowers, supports, and nurtures children's expansion of learning individually and collectively. As Deci and Ryan (2000) noted, to support and motivate children to learn requires that children have a sense of autonomy over their learning (e.g., choice and voice), feel competent that they can complete the task at hand (meaning that the learning situation cannot be "standardized"), and feel a sense of relatedness to those within the learning situation, which reinforces the importance of viewing kindergarten as a supportive democratic learning community (Dewey, 1938/1998).

Children's voices, rather than just the "patriarch's voice" (Lakoff, 2002), also must be a part of the schooling process, including teaching, learning, and assessment. As Phelps et al. (2014) argued, "It would seem . . . that children's perspectives provide immense, largely unutilised potential for educational improvement" (p. 34). The kindergartners I talked with made sense of kindergarten differently from the adults; they were amenable to what kindergarten currently is (Brown & Barry, 2021). Yet they still had clear actionable suggestions for refiguring kindergarten that aligned with much of what the adults and "the research" (e.g., Christopher & Farran, 2020) would like to see changed in kindergarten. Thus, rerouting the Kinder-Race must seek out and incorporate their guidance in moving forward.

Finally, throughout this book, I have referred to Aninyda Kundu's (2020) argument that schools must support as well as develop children's agency and grit. Kundu also noted that the students in his work who have overcome a range of challenges in their lives (e.g., homelessness, incarceration, and/or abuse) to accomplish their goals had consistent role models as a constant presence in their lives. Thus, as Kundu suggested, school personnel and everyone involved in the public education process should consider how they are being allies with and for the children within their communities. For kindergarten teachers, this would require getting to know each child on a personal level and working with their families to ensure that there are such mentors in their lives. To do this would necessitate the school system(s) valuing and supporting teachers in fostering such relationships; that is, the goal must be to replace racing from skill to skill with building a cohesive democratic community. Such actions are necessary to begin to reposition the onus for success in and out of school away from the simplistic framing of a student's level of grit and/or agency and on to the larger community (Clark & Richards, 2017).

Supporting Teachers and Teachers-in-Training

Classroom Teachers. Across the research I have conducted in my career (e.g., Brown, 2007c), almost every individual I have talked with recognizes the importance of supporting teachers in doing their job. Yet teachers consistently are framed by these same stakeholders as either the receivers of the reforms or at the bottom of the policy hierarchy (Ball et al., 2012), which means that teachers' concerns and voices often go unheard.

The kindergarten teachers central to my current work are in a Catch-22. Teachers continually have questioned what they were being asked to do in regard to their teaching and assessment practices, but saw no alternatives to the situation due to the risk of being seen as incompetent or possibly losing their jobs (e.g., Brown & Weber, 2016a). As De Lissovoy (2014) and others (e.g., Lipman, 2013) have noted, the neoliberal system of education has made them disposable commodities that easily are replaced by newly trained and/or untrained teachers (e.g., Teach for America) who are willing to teach as their state or local system dictates (Apple, 2001; Brown, Weber, & Yoon, 2016).

Additionally, simply asking teachers to "close their classroom doors" and not teach the test is unfair to the teachers. They know that taking on the identity of a resistant/defiant teacher might upset school administrators and/or families, or possibly have their students perform poorly on the state exams (Brown, 2018). Arguing that teachers can enact alternative curricular agendas covertly, while still covering the necessary material in their instruction to prepare students for the test, also leaves the system unchanged (Brown, 2015; De Lissovoy, 2014). Furthermore, the "deskilling" of the teaching profession (Keddie et al., 2011) due to the restructuring of teachers as technicians (Lasley, 1994) has negatively impacted many teachers (e.g., Brown & Weber, 2016a, 2016b), including the kindergarten teachers represented in this book.

This necessitates that the act of teaching, alongside the Kinder-Race in general, be reframed through the lens of kindergarten being the expansion of learning. This expansion through such practices as guided play, RIGOROUS

DAP, and CSP would allow teachers to move beyond standardized practices and endless summative assessments so they could engage in practices that positioned the child as the central pivot upon which instructional decisions should be made (Brown, 2009c).

Teachers must be seen as the professionals that they are; in Texas, they manage 22 dynamic and powerful individuals alone on a daily basis for long periods of uninterrupted time, while teaching students a range of new skills and knowledge that impact their immediate and future success in the world (e.g., Reynolds et al., 2018). This also requires continued training and development for them and for teachers-in-training to support the increasingly complex and talented students entering their classrooms on a daily basis.

Teacher Training. The professional development of classroom teachers and teachers-in-training, whom I refer to as preservice teachers (PSTs) in my work (e.g., Brown, 2010a), is essential for the Kinder-Race to be rerouted toward the expansion of learning. While this is an argument that has been made by many (e.g., Kennedy & Heineke, 2014), it is also clear that both practicing and PSTs in high-stakes SBA contexts often frame teaching kindergarten through teacher-centered instruction to prepare children for the academic achievement expectations awaiting them in elementary school (Brown, Feger, & Mowry, 2015; Di Santo et al., 2017), even when professional development and teacher education programs work to challenge such reasoning (Brown & Ku, 2018; Brown, Weber, & Yoon, 2015).

A central form of instruction that was absent from much of what was occurring in Ms. Cutler's classroom was CSP (e.g., Paris & Alim, 2014). The dominant narratives of school readiness, standardization, testing, and accountability appeared to all but squeeze CSP out of her classroom; to be clear, her diverse student body routinely told me they liked Ms. Cutler and felt that she cared about them. Still, engaging in CSP is difficult and requires continued and sustained support, either via professional development or working with collaborative communities of educators, to assist in the process of fostering and maintaining culturally relevant instruction of students (Brown & Weber, 2016a). Such continued support from colleagues and/or administrators can help early educators make sense of the process of engaging in CSP within the standardized teaching context.

Teachers also need educational and administrative support to engage in guided play and/or RIGOROUS DAP. For example, Pyle and Danniels (2017) found, through their investigation into how 15 kindergarten teachers understood and implemented guided play in their classrooms, that the teachers needed support in engaging in as well as understanding the academic benefits of guided play. Thus, asking teachers to engage in and sustain new practices requires them to think about their instruction in more complex ways (Brown et al., 2018). It also requires teachers to be intentional in their intervention in and scaffolding of children's learning so that they support and extend children's cognitive, sociocultural, and emotional development in a manner that prepares them for success in kindergarten and beyond (Toub et al., 2016).

For classroom teachers (CTs) and PSTs, beyond reenvisioning teacher education as a whole, which goes beyond the scope of my argument (e.g., Reid & O'Donoghue, 2004), my other work (Brown, Barry, Ku, & Puckett, 2021) has shown that there needs to be increased collaboration between teacher educators (TEs) and CTs and PSTs (Whitenack & Swanson, 2013). The dialogue between these groups of stakeholders needs to improve so that each recognizes the challenges they have witnessed and are experiencing within the Kinder-Race (Brown et al., 2020a, 2020b). Doing so would allow TEs, CTs, and PSTs not only to understand how each is interpreting the Kinder-Race but also to discuss how they have either attended to policymakers' demands or attempted to teach beyond them. Engaging in these personal and practical conversations is important because empirical studies consistently have found that making teachers'—whether TEs, CTs, or PSTs—beliefs explicit is crucial to their learning process and can lead them to change their teaching practices (Brownlee et al., 2011).

On a more practical level, PSTs also would benefit from engaging in professional development experiences and teacher education programs that make PSTs aware of and support them in responding to the pressure of policymakers' SBA reforms so that they can teach children academics through practices that expand children's learning (Brown et al., 2020a, 2020b). This would include TEs providing CTs and PSTs with both theoretical knowledge and pedagogical practices, such as guided play (e.g., Pyle & Danniels, 2017), to envision and understand how their instructional decisions, which should reflect a continuum of practices (Bredekamp & Rosengrant, 1995), are supporting as well as preparing their students for school success (Brown et al., 2018). In sum, as Williford et al. (2017) found, "a core component that led to change in practices was a teacher's ability to identify, justify, and evaluate high-quality classroom interactions" (p. 116), which means moving past the dominant narratives of school readiness, standardization, testing, and accountability, and requires an in-depth conceptual and practical discussion about engaging in practices that sustain and expand children's learning in and beyond their teacher education programs (e.g., Sherfinski et al., 2019).

Supporting Principals and School Administrators

The principals I talked with throughout this study wanted the Kinder-Race to be rerouted, but the dominant narrative of accountability seemed to detour them from such change. While reframing both assessment and accountability is an important step in this process, policies also must be changed. However, at a practical level, it appears that principals could help reroute the Kinder-Race if they were to spend more time advocating for and supporting change in the kindergarten classrooms they oversee. As these principals and many others I spoke with pointed out, because kindergarten is so far away from the 3rd- and 5th-grade tests, principals often spend the least amount of time at this grade level (Brown, 2011).

Alongside paying more attention to kindergarten, principals and other school administrators might consider how they can implement as well as advocate for instructional change among their teachers (Brown & Mowry, 2013). This might require principals to spend time examining how young children develop and learn (e.g., Kostelnik & Grady, 2009), so that their teachers can engage in child-centered teaching practices that have been shown to improve children's interest in reading and mathematics (Lerkkanen et al., 2012). They also might ask themselves whether they are working with classroom teachers to create learning environments that support children's sociocultural and emotional learning, which has been tied to improving their academic skills (Berk & Meyers, 2013; Bryce et al., 2018).

Additionally, it might be beneficial for principals to seek out and listen to families' and teachers' concerns about the Kinder-Race. Such community collaboration has been shown to improve children's performance in school (e.g., Hampden-Thompson & Galindo, 2017). Thus, the rerouting of the Kinder-Race requires not only the stakeholders within the school building but also those outside.

Supporting Families

All the families I talked with want kindergarten to be rerouted (e.g., Brown, Englehardt, Ku, & Barry, 2019), and thus they are important allies in the process of reframing kindergarten as the expansion of learning—as Pohan and Adams (2007) noted, "Families care deeply about their children's education" (p. 48). Much of what I suggest for principals and school administrators to do to support their teachers also can be applied to families. Still, school personnel need to be aware that "different groups of parents do not have access to the same sets of information, networks, or resources" (Villavicencio, 2013, p. 4). For example, Colegrove (2019) and Colegrove and Krause (2017) found that Latinx immigrant families in Texas and California felt that elementary schoolteachers were unavailable and/or unwilling to discuss academic or social issues as they occurred across the school year.

Accordingly, family involvement should be broadly defined as well as instigated and supported by elementary school personnel (Hornby & Lafaele, 2011). School administrators and teachers must "welcome, value, and respect parents as participants in students' education" (Whitaker & Hoover-Dempsey, 2013, p. 79). This requires all education stakeholders to "better appreciate the many ways that most parents and families display educational care" for their children "outside of schools" (Cooper, 2009, p.

390), as well as engaging families in meaningful ways that go beyond such traditional practices as sending home notes/newsletters to families or talking with them when at school (Doucet, 2011).

This is significant because researchers have shown that parental involvement is both a predictor as well as a supporter of children's academic and social success in school (Topor et al., 2010). For example, as Mitra et al. (2016) articulated, educators who shared information, through web-based and social media sites, with families about what was occurring within the school context were more involved in their children's education in and out of the school context.

Lastly, a range of empirical investigations have documented how families have influenced the implementation of and outcomes resulting from policy changes that altered their children's learning experiences at school (Marsh & Wohlstetter, 2013). For example, Brown (2008b) and Mitra et al. (2016) both documented how families' decisions to opt their children out of their state's testing system influenced the outcome of a state standardized testing system. Such work provides a clear indication that to reroute the Kinder-Race entails recruiting and empowering families as allies within the political process to reform public education (Brown, Englehardt, Ku, & Barry, 2019).

Up to this point, I have outlined a range of ideas as to what framing kindergarten as the expansion of learning might mean at the practical level—reframing learning, teaching, assessments, students, school readiness, teachers, teacher training, school administrators, and families. However, education is more than the practical; it is also a political act (e.g., Apple, 2001).

MOVING INTO THE POLITICAL

While the secretary of education in West Virginia stated, "We need to stop doing policy. If it were up to me, I would burn all the policies!", political and policy changes are needed if the Kinder-Race is to be reframed as the expansion of learning. To move forward politically, and building from Lakoff's (2002) idea that to change the narrative of the Kinder-Race one must put forward new frames that speak to both conservatives and liberals, I contend that kindergarten is the expansion of learning.

To shift the politics of kindergarten, as Majone (1989) argued, requires stakeholders to pay attention to the "ideas, theories, and arguments as well as technology, economics, and politics" that exist within the given policy context (p. 166). The main ideas surrounding the Kinder-Race are school readiness, standardization, testing, and accountability. Majone (1989) added that "a policy idea will not be adopted unless it is communicated persuasively and meets the demands of the political environment" (p. 165).

Moreover, "to have one's ideas and values incorporated in the policymaking process . . . policy actors must alter the values and preferences of the people they represent. They must, in effect, be translated so that they will be recognized, included, and heard in the policy culture" (Marshall et al., 1986, p. 375). For policymakers to be successful in promoting change, "policy actors must rephrase, create, and change the image, symbols, content, and goals of policy preferences if they are to maintain power and have a chance of seeing their needs met" (p. 376). I see employing Lakoff's work and reframing kindergarten as the expansion of learning, which is how public education in general also should be framed, as a politically viable idea that can promote a range of reforms to alter the current framing of schooling rooted in narratives of school readiness, standardization, testing, and accountability.

Nevertheless, I know that policy change is difficult. In fact, my dissertation (Brown, 2004), which included an investigation into how policymakers formulated and implemented Wisconsin's high-stakes education reforms, uncovered four key ideas that I take into any investigation involving education policy. First, all stakeholders want to improve public education; what differs is how they frame the policy problem and potential solutions. Second, policymakers almost always address education issues through a series of peripheral rather than core policy changes (Majone, 1989). As McLaughlin (1987) noted long ago, policymakers often are just "muddling through" various education reforms that offer some change to look like they are trying to support public education. It is this "muddling through" that often makes it difficult for education stakeholders to distinguish whether a reform idea is a tool for change or just more muddling. Nevertheless, and this is the third idea, most reforms are bound by the principles of ensuring that whatever change is being proposed must be cheap and local (Brown, 2008b)—the policies must speak to the demands of those in power within local communities and not be a drain on a limited set of fiscal resources. Lastly, policy change is about speaking to multiple audiences in a manner that each will understand (Brown, 2004).

To reframe and enact political change that leads to kindergarten classrooms centered on expanding children's learning, I outline how education stakeholders might mitigate policy change from the bottom up—moving from the kindergarten classroom to the federal government. Before doing so, I want to reiterate the point that there appears to be a willingness for change at all levels of education reform (Brown, Englehardt, Barry, & Ku, 2019a), and as such, spaces exist for what Kingdon (2003) termed a policy entrepreneur(s), which might include parent/community organizations, professional groups, or other advocates (e.g., Brown, 2007b), to develop and push through education reforms that seek to center kindergarten and public education on the expansion of learning for all children (Brown, Barry, Ku, & Englehardt, 2021).

Kindergarten Classrooms

The kindergarten classroom is inhabited by a range of education stakeholders, and key to effective change within this context is the formation of alliances across these groups that seek to expand the learning of all children (Apple, 2001; Guinier & Torres, 2002). As Chapters 3 and 4 demonstrated, all the stakeholders are aware that all children can succeed in school, but how such success is being demanded and the curriculum implemented to achieve this goal must be changed. Thus, students, teachers, families, and administrators should work together to develop a plan of action that decenters the demands of policymakers' reforms, and instead positions the needs and interests of the learning community to drive the expansion of learning.

To do this requires open conversations across groups about what such expansive teaching and learning might look like. Potential issues that would need to be addressed in these conversations include:

- A clear outline of academic, sociocultural (which includes children's home languages), emotional, and democratic goals all stakeholders are working toward
- The forms of instruction they would like to see employed by teachers in each classroom (e.g., guided play, RIGOROUS DAP, and CSP)
- Appropriate formative "assessments" that would be used to ensure that each child was growing as a learner and community member (Shepard et al., 1998)
- All stakeholders holding and employing a dynamic and positive understanding of learning that is grounded in a growth mindset (Deci & Ryan, 2000; Dweck, 2006; Johnston, 2012)
- All stakeholders recognizing that no two classrooms and possibly no two days of instruction might look the same (Brown, Feger, & Mowry, 2018)
- The understanding that teachers and administrators must ensure that all children feel cared for, see themselves as learners, and are learning things that matter to them and their families

Envisioning and enacting such practices and framings of schooling, as mentioned above, will require not only open lines of communication but also trust across groups in working toward the same goals.

It also requires these stakeholders to possess what Loh and Hu (2014) termed a "neoliberal literacy" (p. 20) that helps them recognize how policymakers' demands for specific forms of instruction, assessment, and accountability are deterring them from expanding the learning of all their students (Brown, Englehardt, Barry, & Ku., 2019b). Understanding not only the limits of these neoliberal reforms but also the economic discourse that empowers these ideas makes it easier to reframe and counter such arguments. For example, simply asking those who employ these neoliberal discourses such questions as, "Do you see my child/students as a financial investment or a budding member of our democratic society?" or "How are you supporting the expansion of my child's learning (or children's learning)?" immediately can shift the dynamics of a conversation around schooling.

Moving Into the Entire School

The conversations outlined above also must be part of the entire schooling process. In this way, the issue of accountability becomes more prominent—school personnel not just being accountable for ensuring that children are growing as learners and community members as they move from grade to grade, but also attending to the demands of district/county and state policymakers. To speak back to demands in a manner that seeks change requires alliances that go beyond the school. While such a task seems daunting, change has occurred throughout the United States (Brown, 2008b). It requires a deep commitment, open lines of communication, and a clear understanding of what the goals of the alliances are; for example, the elimination of a high-stakes test, which many (e.g., McNeil & Valenzuela, 2001) have been fighting for across waves of education reform.

As was demonstrated in Chapters 4 and 5, most of the stakeholders believe that policymakers (at any level) have no idea what's occurring in schools, and thus these alliances should and hold such policymakers accountable for learning what is occurring on a daily basis in the schools they oversee. For example, to expand every child's learning requires policymakers to ensure that they are providing the financial resources, curricula, and training that educators need so that each child's growth is accounted for across their state. In putting forward these suggestions for reform, I recognize that such actions are risky and can endanger teachers' and school administrators' professional careers (e.g., Brown, 2015). Moreover, these local changes, as well as the larger changes I am about to propose, also can "have their own dangers and disciplinary effects" (McLeod, 2001, p. 280) that create unintended consequences (e.g., Brown, 2009a). Thus, all stakeholders need to monitor their reforms and ensure that any enacted policies are not simply creating new problems that impede the goal of creating democratic school communities that expand the learning of all children.

Districts/Counties

When moving outside the immediate school, district and county school boards and administrators impact the policies and procedures of what occurs in classrooms in significant ways (e.g., Sherman, 2008). Besides hiring district/county and school personnel, they make decisions about curricula (e.g., textbooks), assessment practices, and other day-to-day procedures in numerous ways: grade-level promotion policies, teacher tenure, professional development requirements/programs, and family outreach programs. They also are "interpreters" of state and federal policy, and as such, they develop district/county policies designed to adhere to or possibly speak back to such reforms. Thus, it's important to pay attention not only to school board elections but also to school board meeting schedules and to attend when issues of curriculum, assessment, and accountability are discussed.

State Governments

At the state level, it matters who is elected in both houses of the state congress and on state school boards. Both generate policies that affect the day-to-day experiences of schools in numerous ways.

As for state congresses, which elected official sits on the education committee(s) matters. As the Texas House member on the Education Committee noted, thousands of bills are filed each session that affect the education of about 5 million children across the state of Texas. Thus, the interests of the chairs of those committees often dictate which bills will get a full hearing and be passed up to the full house or senate. Almost every state legislature has a webpage that lists its members, committees, policies, and so on.[4] Most states have print and online media that follow the working of state and local governments. By beginning to examine these processes, you can learn the structure of governance in your state, and who appears to be dictating policy and reform. It is through speaking to these folks that real policy change can occur (Brown, 2008b; Valenzuela, 2005); for instance, the No Child Left Behind Act emerged out of Texas's state education policies. Moreover, it is state legislatures that decide whether school personnel will follow such initiatives as the Common Core.

State school boards typically interpret and implement newly passed state or federal laws. Thus, paying attention to who serves on these boards matters, and as with state legislatures, paying attention to "what" they are focusing on in regard to the day-to-day practices of schooling matters. As with state policymakers, it requires school stakeholders like you, whether you are an administrator, teacher, and/or family member, to show up at these meetings, voice your concerns, and provide insight into how these board members can help put in place reforms that support the expansion of learning of all children.

Federal Government

While the federal government often plays a minor role in the day-to-day practices of kindergarten classrooms, federal policies can dictate much of what is "valued" within an education system. Besides NCLB, the Obama administration's RTTT-ELC and the Enhanced Assessment Grants led to the formulation and implementation of kindergarten readiness assessments (Weisenfeld et al., 2020). Moreover, ESSA was supposed to address many of the issues outlined in this book. Passed in 2015, ESSA sought to empower states to rethink schooling, allowing them greater flexibility in developing their own systems of standards and accountability. For example, the law eliminated penalties for struggling schools; it allows school districts to use another nationally recognized assessment in high school instead of a state standards-based exam; and it provided funding for states to streamline and reduce the number of tests given.[5] While many state policymakers have not modified their education systems, ESSA demonstrates that there are opportunities for change out there.

Thus, to alter the politics and policies that shape public education requires public education stakeholders, including myself, to "maintain a stance of constant critical questioning, never allowing ourselves to be too comfortable with the landscape we create, or for our practices and understandings to become taken for granted as part of the status quo" (Evans, 2016, p. 75). To remain critical while being uncomfortable with whatever emerges from these proposed acts of change will require education stakeholders to question constantly how their proposed curricula and forms of instruction might privilege one group and disenfranchise another at any step in the reform process (Cannella, 1997).

Such vigilance creates opportunities for schooling experiences that expand all children's learning so that they become active democratic citizens as they progress through and beyond the education system (Brown, Englehardt, Barry, & Ku, 2019b). Furthermore, finding and capitalizing on the inherent value of community-based acts of inquiry within each classroom (e.g., Katz & Chard, 2000) and devaluing the power of mandated curricula and assessments may lead to a range of instructional practices that neoliberal reforms have eliminated from most public education systems. Finally, to seek out and capitalize on the funds of knowledge all students bring to kindergarten classrooms specifically and public education in general (Moll et al., 1992) could fundamentally alter the day-to-day practices of schools.

RESOURCES TO HELP CREATE SCHOOLS TO EXPAND LEARNING FOR ALL CHILDREN

There are a range of resources that can help you work toward expanding the learning of all children (Brown, 2008c). I would suggest first looking within your local community. For example, Texas has a recent political action group entitled Raise Your Hand Texas (www.raiseyourhandtexas.org). While their work employs much of the neoliberal discourses of which I have been critical throughout this book, they, and many others (e.g., Texas

Legislative Education Equity Coalition[6]) are striving to improve the education of all children in Texas (a state with historically underfunded schools). As Apple (2001) has pointed out, alliances are not perfect, but they can get beyond their differences to achieve meaningful change.

Nationally, there are a range of organizations that are working to improve the education of all children from birth through college. For example, you can find articles and reports at:

- National Institute for Early Education Research (www.nieer.org)
- Foundation for Child Development (www.fcd-us.org)
- New America Foundation (https://www.newamerica.org/education-policy/early-elementary-education-policy/)
- RAND (http://www.rand.org/education.html)
- The Brookings Institute (https://www.brookings.edu/topic/early-childhood-education/)
- The Future of Children, which is run by the Brookings Institute with Princeton University (www.futureofchildren.org)
- The Network for Public Education (https://networkforpubliceducation.org)
- National Education Policy Center (https://nepc.colorado.edu)
- National Center on Education and the Economy (ncee.org)
- Alliance for Early Success (http://earlysuccess.org/)

In terms of high-stakes testing, I would recommend looking at the National Center for Fair and Open Testing (http://fairtest.org/) as well as in your local community (e.g., in Texas, there is Texans Advocating for Meaningful Student Assessment, https://tamsatx.org). You also can gain a more global perspective on early care and education through the World Forum on Early Care and Education (www.worldforumfoundation.org).

Each of these organizations (and there are many more) produces newsletters/emails that offer insight and access to policy and research issues that affect the education of children, and many of these groups either evaluate and analyze education issues or put forward policy plans they feel will improve the status of early childhood education.

MOVING FORWARD IN EXPANDING THE LEARNING OF ALL CHILDREN

Across this book, I have shared what the Kinder-Race entails, how stakeholders make sense of it, and how they want it rerouted. In offering an alternative to this race, I contend that kindergarten must be framed as the expansion of learning. Enacting such a vision not only requires a rethinking of teaching, learning, assessment, accountability, and many other constructs (e.g., school readiness), but also requires active practical and political participation by stakeholders at all levels of governance and implementation.

Such rerouting is necessary so that kindergarten specifically and public education in general can produce the next generation of educated and engaged democratic citizens (Dewey, 1938/1998). Starting small, for example, teachers and/or families simply might ask, "Is my child/student happy in school? Do they see themselves as learners and/or a learning community? Is their learning valued by their classmates and teachers? Where do they want to go in their learning? How can they work with their classmates to achieve such goals?" Such questions can help any stakeholder begin to envision a path forward for change. From there, it's a matter of working collectively to promote and sustain such a vision of learning (e.g., Cohen & Mehta, 2017). Doing nothing, as Guinier and Torres (2002) and others (Apple, 2001; Brown, Englehardt, Barry, & Ku, 2019b; Dahlberg & Moss, 2005) have argued, is "to witness the slow but steady evisceration of American democracy" (p. 167).

Research Design

This book emerged out of an exploratory video-cued multivocal ethnographic study I conducted over 4 years (Adair et al., 2018; Hayashi & Tobin, 2012; Tobin et al., 2009; Valente, 2019). I formulated this study in the summer of 2014. In the fall of that year, both Natalie Weber and Dr. Joanna Englehardt helped me develop a research proposal that I submitted to the Spencer Foundation and the College of Education at The University of Texas at Austin that November.[1] Throughout that fall, I had numerous conversations with personnel from a range of schools and districts in Texas about finding a school and classroom reflective of the common experiences they expected teachers and students in kindergarten to engage in on a daily basis (Patton, 2015). In December, with the assistance of Natalie Weber, I located a school district, school, and school principal, Principal Atwell, willing to work with me for my study. Principal Atwell selected Ms. Cutler's classroom and asked whether she would be willing to work with me. Luckily, after my initial meeting with Ms. Cutler, she said yes.

While I have discussed this process in detail across several publications (e.g., Brown, Barry, Ku, & Englehardt, 2021; Brown, Englehardt, Barry, & Ku, 2019a), it essentially entailed me spending the following spring in Ms. Cutler's classroom. Prior to filming, I visited her class on average 3 days a week. I came in at different times across the school day to get a sense of how the day flowed and what typically happened during the varied scheduled subjects and activities (Graue & Walsh, 1998). I assisted Ms. Cutler in any way that I could and often worked with students in small groups or one-on-one.

In March, I filmed 3 days of Ms. Cutler teaching, using a camera lent to me by Dr. Jennifer Adair and my own camera, which I had used in previous studies documenting the work of public school teachers (e.g., Brown & Lee, 2012). Dr. Adair filmed 1 day with me and brought a different camera to film with that day. For the remaining 2 days, Dr. Joanna Englehardt filmed one day and Natalie Weber filmed the other—each of us using the original two cameras. In generating this film, with the assistance of Ms. Cutler, Robert Donald, and Natalie Weber, my focus was on what typically occurs across the day, which mirrors the work of Tobin et al. (1991, 2009).

THE VCME METHOD

VCME research investigates and compares how informants from various stakeholder groups make sense of the cultural act under investigation (Tobin et al., 2009). The video serves as a "cue to stimulate" a conversation concerning their "beliefs" about the purpose and processes of schooling (Tobin et al., 2009, p. 8). Tobin et al. (2013) stated that the "core assumption of the method is that . . . being able to comment on scenes in a video is [a] more concrete, less daunting task [than] being asked to answer abstract questions," and "by providing a common object for attention . . . the differences in how people respond to our [video] reveal differences in their beliefs and worldviews" (p. 24).

PARTICIPANT RECRUITMENT

Following the practices of VCME research, as outlined by Tobin et al. (2009) and their colleagues (Adair et al., 2018; Valente, 2019), I first recruited stakeholders within the school district in which I shot the video, which included the classroom teacher, other kindergarten teachers in the school, and school and district administrators (*n* = 10).

Then, I recruited stakeholders from two different school districts in Texas (*n* = 30) and two counties in West Virginia (*n* = 19) who were willing to participate in the study. The schools and school districts/counties were selected for their typicality within each state, which Patton (2015) defined as being "not in any major way atypical, extreme, deviant, or intensely unusual" (p. 284), and for their willingness to be a part of the larger study, which required permission from district personnel to allow district administrators, school principals, kindergarten teachers, and families of kindergartners to be interviewed individually or in focus groups (Merriam & Tisdell, 2016).

At the state level, I used a snowball-sampling system (Brown, 2004; Patton, 2015) to identify key informants who had knowledge about kindergarten and public education issues within their state context. I began this process by first reaching out to the lead state administrators who oversaw kindergarten programs in their respective state (Brown, 2008b; Patton, 2015). In conversations with these stakeholders, I asked them who else was knowledgeable about kindergarten within their state; based on their recommendations, I sought other key stakeholders to ask the same question. These participants included state administrators, members of policy advocacy organizations and research institutes, and state policymakers in Texas (*n* = 19) and in West Virginia (*n* = 9). At the national level, I again employed a snowball-sampling system, which began with conversations with representatives from a national early education advocacy group and a representative from an organization representing state officials in early childhood to identify policy analysts, early childhood specialists at a range of national organizations serving early childhood education, and nationally known K–12 education early childhood researchers who have expertise in kindergarten (n = 16).

DATA COLLECTION

Data collection consisted of artifact collection, interviewing participants after they watched the 23-minute video of kindergarten in the current era, memos, and observing and taking fieldnotes in the kindergarten classrooms of participating kindergarten teachers (Adair et al., 2018; Tobin et al., 2009; Valente, 2019).

Artifact Collection

I collected multiple data artifacts such as policy documents at the national, state, and district levels to catalogue the formulation, implementation, and maintenance of kindergarten in the United States (Merriam & Tisdell, 2016).

Interviews

I interviewed all participants either in focus groups (n = 86) or as individuals (n = 42) about their understandings of the types of learning experiences children are having as they begin elementary school. These two types of interviews are different. Individual interviews seek to generate "detailed accounts of participants' thoughts, attitudes, beliefs, and knowledge pertaining to a given phenomenon" (Lambert & Loiselle, 2008, p. 229). Focus groups are socially constructed conversations that allow participants to possibly refine their statements based on what others have stated (Merriam & Tisdell, 2016). Yet each "reveals different parts of the phenomenon of interest (complementary views)," and in doing so, each form of data generation "contributes to a more comprehensive understanding (expanding the breadth and/or depth of the findings)" of how these stakeholders conceptualized how kindergartners are and should be taught in school (Lambert & Loiselle, 2008, p. 230).

For this study, I determined whether to use focus group interviews based on the participant group and the number of participants available at each research site (Brown, Barry, Ku, & Englehardt, 2021). For example, since there were several kindergarten teachers at every school site, the teachers participated in focus groups, and since there was only one principal at each school, each principal participated in an individual interview. In some instances, particularly involving policymakers and their staff, they preferred to participate in individual interviews rather than focus groups (Brown, 2008b). Thus, to ensure that I captured a broad range of stakeholders' perspectives, I conducted individual interviews when necessary. All the interviews were semistructured (Merriam & Tisdell, 2016) and audio-recorded, and each followed the participants' viewing of the 23-minute video (Tobin et al., 2009).

The Video of a Typical Day in Kindergarten

Following the work of Tobin and his colleagues on VCME research, I generated a 23-minute video that represents a day in a kindergarten classroom in Texas where a teacher engaged in the current practices that define kindergarten in this era "to stimulate" a conversation with participants concerning their "beliefs" about the types of learning experiences children should have in kindergarten (Tobin et al., 2009, p. 8). Doing so allowed me to foster a conversation with education stakeholders about their core beliefs and concerns over the types of learning experiences children are and should be having as they begin elementary school (Tobin et al., 2013).

After 3 days of filming (Tobin et al., 1991), I put together a draft of the video, with technical assistance from Robert Donald, which attempted to capture the flow of the 7-hour day; I shared this draft with Ms. Cutler (Adair & Kurban, 2019). Using Ms. Cutler's feedback, I winnowed the movie down to 23 minutes so that it provided "a balance of shots that best reflected the program's approach to working with" kindergartners "and shots that I anticipated would function effectively as cues to stimulate informants to explicate their beliefs and philosophies" about kindergarten (Tobin et al., 2013, p. 25). The video was then shared with other kindergarten teachers in the school to make sure it reflected what happens in kindergarten. From there, I shared the video with other stakeholders within the school district in which it was shot. Then, I shared it with other education stakeholders in Texas and West Virginia, and at the national level.

The Typicality of the Video. As Tobin et al. (2013) noted, the VCME method "inevitably raises questions of typicality: how can I claim that one [kindergarten classroom] was typical . . . or that the day I videotape was typical of other days?" (p. 24). Following Tobin et al. (2009) and their colleagues' suggestions (Adair & Kurban, 2019; Valente, 2019), I was able to address this issue by beginning my investigation with questions for the teacher and administrators at the school in which I shot the video about its typicality. Then I showed this video, which was made in one classroom, "to audiences in many other settings" and "I enlisted our informants with the task of helping us understand in what way the site I chose was typical and then in what ways it reflected regional, audiological, or programmatic variations" (Tobin et al., 2013, p. 24).

The Video Is Data. Unlike Tobin and his colleagues (Adair et al., 2018; Hayashi & Tobin, 2012; Tobin et al., 2009; Valente, 2019), I view the video as data. How the video is made (including the intention of the video maker), who the video is made with (e.g., students in a charter school or students in a Title 1 public school), and verifying that the video reflects the typicality of a classroom all affect the direction of the study and the data collected for it (Merriam & Tisdell, 2016). To simply say it is not data washes away the responsibility of the researcher to verify the typicality of the film, as well as a range of ethical considerations (e.g., Does the researcher have any personal/professional connections to the classroom or school?). Moreover, it unhinges the connection between the participants, such as the teacher and students, in these studies and how they make sense of what they are watching, which end up being key data sources in this or any VCME study.

Interview Protocols

After watching the video, participants engaged in a semistructured interview that lasted between 45 and 90 minutes (Adair & Kurban, 2019; Sherfinski, 2019). All of the participants in both individual and focus group interviews were first asked their general reactions to the film, including such questions as: What did they like about the film? What surprised them? Did it reflect their understanding of kindergarten? From there, they were asked, What did they think about the learning experiences children were having in the film? Did those experiences align with how they thought children develop and learn? Were there experiences they thought kindergartners should have that were not in the film? Why did they think that was? Each participant was then asked: What practices do they think are important for kindergarten children to participate in? Why? What are the goals behind those activities? What do they think the value is of the kindergarten experience for the children? For their families? For society at large? What do they hope others who watch this video learn about kindergarten? Why? If they could alter anything about the kindergarten experience depicted in this video, what would it be and why?

Fieldnotes and Memos

In addition to these interviews, I took fieldnotes at each school site to capture a general sense of the school community; how the kindergarten classrooms were structured, including schedules, classroom organization, and materials available to the students; and what I experienced while at each school (Erlandson et al., 1993). I also generated memos after each interview (Merriam & Tisdell, 2016). Lastly, once the research team (which included Joanna Englehardt, David Barry, Da Hei Ku, and, for a short period of time, Hye Ryung Won) began to meet to transform and analyze the data, memos were generated after each meeting about the data analysis process and the construction of this narrative.

DATA ANALYSIS

The research team analyzed the data for this study using traditional qualitative analytic methods (Erickson, 1986; Graue & Walsh, 1998). For this book, I engaged in this deductive and inductive process again to examine how the stakeholders from a majority of the data set described the Kinder-Race, what they wanted kindergarten to be, why kindergartners should have those experiences, and whether they felt rerouting the Kinder-Race was possible (Graue & Walsh, 1998; Wolcott, 1994). In all, this book represents my intent to "craft a report structure that fits the intellectual and local context of [my] particular study" (Miles et al., 2014, p. 333).

Notes

Chapter 1

1. All names of participants from the research studies I've conducted over the years are pseudonyms. Nevertheless, I'd like to thank all of them for the gift of time they gave me as well as their insight into the issues I care deeply about in education.

Chapter 2

1. Wheelock College is now a part of Boston University.

2. Two other federal policy tools kept the performance of the states at the forefront of the education discourse during the 1980s: the measurements of student achievement enacted by the National Assessment of Educational Progress in 1969; and Secretary Terrell H. Bell's "Wall Chart," implemented in 1984, which ranked states by their educational attainment using such measures as SAT and ACT scores (Vinovskis, 1999). During this time, state governors began to view these comparisons as important and used these data to develop policies that altered their states' education systems. Although the federal government requested such reports as *A Nation at Risk* (NCEE, 1983), overall it took little initiative to implement policy changes during the Reagan years—in fact, Reagan wanted to disband the Department of Education (Ansary, 2007). Instead, the push for education reform took place at the state level.

3. The governors' initiatives traded a decrease in state policymakers' governance over school districts and other academic issues for an increase in the role of academic accountability in ensuring improved student performance (NGA, 1988).

4. Goals 2000 developed out of President George H. W. Bush's failed America 2000 legislation, the reform proposal that emerged from the 1989 Education Summit in Charlottesville, VA (Vinovskis, 1999).

5. http://www.corestandards.org

6. https://www.washingtonpost.com/wp-srv/onpolitics/elections/bushtext071000.htm

Chapter 3

1. Cascio and Schanzenbach (2016), who studied kindergartners in Tennessee, also found that children who were young relative to their kindergarten classmates generally performed no worse on achievement tests, were no more likely to be retained, and were no less likely to take the ACT or SAT. In fact, they found that having older classmates on average improves students' educational outcomes, increasing test scores up to 8 years after kindergarten.

2. I discuss this method of research in detail in the Appendix.

3. This comes from Ladson-Billings (2014) and signifies her argument that there will always be a need "to push forward" so that "new ideas about pedagogy designed to meet the needs of all students" can continue to evolve (p. 81).

4. Currently, only 19 states (AR, CT, DE, HI, LA, MD, NE, NV, NM, OH, OK, PA, RI, SC, SD, TN, VA, WV, WI), plus the District of Columbia, require children to attend kindergarten. All but NE and PA, plus the District of Columbia, require full-day kindergarten, and eight states (AK, FL, ID, MI, MN, NH, NJ, NY) do not require school districts to offer kindergarten.

5. https://tea.texas.gov/sites/default/files/Kinder_TEKS.pdf

6. https://tea.texas.gov/student-assessment/testing/staar/staar-resources

7. https://tea.texas.gov/sites/default/files/digest11-chap01.pdf

8. These terms come from Texas Education Agency documents that provided descriptive statistics of each school within Texas.

9. The specific descriptions of particular activities reflect what occurred in the film that was created.

10. Students in Texas are expected to recite the pledge of allegiance to the U.S. flag and the Texas pledge (see https://texas.public.law/statutes/tex._educ._code_section_25.082)

11. Library is considered one of the three "specials" the students participate in each week. On Mondays, they go to music; Tuesdays, Thursdays, and Fridays, PE; and Wednesdays, the library. Library time, as well as the other specials, is structured in ways similar to their classroom activities and offers limited opportunity for children to have choice or voice in their learning (Brown, Barry, Ku, & Englehardt, 2021). Collectively, the experiences of the kindergartners in this classroom mimic the findings of Bassok et al. (2016) that kindergarten teachers have increased their use of "rote, didactic tasks" to teach children the skills and knowledge covered in kindergarten (p. 10).

12. The TEKS state that students will identify and read at least 25 high-frequency words from a commonly used list by the end of kindergarten (TEA, 2020).

13. DRA stands for Developmental Reading Assessment. This tool assesses a child's reading capabilities, which includes reading level, accuracy, fluency (how fast they can read), and comprehension.

14. https://www.raz-kids.com/

Chapter 4

1. See http://www.corestandards.org/ for more information about the Common Core.

Chapter 5

1. As I went about talking to different stakeholders across these two states, I did strive for "balance" in terms of whom I talked with about the Kinder-Race. However, not all the stakeholders I contacted for my study were willing to participate and/or recommended that a member of their team speak to me rather than the primary stakeholder. Most of the legislators in Texas asked that I speak to their chief of staff or staff members from the committees they oversaw. In terms of lobbying groups, the largest business lobbying group in Texas stated that they did not want to partic-

ipate because no one on their staff worked on issues involving kindergarten (Brown, Englehardt, Barry, & Ku., 2019a).

2. See https://www.dpi.nc.gov/districts-schools/classroom-resources/early-learning-read-achieve/pre-kk-demonstration-program

Chapter 6

1. In this last point, Paris borrows from Tuck's (2009) work in which she contends that researchers need to rethink how they frame their participants who come from communities of color, Indigenous people, and/or those living in poverty. Even though researchers document the "damage" done to these peoples and their communities, Tuck contends that such work often leads to members of these communities thinking they are damaged or broken. Thus, through these five elements, Paris (2016) wants to ensure that teachers do not cause students to feel or see themselves as damaged.

2. See https://nces.ed.gov/nationsreportcard/about/

3. Go to http://www.fairtest.org/k-12/accountability for other examples of accountability systems.

4. Go to https://www.congress.gov/state-legislature-websites to find the website for your state legislature.

5. See https://www.understood.org/en/school-learning/your-childs-rights/basics-about-childs-rights/the-difference-between-the-every-student-succeeds-act-and-no-child-left-behind

6. https://www.idra.org/education_policy/texas-legislative-education-equity-coalition/

Appendix: Research Design

1. Proposal title: *What Should Kindergarten Be? Studying Stakeholders' Conceptions and Understandings of the Purpose, Value, and Practice of Kindergarten* (UT OSP# 201403611).

References

Achinstein, B., & Ogawa, R. (2006). (In)fidelity: What the resistance of new teachers reveals about professional principles and prescriptive educational policies. *Harvard Educational Review, 76*(1), 30–63.

Adair, J. K. (2014). Agency and expanding capabilities in early grade classrooms: What it could mean for young children. *Harvard Educational Review, 84*(2), 217–241.

Adair, J. K., Colegrove, K. S. S., & McManus, M. E. (2018). Troubling messages: Agency and learning in the early schooling experiences of children of Latinx immigrants. *Teachers College Record, 120,* 1–40.

Adair, J. K., & Kurban, F. (2019). Video-cued ethnographic data collection as a tool toward participant voice. *Anthropology & Education Quarterly, 50,* 312–332.

Ailwood, J. (2008). Learning or earning in the "smart state": Changing tactics for governing early childhood. *Childhood, 15,* 535–551.

Alexander, K. L., Entwisle, D. R., & Olson, L. S. (2001). Schools, achievement, and inequality: A seasonal perspective. *Educational Evaluation and Policy Analysis, 23*(2), 171–191.

Alfieri, L., Brooks, P. J., Aldrich, N. J., & Tenenbaum, H. R. (2011). Does discovery-based instruction enhance learning? *Journal of Educational Psychology, 103*(1), 1–18.

Alford, B. L., Rollins, K. B., Padrón, Y. N., & Waxman, H. C. (2016). Using systematic classroom observation to explore student engagement as a function of teachers' developmentally appropriate instructional practices (DAIP) in ethnically diverse pre-kindergarten through second-grade classrooms. *Early Childhood Education Journal, 44,* 623–635.

Alim, H. S. (2005). Critical language awareness in the United States: Revisiting issues and revising pedagogies in a resegregated society. *Educational Researcher, 34*(7), 24–31.

Allen, C. D., & Penuel, W. R. (2015). Studying teachers' sensemaking to investigate teachers' responses to professional development focused on new standards. *Journal of Teacher Education, 66,* 136–149.

Ansary, T. (2007). *Education at risk: Fallout from a flawed report.* Edutopia. https://www.edutopia.org/landmark-education-report-nation-risk

Apple, M. W. (2001). *Educating the "right" way: Markets, standards, god, and inequality.* Routledge.

Apple, M. W. (2007). Ideological success, educational failure? On the politics of No Child Left Behind. *Journal of Teacher Education, 58*(2), 108–116.

Archbald, D. A., & Porter, A. C. (1990). *A retrospective and analysis of roles of mandated testing in education reform.* Office of Technology Assessment.

Argyris, C., & Schon, D. A. (1974). *Theories in practice: Increasing professionalism.* Jossey-Bass.

Ashiabi, G. S. (2007). Play in the preschool classroom: Its socioemotional significance and the teacher's role in play. *Early Childhood Education Journal, 35*(2), 199–207.

Aud, S., Fox, M. A., & Kewal Ramani, A. (2010). *Status and trends in the education of racial and ethnic groups* (NCES 2010-015). U.S. Department of Education, National Center for Education Statistics. http://nces.ed.gov/pubs2010/2010015.pdf

Baker, D. L., Santoro, L., Ware, S., Cuéllar, D., Oldham, A., Cuticelli, M., Coyne, M. D., Loftus-Rattan, S., & McCoach, B. (2015). Understanding and implementing the common core vocabulary standards in kindergarten. *Teaching Exceptional Children, 47*(5), 264–271.

Baker, E. L. (2002). *The struggle to reform education: Exploring the limits of policy metaphors* (CSE Technical Report No. 576). University of California, National Center for Research on Evaluation, Standards, and Student Testing.

Bakhtin, M. M. (1981). *The dialogic imagination: Four essays.* University of Texas Press.

Ball, S. (2003). The teacher's soul and the terrors of performativity. *Journal of Education Policy, 18*(2), 215–228.

Ball, S. J. (2007). *Education plc: Understanding private sector participation in public sector education.* Routledge.

Ball, S., Maguire, M., & Braun, A. (2012). *How schools do policy: Policy enactments in secondary schools.* Routledge.

Ballet, J., Biggeri, M., & Comim, F. (2011). Children's agency and the capability approach: A conceptual framework. In M. Biggeri, J. Ballet, & F. Comim (Eds.), *Children and the capability approach* (pp. 25–45). Palgrave.

Baltodano, M. (2012). Neoliberalism and the demise of public education: The corporatization of schools of education. *International Journal of Qualitative Studies in Education, 25*, 487–507.

Bassok, D., Latham, S., & Rorem A. (2016). Is kindergarten the new first grade? *AERA Open, 4*, 1–31.

Beatty, B. (1995). *Preschool education in America: The culture of young children from the colonial era to the present.* Yale University Press.

Becker, G. S. (1964). *Human capital: A theoretical and empirical analysis, with special reference to education.* National Bureau of Economics Research.

Becker, G. S. (1975). *Human capital: A theoretical and empirical analysis, with special reference to education* (2nd ed.). National Bureau of Economic Research.

Berk, L. E., & Meyers, A. B. (2013). The role of make-believe play in the development of executive function: Status of research and future directions. *American Journal of Play, 6*(1), 98–110.

Bertrand, M., & Marsh, J. A. (2015). Teachers' sensemaking of data and implications for equity. *American Educational Research Journal, 52*, 861–893.

Biesta, G. (2006). What's the point of lifelong learning if lifelong learning has no point? On the democratic deficit of policies for lifelong learning. *European Educational Research Journal, 5*, 169–180.

Bloch, M. N. (1991). Critical science and the history of child development's influence on early education research. *Early Education and Development, 2*(2), 95–108.

Bonawitz, E., Shafto, P., Gweon, H., Goodman, N. D., Spelke, E., & Schulz, L. (2011). The double-edged sword of pedagogy: Instruction limits spontaneous exploration and discovery. *Cognition, 120*(3), 322–330.

Booher-Jennings, J. (2005). Below the bubble: "Educational triage" and the Texas accountability system. *American Educational Research Journal, 42*(2), 231–268.

Brathwaite, J. (2016). Neoliberal education reform and the perpetuation of inequality. *Critical Sociology, 43*(3), 429–448.

Bredekamp, S. (1987). *Developmentally appropriate practice in early childhood programs serving children from birth through age 8*. National Association for the Education of Young Children.

Bredekamp, S., & Rosegrant, T. (Eds.). (1995). *Reaching potentials: Transforming early childhood curriculum and assessment* (Vol. 2). National Association for the Education of Young Children.

Brewer, C., Gasko, J. W., & Miller, D. (2011). Have we been here before? Lessons learned from a microhistory of the policy development of universal kindergarten. *Educational Policy, 25*(1), 9–35.

Britt, C., & Rudolph, S. (2013). "All our hands would tell about the community": Re-imagining (im)possible teacher/student subjectivities in the early years of primary school. *The International Journal of Critical Pedagogy, 4*(2), 35–52.

Brock, L. L., Rimm-Kaufman, S. E., Nathanson, L., & Grimm, K. J. (2009). The contributions of "hot" and "cool" executive function to children's academic achievement, learning-related behaviors, and engagement in kindergarten. *Early Childhood Research Quarterly, 24*(3), 337–349.

Brosterman, N. (1997). *Inventing kindergarten*. New York: Abrams/Times Mirror.

Brown, A. L., & Brown, K. D. (2010). Strange fruit indeed: Interrogating contemporary textbook representations of racial violence toward African Americans. *Teachers College Record, 112*(1), 31–67.

Brown, C. P. (2004). *Analyzing discourses of accountability through Wisconsin's 4th and 8th grade promotion statutes* [Doctoral dissertation, University of Wisconsin-Madison]. ProQuest Dissertations and Theses Global.

Brown, C. P. (2005a). Creating opportunities. *Contemporary Issues in Early Childhood, 6*, 112–127.

Brown, C. P. (2005b). Staking out the successful student. *Education Policy Analysis Archives, 13*(14). https://epaa.asu.edu/ojs/article/view/119

Brown, C. P. (2006). A universal early childhood education system. *Childhood Education, 83*, 44–47.

Brown, C. P. (2007a). It's more than content: Expanding the conception of early learning standards. *Early Childhood Research and Practice, 9*(1). https://ecrp.illinois.edu/v9n1/brown.html

Brown, C. P. (2007b). Examining the streams of a retention policy to understand the politics of high-stakes reform. *Education Policy Analysis Archives, 15*(9). https://epaa.asu.edu/ojs/article/view/57

Brown, C. P. (2007c). Unpacking standards in early childhood education. *Teachers College Record, 109* (3), 635–668.

Brown, C. P. (2008a). Examining how the student "determines" the success and/or failure of education reform. *International Critical Childhood Policy Studies, 1*(1), 1–27.

Brown, C. P. (2008b). Keep it cheap, keep it local, and keep it coming: Standards-based accountability reform in Wisconsin. *Educational Policy, 22*, 250–294.

Brown, C. P. (2008c). Research in review: Advocating for policies to improve practice. *Young Children, 63*(4), 70–77.

Brown, C. P. (2009a). Being accountable for one's own governing: A case study of early educators responding to standards-based early childhood education reform. *Contemporary Issues in Early Childhood, 10*(1), 3–23.

Brown, C. P. (2009b). Confronting the contradictions: A case study of early childhood teacher development in neoliberal times. *Contemporary Issues in Early Childhood, 10*(3), 240–259.

Brown, C. P. (2009c). Pivoting a pre-kindergarten program off the child or the standard? A case study of integrating the practices of early childhood education into elementary school. *The Elementary School Journal, 110*(2), 202–227.

Brown, C. P. (2010a). Children of reform: The impact of high-stakes education reform on preservice teachers. *Journal of Teacher Education, 61*, 477–491.

Brown, C. P. (2010b). *Microwaving the teacher induction process: A case study of first year teachers' experiences in high-stakes contexts* [Paper presentation]. American Educational Research Association annual meeting, Denver, CO, United States.

Brown, C. P. (2011). Searching for the norm in a system of absolutes: A case study of standards-based accountability reform in pre-kindergarten. *Early Education and Development, 22*(1), 151–177.

Brown, C. P. (2013). Reforming preschool to ready children for academic achievement: A case study of the impact of pre-K reform on the issue of school readiness. *Early Education and Development, 24*(4), 554–573.

Brown, C. P. (2015). Conforming to reform: Teaching pre-kindergarten in a neoliberal early education system. *Journal of Early Childhood Research, 13*, 236–251.

Brown, C. P. (2018). Attempting to fracture the neoliberal hold on early educators' practical conceptions of teaching: A case study. *Global Studies of Childhood, 8*(1), 53–74.

Brown, C. P. (2019). Introducing the text and examining the emergence, maintenance, and expansion of gaps, deficits, and risks through early childhood policy. In F. Nxumalo & C. P. Brown (Eds.), *Disrupting and countering deficits in early childhood education* (pp. 1–19). Routledge.

Brown, C. P. (2021). *Ready for kindergarten? Freeing yourself from the readiness trap so that you and your child will succeed in kindergarten.* ADVANCE Publishing.

Brown, C. P., & Barry, D. P. (2021). Make kindergarten "funner": Examining how kindergartners made sense of the changed kindergarten. *Teachers College Record, 123*(6). https://www.tcrecord.org/Content.asp?ContentId=23705

Brown, C. P., & Barry, D. P. (2019). Public policy and early childhood curriculum in the United States. In J. J. Mueller & N. File (Eds.), *Curriculum in early childhood: Re-examined, reclaimed, and renewed* (2nd ed., pp. 17–33). Routledge.

Brown, C. P., Barry, D., & Ku, D. (2021). How education stakeholders made sense of school readiness in and beyond kindergarten. *Journal of Research in Childhood Education, 35*(1), 122–142.

Brown, C. P., Barry, D., Ku, D., & Englehardt, J. (2021). How education stakeholders made sense of the types of learning experiences children are and should be having in kindergarten and why. *Early Education and Development, 32*(2), 291–322.

Brown, C. P., Barry, D., Ku, D., & Puckett, K. (2021). Teach as I say, not as I do: How preservice teachers made sense of the mismatch between how they were expected to teach and how they were taught in their professional training program. *The Teacher Educator*. https://doi.org/10.1080/08878730.2020.1847225

Brown, C. P., Bay-Borelli, D. E., & Scott, J. (2015). Figuring out how to be a teacher in a high-stakes context: A case study of first-year teachers' conceptual and practical development. *Action in Teacher Education, 37*, 45–64.

Brown, C. P., & Englehardt, J. (2016). Conceptions of and early childhood educators' experiences in early childhood professional development programs: A qualitative metasynthesis. *Journal of Early Childhood Teacher Education, 37*(3), 216–244.

Brown, C. P., & Englehardt, J. (2017). A case study of how a sample of preservice teachers made sense of incorporating iPads into their instruction with children. *Journal of Early Childhood Teacher Education, 38*(1), 19–38.

Brown, C. P., Englehardt, J., Barry, D. P., & Ku, D. (2019a). Examining how stakeholders at the local, state, and national level made sense of the changed kindergarten. *American Educational Research Journal, 56*, 822–867.

Brown, C. P., Englehardt, J., Barry, D., & Ku, D. (2019b). Questioning democratic notions of governance: A case study examining how a kindergarten teacher and her students give voice to and enact a neoliberal framing of schooling. *Contemporary Issues in Early Childhood, 20*(3), 236–252.

Brown, C. P., Englehardt, J., Ku, D., & Barry, D. P. (2019). "Where's the joy in the classroom?": Families' sensemaking of the changed kindergarten. *The Elementary School Journal, 120*(2), 319–346.

Brown, C. P., Englehardt, J., & Mathers, H. (2016). Examining preservice teachers' conceptual and practical understandings of adopting iPads into their teaching of young children. *Teaching and Teacher Education, 60*, 179–190.

Brown, C. P., & Feger, B. (2010). Examining the challenges early childhood teacher candidates face in figuring their roles as early educators. *Journal of Early Childhood Teacher Education, 31*, 286–306.

Brown, C. P., Feger, B. S., & Mowry, B. N. (2015). Helping others understand academic rigor in teachers' developmentally appropriate practices. *Young Children, 70*(4), 62–69.

Brown, C. P., Feger, B. S., & Mowry, B. N. (2018). *RIGOROUS DAP in the early years: From theory to practice*. Redleaf Press.

Brown, C. P., & Gasko, J. W. (2012). Why should pre-K be more like elementary school? A case study of pre-K reform. *Journal of Research in Childhood Education, 26*, 264–290.

Brown, C. P., & Ku, D. (2018). Putting theories into action: A case of study of how early educators made sense of teaching lessons that reflected their students' sociocultural worlds. *Journal of Early Childhood Teacher Education, 39*, 382–405.

Brown, C. P., Ku, D., & Barry, D. P. (2020a). "Kindergarten isn't fun anymore. Isn't that so sad?": Examining how kindergarten teachers in the US made sense of the changed kindergarten. *Teaching and Teacher Education, 90*. https://doi.org/10.1016/j.tate.2020.103029

Brown, C. P., Ku, D., & Barry, D. P. (2020b). Making sense of instruction within the changed kindergarten: Perspectives from preservice early childhood educators and teacher educators. *Journal of Early Childhood Teacher Education*. https://doi.org/10.1080/10901027.2020.1726532

Brown, C. P., & Lan, Y. C. (2013). The influence of developmentally appropriate practice on children's cognitive development: A qualitative metasynthesis. *Teachers College Record, 115*(12), 1–36.

Brown, C. P., & Lan, Y. C. (2015a). A qualitative metasynthesis of how early educators in international contexts address cultural matters that contrast with developmentally appropriate practices. *Early Education and Development, 26*(1), 22–45.

Brown, C. P., & Lan, Y. C. (2015b). A qualitative metasynthesis comparing U.S. teachers' conceptions of school readiness prior to and after the implementation of NCLB. *Teaching and Teacher Education, 45*(1), 1–13.

Brown, C. P., & Lan, Y. C. (2018). Understanding families' conceptions of school readiness in the United States: A qualitative metasynthesis. *International Journal of Early Years Education, 26*, 403–421.

Brown, C. P., & Lee, J. E. (2012). How to teach to the child when the stakes are high: Examples of implementing developmentally appropriate and culturally relevant practices in pre-kindergarten. *Journal of Early Childhood Teacher Education, 33*(4), 322–348.

Brown, C. P., & Mowry, B. (2009). Preparing for change: A case study of successful alignment between a PreK program and a K–12 education system. *Childhood Education, 85*(3), 173–178.

Brown, C. P., & Mowry, B. (2013). Balancing preschool and academic rigor. *Principal, 92*(5), 52–53.

Brown, C. P., & Mowry, B. (2015). Close early learning gaps with RIGOROUS DAP. *Phi Delta Kappan, 96*(7), 53–57.

Brown, C. P., & Weber, N. B. (2016a). Struggling to overcome the state's prescription for practice: A study of a sample of early educators' professional development and action-research projects in a high-stakes teaching context. *Journal of Teacher Education, 67*, 183–202.

Brown, C. P., & Weber, N. B. (2016b). Working with practicing teachers in a high-stakes teaching context to rethink their pedagogical practices with children of diverse backgrounds. *Action in Teacher Education, 38*(3), 259–277.

Brown, C. P., & Weber, N. B. (2019). Bringing being into professional development: A qualitative investigation into teachers' struggles moving beyond an epistemological framing of teaching and learning. *Early Child Development and Care, 188*(5), 763–776.

Brown, C. P., Weber, N. B., & Yoon, Y. (2015). The practical difficulties for early educators who tried to address children's realities in their high-stakes teaching context. *Journal of Early Childhood Teacher Education, 36*(1), 3–23.

Brown, C. P., Weber, N. B., & Yoon, Y. (2016). Reluctantly governed: The struggles of early educators in a professional development course that challenged their teaching in a high-stakes neoliberal early education context. *Contemporary Issues in Early Childhood, 17*(2), 210–234.

Brownlee, J., Petriwskyj, A., Thorpe, K., Stacey, P., & Gibson, M. (2011). Changing personal epistemologies in early childhood pre-service teachers using an integrated teaching program. *Higher Education Research & Development, 30*, 477–490.

Bryant, D. M., Clifford, R. M., & Peisner, E. S. (1991). Best practices for beginners: Developmental appropriateness in kindergarten. *American Educational Research Journal*, *28*(4), 783–803.

Bryce, C. I., Goble, P., Swanson, J., Fabes, R. A., Hanish, L. D., & Martin, C. L. (2018). Kindergarten school engagement: Linking early temperament and academic achievement at the transition to school. *Early Education and Development*, *29*(5), 780–796.

Burchinal, M., Foster, T. J., Bezdek, K. G., Bratsch-Hines, M., Blair, C., Vernon-Feagans, L., & Family Life Project Investigators. (2020). School-entry skills predicting school-age academic and social-emotional trajectories. *Early Childhood Research Quarterly*, *51*, 67–80.

Burger, K. (2010). How does early childhood care and education affect cognitive development? An international review of the effects of early interventions for children from different social backgrounds. *Early Childhood Research Quarterly*, *25*(2), 140–165.

Burman, E. (1994). *Deconstructing developmental psychology*. Routledge.

Bustamante, A. S., & Hindman, A. H. (2019). Classroom quality and academic school readiness outcomes in Head Start: The indirect effect of approaches to learning. *Early Education and Development*, *30*, 19–35.

Campbell, F. A., Ramey, C. T., Pungello, E., Sparling, J., & Miller-Johnson, S. (2002). Early childhood education: Young adult outcomes from the Abecedarian Project. *Applied Developmental Science*, *6*(1), 42–57.

Cannella, G. S. (1997). *Deconstructing early childhood education: Social justice and revolution*. Peter Lang.

Cascio, E. U., & Schanzenbach, D. W. (2016). First in the class? Age and the education production function. *Education Finance and Policy*, *11*(3), 225–250.

Castro, A. J. (2010). Challenges in teaching for critical multicultural citizenship: Student teaching in an accountability-driven context. *Action in Teacher Education*, *32*, 97–109.

Cheruvu, R. (2019). Disrupting standardized early education through culturally sustaining pedagogies with young children. In F. Nxumalo & C. P. Brown (Eds.), *Disrupting and countering deficits in early childhood education and care* (pp. 103–118). Routledge.

Chetty, R., Friedman, J. N., Hilger, N., Saez, E., Schanzenbach, D. W., & Yagan, D. (2011). How does your kindergarten classroom affect your earnings? Evidence from Project STAR. *The Quarterly Journal of Economics*, *126*(4), 1593–1660.

Cho, H. (2017). Navigating the meanings of social justice, teaching for social justice, and multicultural education. *International Journal of Multicultural Education*, *19*(2), 1–19.

Christopher, C., & Farran, D. (2020). Academic gains in kindergarten related to eight classroom practices. *Early Childhood Research Quarterly*, *53*, 638–649.

Cibulka, J. G. (1999). Moving toward an accountable system of K–12 education: Alternative approaches and challenges. In G. J. Cizek (Ed.), *Handbook of educational policy* (pp. 183–211). Academic Press.

Claessens, A., Duncan, G. J., & Engel, M. (2009). Kindergarten skills and fifth-grade achievement: Evidence from the ECLS-K. *Economics of Education Review*, *28*, 415–427.

Claessens, A., Engel, M., & Curran, F. C. (2014). Academic content, student learning, and the persistence of preschool effects. *American Educational Research Journal, 51*(2), 403–434.

Clark, J., & Richards, S. (2017). The cherished conceits of research with children: Does seeking the agentic voice of the child through participatory methods deliver what it promises? *Sociological Studies of Children and Youth, 22*(1), 127–147.

Clements, D. H. (1999). Subitizing: What is it? Why teach it? *Teaching Children Mathematics, 5*, 400–405.

Coburn, C. E. (2001). Collective sensemaking about reading: How teachers mediate reading policy in their professional communities. *Educational Evaluation and Policy Analysis, 23*, 145–170.

Coburn, C. E. (2004). Beyond decoupling: Rethinking the relationship between the institutional environment and the classroom. *Sociology of Education, 77*(3), 211–244.

Cohen, D. K., & Mehta, J. D. (2017). Why reform sometimes succeeds: Understanding the conditions that produce reforms that last. *American Educational Research Journal, 54*, 644–690.

Cohen, D. K., & Spillane, J. P. (1993). Policy and practice: The relationship between governance and instruction. In S. H. Fuhrman (Ed.), *Designing coherent education policy: Improving the system* (pp. 35–95). Jossey-Bass.

Cohen-Vogel, L., Little, M., Jang, W., Burchinal, M., & Bratsch-Hines, M. (2021). A missed opportunity? Instructional content redundancy in pre-K and kindergarten. *AERA Open*, *7*(1), 1–15.

Cohen-Vogel, L., Sadler, J. R., Little, M., & Merrill, B. (2020). (Mis)alignment of instructional policy supports in pre-K and kindergarten: Evidence from rural districts in North Carolina. *Early Childhood Research Quarterly, 52*, 3–43.

Colegrove, K. S. S. (2019). Working with diverse families. In C. P. Brown, M. McMullen, & N. File (Eds.), *The Wiley handbook of early childhood care and education* (pp. 219–238). Wiley.

Colegrove, K. S. S., & Krause, G. (2017). "Lo hacen tan complicado": Bridging the perspectives and expectations of mathematics instruction of Latino immigrant parents. *Bilingual Research Journal, 40*, 187–204.

Cooper, C. W. (2009). Parent involvement, African American mothers, and the politics of educational care. *Equity & Excellence in Education, 42*, 379–394.

Copple, C., & Bredekamp, S. (2009). *Developmentally appropriate practice in early childhood programs serving children from birth through age 8* (3rd ed.). National Association for the Education of Young Children.

Cruse, K. L., & Twing, J. S. (2000). The history of statewide achievement testing in Texas. *Applied Measurement in Education, 13*, 327–331.

Cuban, L. (1988). A fundamental puzzle of school reform. *Phi Delta Kappan, 69*, 341–344.

Cuban, L. (1992). Why some reforms last: The case of the kindergarten. *American Journal of Education, 100*, 166–194.

Dagli, U. Y., & Jones, I. (2013). The longitudinal effects of kindergarten enrollment and relative age on children's academic achievement. *Teachers College Record, 115*(3), 1–40.

Dahlberg, G., & Moss, P. (2005). *Ethics and politics in early childhood education.* Routledge Falmer.

Darling-Hammond, L. (2003). Standards and assessments: Where we are and what we need. *TCRecord.org*. http://www.tcrecord.org/Content.asp?ContentID-11109

Davies, B., & Bansel, P. (2007). Neoliberalism and education. *International Journal of Qualitative Studies in Education, 20*, 247–259.

Deci, E. L., & Ryan, R. M. (2000). The "what" and "why" of goal pursuits: Human needs and the self-determination of behavior. *Psychological Inquiry, 11*(4), 227–268.

De Lissovoy, N. (2014). Pedagogy of the impossible: Neoliberalism and the ideology of accountability. *Policy Futures in Education, 11*, 423–435.

De Lissovoy, N. (2018). Pedagogy of the anxious: Rethinking critical pedagogy in the context of neoliberal autonomy and responsibilization. *Journal of Education Policy, 33*, 187–205.

Delgado, R. (1989). Storytelling for oppositionists and others: A plea for narrative. *Michigan Law Review, 87*(8), 2411–2441.

Delpit, L. D. (2012). *"Multiplication is for white people": Raising expectations for other people's children*. New Press.

DeMatthews, D., & Knight, D. S. (2018, October 9). Texas needs to fund its schools differently. *UT News*. https://news.utexas.edu/2018/10/09/texas-needs-to-fund-its-public-schools-differently/

Dewey, J. (1998). *Experience and education: The 60th anniversary edition*. Kappa Delta Pi. (Original work published 1938)

Diamond, A. (2013). Executive functions. *Annual Review of Psychology, 64*, 135–168.

Di Santo, A., Timmons, K., & Lenis, A. (2017). Preservice early childhood educators' pedagogical beliefs. *Journal of Early Childhood Teacher Education, 38*(3), 223–241.

Djonko-Moore, C. M. (2016). An exploration of teacher attrition and mobility in high poverty racially segregated schools. *Race Ethnicity and Education, 19*(5), 1063–1087.

Dombkowski, K. (2001). Will the real kindergarten please stand up? Defining and redefining the twentieth-century U.S. kindergarten. *History of Education, 30*, 527–545.

Doucet, F. (2011). Parent involvement as ritualized practice. *Anthropology & Education Quarterly, 42*(4), 404–421.

Doucet, F., & Adair, J. K. (2013). Addressing race and inequity in the classroom. *Young Children, 68*(5), 88–92, 94–97.

Douglass, A., Taj, K., Coonan, M., & Friedman, D. H. (2017). Lessons from an urban school readiness initiative: Including family, friend, and neighbor care providers. *Early Education and Development, 28*(6), 640–654.

Drake, S. M., & Savage, M. F. (2016). Negotiating accountability and integrated curriculum in a global context. *International Journal of Learning, Teaching and Educational Research, 15*, 127–144.

DuCharme, C. C. (2000). Lucy Wheelock: Her life and work. *Childhood Education, 76*(3), 164–169.

Duckworth, A. (2016). *Grit: The power of passion and perseverance*. Scribner.

Dumas, M. J., & Nelson, J. D. (2016). (Re)imagining Black boyhood: Toward a critical framework for educational research. *Harvard Educational Review, 86*(1), 27–47.

Duncan, G. J., Dowsett, C. J., Claessens, A., Magnuson, K., Huston, A. C., Klebanov, P., Pagani, L. S., Feinstein, L., Engel, M., Brooks-Gunn, J., Sexton, H.,

Duckworth, K., & Japel, C. (2007). School readiness and later achievement. *Developmental Psychology, 43*, 1428–1446.

Dunn, A. H. (2018). Leaving a profession after it's left you: Teachers' public resignation letters as resistance amidst neoliberalism. *Teachers College Record, 120*(9), 1–34.

Dweck, C. (2006). *Mindset.* Ballantine.

Edwards, S. (2011). Developing diversity dispositions for white culturally responsive teachers. *Action in Teacher Education, 33*, 493–508.

Ehri, L. C. (2012). Why is it important for children to begin learning to read in kindergarten? In S. Suggate & E. Reese (Eds.), *Contemporary debates in childhood education and development* (pp. 171–180). Routledge.

Einboden, R., Rudge, T., & Varcoe, C. (2013). Producing children in the 21st century: A critical discourse analysis of the science and techniques of monitoring early child development. *Health, 17*, 549–566.

Eizadirad, A. (2019). *Decolonizing educational assessment: Ontario elementary students and the EQAO.* Palgrave Macmillan.

Engel, M., Claessens, A., Watts, T., & Farkas, G. (2016). Mathematics content coverage and student learning in kindergarten. *Educational Researcher, 45*(5), 293–300.

Erickson, F. (1986). Qualitative methods in research on teaching. In M. Whittrock (Ed.), *Handbook of research on teaching* (pp. 119–161). Macmillan.

Erickson, F. (2014). Scaling down: A modest proposal for practice-based policy research in teaching. *Education Policy Analysis Archives, 22*, 1–14.

Erlandson, D. A., Harris, E. L., Skipper, B. L., & Allen, S. D. (1993). *Doing naturalistic inquiry: A guide to methods.* Sage.

Evans, A. E. (2007). School leaders and their sensemaking about race and demographic change. *Educational Administration Quarterly, 43*(2), 159–188.

Evans, K. (2016). Beyond a logic of quality: Opening space for material-discursive practices of "readiness" in early years education. *Contemporary Issues in Early Childhood, 17*, 65–77.

Evans, L., Turner, C. R., & Allen, K. R. (2020). "Good teachers" with "good intentions": Misappropriations of culturally responsive pedagogy. *Journal of Urban Learning, Teaching and Research, 15*(1), 1–24.

Fantilli, R. D., & McDougall, D. E. (2009). A study of novice teachers: Challenges and supports in the first years. *Teaching and Teacher Education, 25*, 814–825.

Fine, M. (1988). Of kitsch and caring. The illusion of students at risk. *School Administrator, 45*(8), 16–18, 23.

Finn, C. E., Jr. (1990). The biggest reform of all. *Phi Delta Kappan, 71*(8), 584–592.

Fisher, B. (1991). *Joyful learning: A whole language kindergarten.* Heinemann.

Fletcher, J., & Kim, T. (2016). The effects of changes in kindergarten entry age policies on educational achievement. *Economics of Education Review, 50*, 45–62.

Foucault, M. (1982). The subject and power. *Critical Inquiry, 8*, 777–795.

Foucault, M. (2008). *The birth of biopolitics: Lectures at the Collège de France, 1978–1979* (G. Burchell, Trans.). Palgrave Macmillan.

Fox, S. E., Levitt, P., & Nelson, C. A. (2010). How the timing and quality of early experiences influence the development of brain architecture. *Child Development, 81*, 28–40.

Freeman, E. B., & Hatch, J. A. (1989). What schools expect young children to know and do: An analysis of kindergarten report cards. *The Elementary School Journal, 89*, 594–605.

Fregoso Bailón, R. O., & De Lissovoy, N. (2019). Against coloniality: Toward an epistemically insurgent curriculum. *Policy Futures in Education, 17*, 355–369.

Freire, P. (1974). *Pedagogy of the oppressed* (M. B. Ramos, Trans.). Seabury Press.

Freire, P. (2006). The banking model of education. In E. F. Provenzo (Ed.), *Critical issues in education: An anthology of readings* (pp. 105–117). Sage. (Original work published 1970)

Friedman-Krauss, A. H., Barnett, W. S., Garver, K. A., Hodges, K. S., Weisenfeld, G. G., & Gardiner, B. A. (2020). *The state of preschool 2019: State preschool yearbook*. National Institute for Early Education Research.

Froebel, F. (1902). *The education of man*. D. Appleton.

Gaskins, S., Miller, P. J., & Corsaro, W. A. (1992). Theoretical and methodological perspectives in the interpretive study of children. *New Directions for Child and Adolescent Development, 1992*(58), 5–23.

Gay, G. (2000). *Culturally responsive teaching: Theory, research, and practice.* Teachers College Press.

Gnezda, M. T., & Bolig, R. (1988). *A national survey of public school testing of pre- kindergarten and kindergarten children.* National Forum on the Future of Children and Families, National Research Council.

Goble, P., & Pianta, R. C. (2017). Teacher–child interactions in free choice and teacher-directed activity settings: Prediction to school readiness. *Early Education and Development, 28*(8), 1035–1051.

Goertz, M. (2001). Standards-based accountability: Horse trade or horse whip? In S. Fuhrman (Ed.), *From the capitol to the classroom: Standards-based reforms in the states* (pp. 39–60). University of Chicago Press.

Goff, P. A., Jackson, M. C., Di Leone, B. A. L., Culotta, C. M., & DiTomasso, N. A. (2014). The essence of innocence: Consequences of dehumanizing black children. *Journal of Personality and Social Psychology, 106*(4), 526–545.

Goldstein, L. S. (2007). Beyond the DAP versus standards dilemma: Examining the unforgiving complexity of kindergarten teaching in the United States. *Early Childhood Research Quarterly, 22*(1), 39–54.

Goldstein, L. S. (2008). Kindergarten teachers making "street-level" education policy in the wake of No Child Left Behind. *Early Education and Development, 19*(3), 448–478.

Goodwin, A. L., Cheruvu, R., & Genishi, C. (2008). Responding to multiple diversities in early childhood education. In C. Genishi & A. L. Goodwin (Eds.), *Diversities in early childhood education: Rethinking and doing* (pp. 3–10). Routledge.

Gopnik, A. (2012). Scientific thinking in young children: Theoretical advances, empirical research, and policy implications. *Science, 337*(6102), 1623–1627.

Gopnik, A., Meltzoff, A. N., & Kuhl, P. K. (2000). *The scientist in the crib: What early learning tells us about the mind.* William Morrow Paperbacks.

Gracey, H. L. (1975). Learning the student role: Kindergarten as academic boot camp. In H. R. Stub (Ed.), *The sociology of education: A source book* (pp. 82–95). Dorsey Press.

Grande, S. (2018). Aging, precarity, and the struggle for Indigenous elsewhere. *International Journal of Qualitative Studies in Education, 31*, 168–176.

Graue, M. E. (1993). *Ready for what? Constructing meanings of readiness for kindergarten.* State University of New York Press.

Graue, E. (2005). Theorizing and describing preservice teachers' images of families and schooling. *Teachers College Record, 107*(1), 157–185.

Graue, E. (2006). The answer is readiness—now what is the question? *Early Education and Development, 17*(1), 43–56.

Graue, E. (2009). Reimagining kindergarten. *The School Administrator, 66*, 10–15.

Graue, E. (2011). Are we paving paradise? *Educational Leadership, 68*(7) 12–17.

Graue, M. E., & Walsh, D. J. (1998). *Studying children in context: Theories, methods, and ethics.* Sage.

Graue, M. E., Whyte, K. L., & Karabon, A. E. (2015). The power of improvisational teaching. *Teaching and Teacher Education, 48*, 13–21.

Grissom, J. A., & Mitani, H. (2016). Salary, performance, and superintendent turnover. *Educational Administration Quarterly, 52*(3), 351–391.

Guinier, L., & Torres, G. (2002). *The miner's canary: Enlisting race, resisting power, transforming democracy.* Harvard University Press.

Guthrie, J. T., Wigfield, A., & VonSecker, C. (2000). Effects of integrated instruction on motivation and strategy use in reading. *Journal of Educational Psychology, 92*(2), 331.

Hall, P. M., & McGinty, P. J. (1997). Policy as the transformation of intentions: Producing program from statute. *Sociological Quarterly, 38*(3), 439–467.

Halle, T. G., Hair, E. C., Wandner, L. D., & Chien, N. C. (2012). Profiles of school readiness among four-year-old Head Start children. *Early Childhood Research Quarterly, 27*(4), 613–626.

Hampden-Thompson, G., & Galindo, C. (2017). School–family relationships, school satisfaction and the academic achievement of young people. *Educational Review, 69*(2), 248–265.

Hamre, B. K., & Pianta, R. C. (2005). Can instructional and emotional support in the first-grade classroom make a difference for children at risk of school failure? *Child Development, 76*(5), 949–967.

Hargreaves, A., & Tucker, E. (1991). Teaching and guilt: Exploring the feelings of teaching. *Teaching and Teacher Education, 7*(5–6), 491–505.

Harvey, D. (2005). *A brief history of neoliberalism.* Oxford University Press.

Hatch, J. A. (2002). Accountability shovedown: Resisting the standards movement in early childhood education. *Phi Delta Kappan, 83*, 457–463.

Hatch, J. A. (2015). *Reclaiming the teaching profession: Transforming the dialogue on public education.* Rowman & Littlefield.

Hatch, J. A., & Freeman, E. B. (1988). Kindergarten philosophies and practices: Perspectives of teachers, principals, and supervisors. *Early Childhood Research Quarterly, 3*(2), 151–166.

Hayashi, A., & Tobin, J. (2012). Reframing a visual ethnography of a Japanese preschool classroom. *Visual Anthropology Review, 28*(1), 13–31.

Heckman, J. J. (2000). Policies to foster human capital. *Research in Economics, 54*, 3–56.

Heckman, J. J., Moon, S. H., Pinto, R., Savelyev, P. A., & Yavitz, A. Q. (2010). The rate of the return to the High/Scope Perry Preschool Program. *Journal of Public Economics, 94*, 114–128.

Heimer, L. G., & Ramminger, A. E. (2019). *Reshaping universal preschool: Critical perspectives on power and policy*. Teachers College Press.

Helm, J. H. (2015). *Becoming young thinkers: Deep project work in the classroom*. Teachers College Press.

Hemelt, S. W., & Jacob, B. A. (2020). How does an accountability program that targets achievement gaps affect student performance? *Education Finance and Policy, 15*(1), 45–74.

Holland, D., Lachicotte, W., Skinner, D., & Cain, C. (1998). *Identity and agency in cultural worlds*. Harvard University Press.

Holland, D., & Lave, J. (2009). Social practice theory and the historical production of persons. *Actio: An International Journal of Human Activity Theory, 2*(1), 1–15.

Hornby, G., & Lafaele, R. (2011). Barriers to parental involvement in education: An explanatory model. *Educational Review, 63*(1), 37–52.

Hubble, E. (1929). A relation between distance and radial velocity among extra-galactic nebulae. *Proceedings of the National Academy of Sciences of the United States of America, 15*(3), 168–173.

Huber, J., Caine, V., Murphy, S., Lessard, S., Menon, J., & Clandlin, D. J. (2018). A narrative inquiry into the experiences of urban Indigenous families as they ready their children for, and during, kindergarten. *Journal of Childhood Studies, 43*(3), 46–57.

Hursh, D. (2005). Neo-liberalism, markets and accountability: Transforming education and undermining democracy in the United States and England. *Policy Futures in Education, 3*(1), 3–15.

Hursh, D. (2007). Assessing No Child Left Behind and the rise of neoliberal education policies. *American Educational Research Journal, 44*(3), 493–518.

Hustedt, J. T., Buell, M. J., Hallam, R. A., & Pinder, W. M. (2018). While kindergarten has changed, some beliefs stay the same: Kindergarten teachers' beliefs about readiness. *Journal of Research in Childhood Education, 32*, 52–66.

Hyson, M. (2008). *Enthusiastic and engaged learners: Approaches to learning in the early childhood classroom*. Teachers College Press.

Ilgaz, H., Hassinger-Das, B., Hirsh-Pasek, K., & Golinkoff, R. M. (2018). Making the case for playful learning. In M. Fleer & B. van Oers (Eds.), *International handbook of early childhood education* (pp. 1245–1263). Springer.

Inden, R. (1990). *Imagining India*. Blackwell.

Ingersoll, R., & Strong, M. (2011). The impact of induction and mentoring programs for beginning teachers: A critical review of the research. *Review of Educational Research, 81*, 201–233.

Jalongo, M. R. (2007). Beyond benchmarks and scores: Reasserting the role of motivation and interest in children's academic achievement an ACEI position paper. *Childhood Education, 83*(6), 395–407.

James, A., Jenks, C., & Prout, A. (1998). *Theorizing childhood*. Teachers College Press.

Johnston, P. H. (2004). *Choice words: How our language affects children's learning*. Stenhouse.

Johnston, P. H. (2012). *Opening minds: Using language to change lives*. Stenhouse.

Jones, E., & Nimmo, J. (1994). *Emergent curriculum*. National Association for the Education of Young Children.

Kagan, S. L., Moore, E., & Bredekamp, S. (Eds.). (1995). Reconsidering children's early learning and development: Toward shared beliefs and vocabulary. National Education Goals Panel.

Katz, L. G. (1987). *Current issues in early childhood education* (ED 281 908). ERIC Clearinghouse on Early Childhood Education.

Katz, L. G., & Chard, S. C. (2000). *Engaging children's minds: The project approach.* Greenwood.

Keddie, A., Mills, M., & Pendergast, D. (2011). Fabricating an identity in neo-liberal times: Performing schooling as "number one". *Oxford Review of Education, 37*(1), 75–92.

Kelley, B., Weyer, M., McCann, M., Brown, S., & Keily, T. (2020). *50 state comparison: State K-3 policies.* Education Commission of the States. http://www.ecs.org/kindergarten-policies/

Kennedy, A. S., & Heineke, A. (2014). Re-envisioning the role of universities in early childhood teacher education: Community partnerships for 21st-century learning. *Journal of Early Childhood Teacher Education, 35*, 226–243.

Kingdon, J. W. (2003). *Agendas, alternatives, and public policies* (2nd ed.). Longman.

Kornrich, S., & Furstenberg, F. (2013). Investing in children: Changes in parental spending on children, 1972–2007. *Demography, 50*, 1–23.

Kostelnik, M. J., & Grady, M. L. (2009). *Getting it right from the start: The principal's guide to early childhood education.* Corwin Press.

Kundu, A. (2020). *The power of student agency: Looking beyond grit to close the opportunity gap.* Teachers College Press.

Ladd, H. F. (2017). No Child Left Behind: A deeply flawed federal policy. *Journal of Policy Analysis and Management, 36*, 461–468.

Ladson-Billings, G. (1994). *The dream-keepers: Successful teachers of African American children.* Jossey-Bass.

Ladson-Billings, G. (2006a). From the achievement gap to the education debt: Understanding achievement in U.S. schools. *Educational Researcher, 35*, 3–12.

Ladson-Billings, G. (2006b). Yes, but how do we do it? Practicing culturally relevant pedagogy. In J. Landsman & C. W. Lewis (Eds.), *White teachers/diverse classrooms: A guide to building inclusive schools, promoting high expectations, and eliminating racism* (pp. 29–42). Stylus.

Ladson-Billings, G. (2014). Culturally relevant pedagogy 2.0: The remix. *Harvard Educational Review, 84*(1), 74–84.

Lakoff, G. (2002). *Moral politics: How liberals and conservatives think* (2nd ed.). University of Chicago Press.

Lakoff, G. (2004). *Don't think of an elephant! Know your values and frame the debate.* Chelsea Green.

Lambert, S. D., & Loiselle, C. G. (2008). Combining individual interviews and focus groups to enhance data richness. *Journal of Advanced Nursing, 62*(2), 228–237.

Landers, C. (2013). *Getting ready for school: A child-to-child approach: Strategic framework.* United Nations Children's Fund.

Lasley, T. J. (1994). Teacher technicians: A "new" metaphor for new teachers. *Action in Teacher Education, 16*(1), 11–19.

Lee, V. E., & Burkham, D. (2002). *Neighborhood poverty: Inequality at the starting gate.* Economic Policy Institute.

Lefstein, A., & Perath, H. (2014). Empowering teacher voices in an education policy discussion: Paradoxes of representation. *Teaching and Teacher Education, 38*, 33–43.

Lemke, T. (2001). "The birth of bio-politics": Michel Foucault's lecture at the Collège de France on neo-liberal governmentality. *Economy and Society, 30*, 190–207.

Lerkkanen, M. K., Kiuru, N., Pakarinen, E., Poikkeus, A.-M., Rasku Puttonen, H., Siekkinen, M., & Nurmi, J.-E. (2016). Child-centered versus teacher-directed teaching practices: Associations with the development of academic skills in the first grade at school. *Early Childhood Research Quarterly, 36*, 145–156.

Lerkkanen, M.-K., Kiuru, N., Pakarinen, E., Viljaranta, J., Poikkeus, A.-M., Rasku-Puttonen, H., & Nurmi, J.-E. (2012). The role of teaching practices in the development of children's interest in reading and mathematics in kindergarten. *Contemporary Educational Psychology, 37*, 266–279.

Lewis, S., & Holloway, J. (2019). Datafying the teaching "profession": Remaking the professional teacher in the image of data. *Cambridge Journal of Education, 49*, 35–51.

Linn, R. L. (2005). Conflicting demands of No Child Left Behind and state systems: Mixed messages about school performance. *Education Policy Analysis Archives, 13*(33), 1–20.

Lipman, P. (2013). Economic crisis, accountability, and the state's coercive assault on public education in the USA. *Journal of Education Policy, 28*, 557–573.

Lipsky, M. (1980). *Street-level bureaucracy: Dilemmas of the individual in public services*. Russell Sage Foundation.

Loh, J., & Hu, G. (2014). Subdued by the system: Neoliberalism and the beginning teacher. *Teaching and Teacher Education, 41*, 13–21.

Lynch, M. (2015). More play please: The perspectives of kindergarten teachers on play in the classroom. *American Journal of Play, 7*, 347–370.

Mackenzie, C. (1886, July). *Free kindergartens*. Social Welfare History Project. http://socialwelfare.library.vcu.edu/programs/education/kindergartens-a-history-1886/

MacLean, N. (2017). *Democracy in chains: The deep history of the radical right's stealth plan for America*. Penguin.

Majone, G. (1989). *Evidence, argument, and persuasion in the policy process*. Yale University Press.

Marsh, J. A., & Wohlstetter, P. (2013). Recent trends in intergovernmental relations: The resurgence of local actors in education policy. *Educational Researcher, 42*, 276–283.

Marshall, C., Mitchell, D., & Wirt, F. (1986). The context of state-level policy formation. *Educational Evaluation and Policy Analysis, 8*(4), 347–378.

Martin, A. (1985). Back to kindergarten basics. *Harvard Educational Review, 55*, 318–320.

Mashburn, A. J., Pianta, R. C., Hamre, B. K., Downer, J. T., Barbarin, O. A., Bryant, D., Burchinal, M., Early, D. M., & Howes, C. (2008). Measures of classroom quality in prekindergarten and children's development of academic, language, and social skills. *Child Development, 79*(3), 732–749.

Mayall, B. (2002). *Towards a sociology for childhood: Thinking from children's lives*. Open University Press.

McFarland, J., Hussar, B., Wang, X., Zhang, J., Wang, K., Rathbun, A., Barmer, A., Forrest Cataldi, E., & Bullock Mann, F. (2018). *The condition of education 2018* (NCES 2018-144). National Center for Education Statistics.

McLaughlin, M. W. (1987). Learning from experience: Lessons from policy implementation. *Educational Evaluation and Policy Analysis, 9*(2), 171–178.

McLeod, J. (2001). When post-structuralism meets gender. In K. Hultqvist & G. Dahlberg (Eds.), *Governing the child in the new millennium* (pp. 259–289). Routledge.

McNeil, L. M. (2000). *Contradictions of school reform: Educational costs of standardized testing*. Routledge.

McNeil, L. M., & Valenzuela, A. (2001). The harmful impact of the TAAS system of testing in Texas: Beneath the accountability rhetoric. In G. Orfield & M. L. Kornhaber (Eds.), *Raising standards or raising barriers? Inequality and high-stakes testing in public education*. The Century Foundation Press.

Meier, D., & Knoester, M. (2017). *Beyond testing: Seven assessments of students and schools more effective than standardized tests*. Teachers College Press.

Meisels, S. J. (1989). High stakes testing in kindergarten. *Educational Leadership, 46*(7), 16–22.

Meisels, S. J. (1999). Assessing readiness. In R. C. Pianta & M. J. Cox (Eds.), *The transition to kindergarten* (pp. 39–63). Brookes.

Menken, K. (2006). Teaching to the test: How No Child Left Behind impacts language policy, curriculum, and instruction for English language learners. *Bilingual Research Journal, 30*(2), 521–546.

Merriam, S. B., & Tisdell, E. J. (2016). *Qualitative research: A guide to design and implementation* (4th ed.). Jossey-Bass.

Miles, M. B., Huberman, A. M., & Saldaña, J. (2014). *Qualitative data analysis: A methods sourcebook* (3rd ed.). Sage.

Miller, E., & Almon, J. (2009). *Crisis in the kindergarten: Why children need to play in school*. Alliance for Childhood.

Miller, L. J., & Smith, S. C. (2011). Did the No Child Left Behind Act miss the mark? Assessing the potential benefits from an accountability system for early childhood education. *Educational Policy, 25*(1), 193–214.

Mincer, J. (1958). Investment in human capital and personal income distribution. *Journal of Political Economy, 66*(4), 281–302.

Minicozzi, L. L. (2016). The garden is thorny: Teaching kindergarten in the age of accountability. *Global Studies of Childhood, 6*, 299–310.

Mitra, D., Mann, B., & Hlavacik, M. (2016). Opting out: Parents creating contested spaces to challenge standardized tests. *Education Policy Analysis Archives, 24*, 1–19.

Miyake, A., Friedman, N. P., Emerson, M. J., Witzki, A. H., Howerter, A., & Wager, T. D. (2000). The unity and diversity of executive functions and their contributions to complex "frontal lobe" tasks: A latent variable analysis. *Cognitive Psychology, 41*(1), 49–100.

Moll, L. C., Amanti, C., Neff, D., & González, N. (1992). Funds of knowledge for teaching: Using a qualitative approach to connect homes and classrooms. *Theory Into Practice, 31*, 132–141.

Morrison, K. A., Robbins, H. H., & Rose, D. G. (2008). Operationalizing culturally relevant pedagogy: A synthesis of classroom-based research. *Equity & Excellence in Education, 41*, 433–452.

Moss, P. (2014). *Transformative change and real utopias in early childhood education*. Routledge.

Moss, P. (2017). Power and resistance in early childhood education: From dominant discourse to democratic experimentalism. *Journal of Pedagogy, 8*(1), 11–32.

National Association for the Education of Young Children. (1995). *School readiness: A position statement of the NAEYC*. http://www.naeyc.org/files/naeyc/file/positions/PSREADY98.PDF

National Center for Education Statistics. (2019). *The condition of education 2019* (NCES 2019-144). U.S. Department of Education.

National Commission on Excellence in Education. (1983). *A nation at risk: The full account*. Author.

National Education Goals Panel. (1991). *Measuring progress toward the National Education Goals: Potential indicators and measurement strategies*. Discussion document. ERIC Clearinghouse.

National Governors Association. (1988). *Restructuring the education system*. Author.

National Research Council. (2000). *How people learn: Brain, mind, experience, and school* (Expanded ed.). National Academy Press.

Nieto, S. (2002). *Language, culture, and teaching: Critical perspectives for a new century*. Erlbaum.

Nxumalo, F. (2019). Disrupting racial capitalist formations in early childhood education. In F. Nxumalo & C. P. Brown (Eds.), *Disrupting and countering deficits in early childhood education* (pp. 164–178). Routledge.

Nxumalo, F., & Adair, J. K. (2019). Social justice and equity in early childhood education. In C. P. Brown, M. McMullen, & N. File (Eds.), *The Wiley handbook of early childhood care and education* (pp. 661–682). Wiley.

Nxumalo, F., & Brown, C. P. (2019). *Disrupting and countering deficits in early childhood education*. Routledge.

O'Day, J. A. (2002). Complexity, accountability, and school improvement. *Harvard Educational Review, 72*(3), 293–329.

Office of the White House. (2002). *Good start, grow smart: The Bush administration's early childhood initiative*. https://georgewbush-whitehouse.archives.gov/infocus/earlychildhood/earlychildhood.html

Olssen, M., & Peters, M. A. (2005). Neoliberalism, higher education and the knowledge economy: From the free market to knowledge capitalism. *Journal of Education Policy, 20*, 313–345.

Pakarinen, E., Kiuru, N., Lerkkanen, M. K., Poikkeus, A. M., Ahonen, T., & Nurmi, J. E. (2011). Instructional support predicts children's task avoidance in kindergarten. *Early Childhood Research Quarterly, 26*(3), 376–386.

Paley, V. G. (2009). *You can't say you can't play*. Harvard University Press.

Pan, Q., Trang, K., Love, H. R., Templin, J. L., Hill, C., Kivlighan, D. M., . . . & Jones, D. D. (2019). School readiness profiles and growth in academic achievement. *Frontiers in Education, 4*, 1–17.

Paris, D. (2012). Culturally sustaining pedagogy: A needed change in stance, terminology, and practice. *Educational Researcher, 41*, 93–97.

Paris, D. (2016). *On educating culturally sustaining teachers* (TeachingWorks working paper). University of Michigan. https://www.teachingworks.org/images/files/TeachingWorks_Paris.pdf

Paris, D., & Alim, H. S. (2014). What are we seeking to sustain through culturally sustaining pedagogy? A loving critique forward. *Harvard Educational Review, 84*(1), 85–100.

Paris, D., & Alim, H. S. (Eds.). (2017). *Culturally sustaining pedagogies: Teaching and learning for justice in a changing world*. Teachers College Press.

Parker, A., & Neuharth-Pritchett, S. (2006). Developmentally appropriate practice in kindergarten: Factors shaping teacher beliefs and practice. *Journal of Research in Childhood Education, 21*(1), 65–78.

Parson, E. C., & Wall, S. (2011). Unpacking the critical in culturally relevant pedagogy: An illustration involving African Americans and Asian Americans. In L. Scherff & K. Spector (Eds.), *Culturally relevant pedagogy: Clashes and confrontations* (pp. 15–34). Rowman & Littlefield.

Patton, M. Q. (2015). *Qualitative research and methods: Integrating theory and practice*. Sage.

Payne, K. A. (2018). Democratic teachers mentoring novice teachers: Enacting democratic practices and pedagogy in teacher education. *Action in Teacher Education, 40*(2), 133–150.

Pennington, J. L. (2007). Re-viewing NCLB through the figured worlds of policy and teaching: Creating a space for teacher agency and improvisation. *Language Arts, 84*, 465–474.

Penttinen, V., Pakarinen, E., von Suchodoletz, A., & Lerkkanen, M. K. (2020). Relations between kindergarten teachers' occupational well-being and the quality of teacher–child interactions. *Early Education and Development, 31*(7), 994–1010.

Penuel, W. R., Fishman, B. J., Yamaguchi, R., & Gallagher, L. P. (2007). What makes professional development effective? Strategies that foster curriculum implementation. *American Educational Research Journal, 44*(4), 921–958.

Pérez, M. S. (2019). Dismantling racialized discourses in early childhood education and care: A revolution towards reframing the field. In F. Nxumalo & C. P. Brown (Eds.), *Disrupting and countering deficits in early childhood education* (pp. 20–36). Routledge.

Pérez, M. S., & Cahill, B. (2016). "Readiness" as central to the (re)production of quality discourses in the United States. In G. S. Cannella, M. S. Pérez, & I. F. Lee (Eds.), *Critical examinations in quality in early education and care: Regulation, disqualification, and erasure* (pp. 11–25). Peter Lang.

Pérez, M. S., & Saavedra, C. M. (2017). A call for onto-epistemological diversity in early childhood education and care: Centering global south conceptualizations of childhood/s. *Review of Research in Education, 41*, 1–29.

Phelps, R., Graham, A., Tuyet N. H. T., & Geeves, R. (2014). Exploring Vietnamese children's experiences of, and views on, learning at primary school in rural and remote communities. *International Journal of Educational Development, 36*, 33–43.

Pohan, C. A., & Adams, C. (2007). Increasing family involvement and cultural understanding through a university–school partnership. *Action in Teacher Education, 29*(1), 42–50.

Powell, K. S. (1969). Kindergarten is not sitting at a desk with a workbook and sharpened pencil. In D. K. Osborn (Ed.), *Kindergarten: Who? what? where?* (pp. 34–35). Southern Association on Children Under Six.

Power, M. (1997). *The audit society: Rituals of verification*. Oxford University Press.

Pyle, A., & Danniels, E. (2017). A continuum of play-based learning: The role of the teacher in play-based pedagogy and the fear of hijacking play. *Early Education and Development, 28*(3), 274–289.

Pyle, A., & DeLuca, C. (2017). Assessment in play-based kindergarten classrooms: An empirical study of teacher perspectives and practices. *Journal of Educational Research, 110*, 457–466.

Quirk, M., Dowdy, E., Goldstein, A., & Carnazzo, K. (2017). School readiness as a longitudinal predictor of social–emotional and reading performance across the elementary grades. *Assessment for Effective Intervention, 42*(4), 248–253.

Quirk, M., Nylund-Gibson, K., & Furlong, M. (2013). Exploring patterns of Latino/a children's school readiness at kindergarten entry and their relations with grade 2 achievement. *Early Childhood Research Quarterly, 28*(2), 437–449.

Qvortrup, J. (2009). Are children human beings or human becomings? A critical assessment of outcome thinking. *Vita e Pensiero, 117*, 631–653.

Reid, A., & O'Donoghue, M. (2004). Revisiting enquiry-based teacher education in neo-liberal times. *Teaching and Teacher Education, 20*, 559–570.

Reyes, R., III. (2016). In a world of disposable students: The humanizing elements of border pedagogy in teacher education. *The High School Journal, 99*(4), 337–350.

Reynolds, A. J., Ou, S., & Temple, J. (2018). A multicomponent, preschool to third grade preventive intervention and educational attainment at 35 years of age. *Journal of the American Medical Association Pediatrics, 172*, 247–256.

Rist, R. C. (2000). Influencing the policy process with qualitative research. In N. Denzin & Y. Lincoln (Eds.), *The handbook of qualitative research* (2nd ed., pp. 1001–1017). Sage.

Ritchie, S., Phillips, E. C., & Garrett, C. G. (2016). Professional development at its best: North Carolina's pre-K and kindergarten demonstration program. *Young Children, 71*(4), 8–13.

Roberts-Holmes, G. (2015). The "datafication" of early years pedagogy: "If the teaching is good, the data should be good and if there's bad teaching, there is bad data". *Journal of Education Policy, 30*(3), 302–315.

Robertson, S., & Dale, R. (2002). Local states of emergency: The contradictions of neo-liberal governance in education in New Zealand. *British Journal of Sociology of Education, 23*(3), 463–482.

Roeber, E. D. (1999). Standards initiatives and American educational reform. In G. J. Cizek (Ed.), *Handbook of educational policy* (pp. 151–181). Elsevier.

Rogoff, B. (2003). *The cultural nature of human development*. Oxford University Press.

Rose, N. (1996). Governing "advanced" liberal democracies. In A. Barry, T. Osborne, & N. Rose (Eds.), *Foucault and political reason: Liberalism, neo-liberalism, and rationalities of government* (pp. 37–64). University of Chicago Press.

Rose, N. (1999). *Powers of freedom: Reframing political thought*. Cambridge University Press.

Ross, E. D. (1976). *The kindergarten crusade: The establishment of preschool education in the United States*. Ohio University Press.

Russell, J. L. (2011). From child's garden to academic press: The role of shifting institutional logics in redefining kindergarten education. *American Educational Research Journal, 48*, 236–267.

Ryan, S. V., Nathaniel, P., Pendergast, L. L., Saeki, E., Segool, N., & Schwing, S. (2017). Leaving the teaching profession: The role of teacher stress and educational accountability policies on turnover intent. *Teaching and Teacher Education, 66*, 1–11.

Schmidt, M., & Allsup, R. E. (2019). John Dewey and teacher education. In *Oxford Research Encyclopedia of Education*. https://doi.org/10.1093/acrefore/9780190264093.013.475

Schmidt, M., & Datnow, A. (2005). Teachers' sense-making about comprehensive school reform: The influence of emotions. *Teaching and Teacher Education, 21*(8), 949–965.

Schweinhart, L. J. (2005). *Lifetime effects: The High/Scope Perry Preschool study through age 40* (No. 14). High/Scope Foundation.

Shepard, L. A. (1994). The challenge of assessing young children appropriately. *Phi Delta Kappan, 76*, 206–212.

Shepard, L. A., Kagan, S. L., & Wurtz, E. (Eds.). (1998). *Principles and recommendations for early childhood assessments*. National Education Goals Panel.

Sherfinski, M. (2013). Class and parents' agency in West Virginia: Between choices and rights. *Education Policy Analysis Archives, 21*(78), 1–35.

Sherfinski, M. (2019). Culture matters: A comparative study of teachers' views of universal pre-kindergarten in two state regions. *Early Child Development and Care, 189*(8), 1325–1338.

Sherfinski, M., Hayes, S., Zhang, J., & Jalalifard, M. (2019). "Do it all but don't kill us": (Re)positioning teacher educators and preservice teachers amidst edTPA and the teacher strike in West Virginia. *Education Policy Analysis Archives, 27*(151), 1–43.

Sherman, W. H. (2008). No Child Left Behind: A legislative catalyst for superintendent action to eliminate test-score gaps? *Educational Policy, 22*(5), 675–704.

Slater, G. B. (2015). Education as recovery: Neoliberalism, school reform, and the politics of crisis. *Journal of Education Policy, 30*, 1–20.

Smagorinsky, P., Lakly, A., & Johnson, T. S. (2002). Acquiescence, accommodation, and resistance in learning to teach within a prescribed curriculum. *English Education, 34*(3), 187–213.

Smith, M. L. (1991). Put to the test: The effects of external testing on teachers. *Educational Researcher, 20*(5), 8–11.

Smith, M. L., Miller-Kahn, L., Heinecke, W., & Jarvis, P. F. (2004). *Political spectacle and the fate of American schools*. Routledge.

Snodgrass Rangel, V. (2018). A review of the literature on principal turnover. *Review of Educational Research, 88*(1), 87–124.

Sonnenschein, S., Stapleton, L. M., & Benson, A. (2010). The relation between the type and amount of instruction and growth in children's reading competencies. *American Educational Research Journal, 47*(2), 358–389.

Sonu, D., & Benson, J. (2016). The quasi-human child: How normative conceptions of childhood enabled neoliberal school reform in the United States. *Curriculum Inquiry, 46*(3), 230–247.

Souto-Manning, M. (2017). Generative text sets: Tools for negotiating critically inclusive early childhood teacher education pedagogical practices. *Journal of Early Childhood Teacher Education, 38*, 79–101.

Souto-Manning, M. (2018). Disrupting Eurocentric epistemologies: Re-mediating transitions to centre intersectionally-minoritised immigrant children, families and communities. *European Journal of Education, 53*, 456–468.

Souto-Manning, M., & Rabadi-Raol, A. (2018). (Re)centering quality in early childhood education: Toward intersectional justice for minoritized children. *Review of Research in Education, 42*(1), 203–225.

Spillane, J. P., Reiser, B. J., & Reimer, T. (2002). Policy implementation and cognition: Reframing and refocusing implementation research. *Review of Educational Research Quarterly, 72*, 387–433.

Stipek, D. (2006). No Child Left Behind comes to preschool. *The Elementary School Journal, 106*(5), 455–466.

Stipek, D., Feiler, R., Daniels, D., & Milburn, S. (1995). Effects of different instructional approaches on young children's achievement and motivation. *Child Development, 66*(1), 209–223.

Stone, S. J., & Christie, J. F. (1996). Collaborative literacy learning during sociodramatic play in a multiage (K–2) primary classroom. *Journal of Research in Childhood Education, 10*(2), 123–133.

Strauss, V. (2016, January 19). Kindergarten the new first grade? It's actually worse than that. *The Washington Post*. https://www.washingtonpost.com/news/answer-sheet/wp/2016/01/19/kindergarten-the-new-first-grade-its-actually-worse-than-that/

Street, B. V. (1993). Culture is a verb. In D. Graddol, L. Thompson, & M. Byram (Eds.), *Language and culture* (pp. 23–43). BAAL/Multilingual Matters.

Suggate, S. P. (2012). Watering the garden before a rainstorm. In S. Suggate & E. Reese (Eds.), *Contemporary debates in childhood education and development* (pp. 181–190). Routledge.

Swadener, B. B., & Lubeck, S. (Eds.). (1995). *Children and families "at promise": Deconstructing the discourse of risk*. State University of New York Press.

Tavassolie, T., & Winsler, A. (2019). Predictors of mandatory 3rd grade retention from high-stakes test performance for low-income, ethnically diverse children. *Early Childhood Research Quarterly, 48*, 62–74.

Texas Education Agency. (2020). *Texas essential knowledge and skills for kindergarten*. https://tea.texas.gov/sites/default/files/Kinder_TEKS.pdf

Thomas, G. (2016). *How to do your case study* (2nd ed.). Sage.

Tobin, J., Arzubiaga, A. E., & Adair, J. K. (2013). *Children crossing borders: Immigrant parent and teacher perspectives on preschool*. Russell Sage Foundation.

Tobin, J., Hseuh, Y., & Karasawa, M. (2009). *Preschool in three cultures revisited: China, Japan, and the United States*. University of Chicago Press.

Tobin, J., Wu, D., & Davidson, D. (1991). *Preschool in three cultures: Japan, China, and the United States*. Yale University Press.

Topor, D. R., Keane, S. P., Shelton, T. L., & Calkins, S. D. (2010). Parent involvement and student academic performance: A multiple mediational analysis. *Journal of Prevention & Intervention in the Community, 38*(3), 183–197.

Toub, T. S., Rajan, V., Golinkoff, R. M., & Hirsh-Pasek, K. (2016). Guided play: A solution to the play versus learning dichotomy. In D. C. Geary & D. B. Berch (Eds.), *Evolutionary perspectives on child development and education* (pp. 117–141). Springer.

Tsao, Y. L. (2008). Using guided play to enhance children's conversation, creativity and competence in literacy. *Education, 128*, 515–520.

Tuck, E. (2009). Suspending damage: A letter to communities. *Harvard Educational Review, 79*(3), 409–427.

Ukpokodu, O. (2011). Developing teachers' cultural competence: One teacher educator's practice of unpacking student culturelessness. *Action in Teacher Education, 33*, 432–454.

Uphoff, J. K., & Gilmore, J. (1986). Viewpoint 2. Pupil age at school entrance—how many are ready for success? *Young Children, 41*(2), 11–16.

Uprichard, E. (2008). Children as "being and becomings": Children, childhood and temporality. *Children in Society, 22*, 303–313.

Urrieta, L. J. (2007). Identity production in figured worlds: How some Mexican Americans become Chicana/o activist educators. *The Urban Review, 39*, 117–144.

Valencia, R. R. (1997). *The evolution of deficit thinking: Educational thought and practices.* Routledge.

Valente, J. M. (2019). A deaf lens: Adapting video-cued multivocal ethnography for the "kindergartens for the deaf in three countries" project. *Anthropology & Education Quarterly, 50*, 340–347.

Valenzuela, A. (Ed.). (2005). *Leaving children behind: How "Texas-style" accountability fails Latino youth.* State University of New York Press.

Van Oers, B., & Duijkers, D. (2013). Teaching in a play-based curriculum: Theory, practice and evidence of developmental education for young children. *Journal of Curriculum Studies, 45*, 511–534.

VanSchyndel, S. K., Eisenberg, N., Valiente, C., & Spinrad, T. L. (2017). Relations from temperamental approach reactivity and effortful control to academic achievement and peer relations in early elementary school. *Journal of Research in Personality, 67*, 15–26.

Varenne, H., & McDermott, R. (1998). *Successful failure: The school America builds.* Westview Press.

Villavicencio, A. (2013). "It's our best choice right now": Examining the choice options of charter school parents. *Education Policy Analysis Archives, 21*, 1–19.

Villegas, A. M., & Lucas, T. (2002). *Educating culturally responsive teachers: A coherent approach.* State University of New York Press.

Vinovskis, M. (1999). *The road to Charlottesville: The 1989 education summit.* National Education Goals Panel.

Virtanen, T. E., Kiuru, N., Lerkkanen, M. K., Poikkeus, A. M., & Kuorelahti, M. (2016). Assessment of student engagement among junior high school students and associations with self-esteem, burnout, and academic achievement. *Journal for Educational Research Online, 8*(2), 136–157.

Vygotsky, L. S. (1980). *Mind in society: The development of higher psychological processes.* Harvard University Press.

Wagner, T. (2008). Rigor redefined. *Educational Leadership, 66*(2), 20–24.

Walker, M. (2006). Towards a capability-based theory of social justice for education policymaking. *Journal of Education Policy, 21*, 163–185.

Wallerstedt, C., & Pramling, N. (2012). Learning to play in a goal-directed practice. *Early Years, 32*(1), 5–15.

Waring, G. (2008). *Oscar and the frog: A book about growing.* Candlewick.

Washor, E., & Mojkowski, C. (2007). What do you mean by rigor? *Educational Leadership, 64*(4), 84–87.

Weber, E. (1969). *The kindergarten: Its encounter with educational thought in America*. Teachers College Press.
Weick, K. E. (1995). *Sensemaking in organizations* (Vol. 3). Sage.
Weiner, L. (2007). A lethal threat to U.S. teacher education. *Journal of Teacher Education, 58*(4), 274–286.
Weisberg, D. S., Hirsh-Pasek, K., & Golinkoff, R. M. (2013). Guided play: Where curricular goals meet a playful pedagogy. *Mind, Brain, and Education, 7*, 104–112.
Weisenfeld, G. G., Garver, K., & Hodges, K. (2020). Federal and state efforts in the implementation of kindergarten entry assessments (2011–2018). *Early Education and Development, 31*(5), 632–652.
Wells, K. (2016). Governing the global child: Biopolitics and liberal subjectivities. In J. W. Cahill, *Handbook of children and youth studies* (pp. 237–255). Springer Science+Business Media.
Wesley, P. W., & Buysse, V. (2003). Making meaning of school readiness in schools and communities. *Early Childhood Research Quarterly, 18*, 351–375.
West Virginia Board of Education. (2014). *West Virginia early learning readiness: Kindergarten resource guide*. http://wvde.state.wv.us/oel/docs/workbook2.pdf
Whitaker, M., & Hoover-Dempsey, K. (2013). School influences on parents' role beliefs. *The Elementary School Journal, 114*, 73–99.
Whitenack, D. A., & Swanson, P. E. (2013). The transformative potential of boundary spanners: A narrative inquiry into preservice teacher education and professional development in an NCLB-impacted context. *Education Policy Analysis Archives, 21*(57), 1–19.
Williford, A. P., Carter, L. M., Maier, M. F., & Hamre, B. K., Cash, A., Pianta, R. C., & Downer, J. T. (2017). Teacher engagement in core components of an effective, early childhood professional development course: Links to changes in teacher–child interactions. *Journal of Early Childhood Teacher Education, 38*, 102–118.
Wolcott, H. F. (1994). *Transforming qualitative data: Description, analysis, and interpretation*. Sage.
Wynter-Hoyte, K., Braden, E. G., Rodriguez, S., & Thornton, N. (2019). Disrupting the status quo: Exploring culturally relevant and sustaining pedagogies for young diverse learners. *Race Ethnicity and Education, 22*(3), 428–447.
Yin, X., & Buck, G. A. (2019). Using a collaborative action research approach to negotiate an understanding of formative assessment in an era of accountability testing. *Teaching and Teacher Education, 80*, 27–38.
Yosso, T. J. (2005). Whose culture has capital? A critical race theory discussion of community cultural wealth. *Race Ethnicity and Education, 8*, 69–91.

Index

About the Author

Christopher P. Brown is a former preschool, kindergarten, and 1st-grade teacher. He is also an award-winning researcher, teacher educator, and professor of early childhood education in the Department of Educational Leadership and Policy at The University of Texas at Austin. His research centers on how education stakeholders across a range of political and educational contexts make sense of and respond to policymakers' reforms. He has looked at these issues using multiple theoretical and practitioner-based perspectives that span the fields of early childhood and elementary education, curriculum and instruction, teacher education, and policy analysis. Through this work, his goal is to understand and advocate for early learning environments that foster, sustain, and extend the complex educational, sociocultural, and individual goals and aspirations of teachers, children, and their families.